T0277604

DUAL JURISDICTION YOUTH

AMERICANBARASSOCIATION

Criminal Justice Section

Cover design by Rabiah Burks

The materials contained herein represent the opinions of the authors and/or the editors, and should not be construed to be the views or opinions of the law firms or companies with whom such persons are in partnership with, associated with, or employed by, nor of the American Bar Association or the Criminal Justice Section unless adopted pursuant to the bylaws of the Association.

Nothing in this book is to be considered as the rendering of legal advice for specific cases, and readers are responsible for obtaining such advice from their own legal counsel. This book is intended for educational and informational purposes only.

Printed in the United States of America.

27 26 25 24 23   5 4 3 2 1

Library of Congress Cataloging-in-Publication Data
Names: American Bar Association. Section of Criminal Justice, issuing body.
Title: Dual jurisdiction youth / ABA Criminal Justice Section.
Description: First edition. | Chicago : American Bar Association, Criminal
   Justice Section, 2023. | Summary: "This book is a commentary on the
   Black Letter Standards"— Provided by publisher.
Identifiers: LCCN 2023025841 (print) | LCCN 2023025842 (ebook) | ISBN
   9781639051731 (paperback) | ISBN 9781639051748 (epub)
Subjects: LCSH: Juvenile justice, Administration of—United States. |
   Juvenile courts--United States. | Children—Services for—Government
   policy—United States. | Children—Legal status, laws, etc.—United
   States. | Child welfare—United States.
Classification: LCC KF9779 .D83 2023 (print) | LCC KF9779 (ebook) | DDC
   345.73/081—dc23/eng/20230601
LC record available at https://lccn.loc.gov/2023025841
LC ebook record available at https://lccn.loc.gov/2023025842

Discounts are available for books ordered in bulk. Special consideration is given to state bars, CLE programs, and other bar-related organizations. Inquire at Book Publishing, ABA Publishing, American Bar Association, 321 N. Clark Street, Chicago, Illinois 60654-7598.

www.ShopABA.org

ABA Standards for Criminal Justice
Fourth Edition

Task Force on Dual Jurisdiction Youth

Leadership during Project
Justin Bingham, 2022–2023
Wayne McKenzie, 2021–2022
April Frazier Camara, 2020–2021
Kim T. Parker, 2019–2020
Lucian Dervan, 2018–2019
Morris "Sandy" Weinberg, 2017–2018
Matthew Redle, 2016–2017
Bernice Donald, 2015–2016
James Felman and Cynthia Orr, 2014–2015
Mathis H. Heck Jr., 2013–2014
William Shepherd, 2012–2013
Janet Levine, 2011–2012
Bruce Green, 2010–2011
Charles "Joe" Hynes, 2009–2010
Anthony Joseph, 2008–2009
Stephen Saltzburg, 2007–2008

Criminal Justice Standards Committee Chairs
Sam Kamin, 2021–
Bruce Green, 2017–2021
John Cline, 2014–2017
Mark Dwyer, 2011–2014
The Hon. Martin Marcus, 2008–2011

Task Force on Dual Jurisdiction Youth
The Hon. Ernestine Gray, Ret., Chair
Robert R. Schwartz, Vice Chair
Kristin N. Henning, Reporter

"Black Letter" Standards approved by ABA House of Delegates, August 2017

Commentary approved by the Standards Committee, October 2020

ABA Criminal Justice
Standards Committee
2022–2023

Chair

Sam Kamin
Professor of Law, Sturm College of Law, University of Denver
Denver, Colorado

Members

Kimberly M. Foxx
Cook County State's Attorney
Chicago, Illinois

Randy Gioia (ret.)
Deputy Chief Counsel, Public Defender Division
Committee for Public Counsel Services
Boston, Massachusetts

The Hon. Abdul Kallon (ret.)
U.S. District Court, Northern District of Alabama,
Birmingham, Alabama
Private Practitioner, Perkins & Coie
Seattle, Washington

Nina Marino
Private Practitioner, Kaplan & Marino PC
Los Angeles, California

Kimberly N. Overton
Chief Resource Prosecutor, North Carolina Conference
of District Attorneys
Cary, North Carolina

Kim Parker (ret.)
Chief Deputy District Attorney, Sedgwick County, Kansas
Boise, Idaho

Travis Stearns
Attorney, Washington Appellate Project
Seattle, Washington

The Hon. Mary Yu
Justice, Washington State Supreme Court
Olympia, Washington

Liaisons

Mark E. Schamel
National Association of Criminal Defense Lawyers
Washington, D.C.

Eric Olsen
National District Attorneys Association
Bel Air, Maryland

Jonathan Wroblewski
U.S. Department of Justice
Washington, D.C.

Lesli Caldwell Houston
National Legal Aid and Defender Association
Washington, D.C.

Standards Committee Staff
Linda Britton, Director
Shamika Dicks
Washington, D.C.

The commentary to the Dual-Status Youth Standards was approved by this Committee in October 2020. During the Standards Committee consideration of this edition, the Committee was also chaired by Bruce Green (2017–2021) of New York; John Cline (2014–2017) of San Francisco, California; and Mark Dwyer (2011–2014) of Brooklyn, New York. Susan Hillenbrand served as Standards Director from 2008–2016, Sara Elizabeth Dill served as Standards Project Director from 2016–2017, and Kevin Scruggs served as Standards Project Director until May 2016.

Task Force on Dual Jurisdiction Youth

Position and affiliation are as of the time of membership in the
Task Force and may no longer be accurate at publication.

Chair

The Hon. Ernestine Gray (ret.)
Judge, Orleans Parish Juvenile Court
New Orleans, Louisiana

Vice Chair

Robert Schwartz (ret.)
Executive Director Emeritus, Juvenile Law Center
Philadelphia, Pennsylvania

Reporters

Robert E. Shepard (1937–2008)
Professor of Law, University of Richmond Law School
Richmond, Virginia

Kristin N. Henning
Blume Professor of Law; Director, Juvenile Justice Clinic
and Initiative
Georgetown University Law Center
Washington, D.C.

Members

Jay Elliott
Private Practitioner
Columbia, South Carolina

George Mosee Jr.
Deputy District Attorney, Philadelphia District Attorney's
Office
Philadelphia, Pennsylvania

Mryna Raeder
Southwestern Law School
Los Angeles, California

Kate Richtman (ret.)
Ramsey County Attorney's Office
St. Paul, Minnesota

Liaisons

Susan Broderick
National District Attorneys Association
Bel Air, Maryland

Howard Davidson
ABA Center on Children and the Law
Washington, D.C.

Patricia Puritz
National Juvenile Defender Center (now The Gault Center)
Washington, D.C.

Rosa Hirji
Dignity in Schools Campaign
Washington, D.C.

Deborah St. Jean
Office of the Public Defender
Baltimore, Maryland

Task Force Staff

ABA CJS Standards Project Directors
Susan Hillenbrand
Kevin Scruggs
Sara Elizabeth Dill
Linda Britton

Staff Attorneys
Sarina Cox
Christopher Gowen
Kristie Kennedy

Administrative Assistant
Shamika Dicks

Current Published ABA Criminal Justice Standards

Collateral Sanctions and Discretionary Disqualification of Convicted Persons, ©2004
Criminal Appeals, ©1980, 1986 supp. (out of print)
Discovery and Trial by Jury, ©1996
DNA Evidence, ©2007
Electronic Surveillance: Section A: Private Communications, ©2002
Electronic Surveillance: Section B: Technologically Assisted Physical Surveillance,
    ©1999
Fair Trial and Public Disclosure, ©2016
Joinder and Severance, ©1980, 1986 supp. (out of print)
Juvenile Justice, ©1996
Law Enforcement Access to Third Party Records, ©2013
Mental Health, ©1986, 1989 (being updated)
Monitors and Monitoring, ©2019
Pleas of Guilty, ©1999
Postconviction Remedies, ©1980, 1986 supp. (out of print)
Pretrial Release, ©2007
Prosecution Function and Defense Function, ©1993 (being updated)
Prosecutorial Investigations, ©2014
Providing Defense Services, ©1992
Sentencing, ©1994 (being updated)
Special Functions of the Trial Judge, ©2000
Speedy Trial and Timely Resolution of Criminal Cases, ©2006
Treatment of Prisoners, ©2011

Current Standards Drafting Projects

Discovery (update)
Diversion (new)
Juvenile Justice (update)
Mental Health (update)
Prosecution Function and Defense Function (update)
Victims of Crime (new)

Order information, online access to the current Standards, and other information about the Standards project can be found at http://americanbar.org/groups/criminal_justice/standards.html.

ABA Standards for Criminal Justice

Dual Jurisdiction Youth

Table of Contents

BLACKLETTER AND COMMENTARY

PREFACE AND ACKNOWLEDGMENTS

The Criminal Justice Section commissioned the dual jurisdiction standards task force, which convened for the first time in March 2008. Its charge was to "examine how the juvenile justice system should interact with other child serving systems, such as education, child welfare (child protection), mental health. Those systems refer youth to the justice system, serve youth while they are in the juvenile justice system, and receive youth who are re-entering society from the system."

Ably led by Judge Ernestine Gray, the task force met regularly to produce the Black Letter Standards that the ABA adopted in 2017. Professor Bob Shepherd, a juvenile justice expert at the University of Richmond School of Law, was the task force's first Reporter. Bob Shepherd had been a mentor to so many of us in the juvenile justice community. Bob died in December 2008; his death was a blow to the task force's work. Good fortune beckoned, however, when Georgetown professor Kristin Henning agreed to step in as Reporter. Prof. Henning brilliantly synthesized the results of task force meetings, and her work was key to the task force's success.

The commentary to the Black Letter Standards was completed in the fall of 2020, after approval by the Section's Standards Committee. Before going to the Committee for final review, several outside readers provided thoughtful critique. These included Judge Gray and retired Minnesota prosecutor Kate Richtman, both of whom were on the standards task force; Kim Dvorchak of the National Association of Counsel for Children; and Shay Bilchik of the Center for Juvenile Justice Reform. Kris Henning also reviewed the final commentary. I am indebted to those who reviewed the commentary.Decisions about tone and content are mine in the end. This final draft is "current" as of 2020.

The standards task force was ably served by many ABA staff. I am particularly grateful to Linda Britton for her support as I worked on the commentary. Linda ably guided my drafts through the ABA process.

Bob Schwartz
Philadelphia
December 2022

Juvenile Justice Standards Relating to Dual Jurisdiction Youth

Kristin N. Henning,[1] Reporter
Commentary by Robert G. Schwartz[2]

Introduction

Youth are referred to delinquency court through numerous routes. These pathways vary by jurisdiction. Some youth are referred by prosecutors following an investigation by police; some are referred by parents; many are referred by other youth-serving systems, such as schools, child welfare agencies, mental health providers, or drug or alcohol treatment providers. Many of these youth have needs that can and should be addressed by one or more of these other systems without courts exercising delinquency jurisdiction.

Youth referred by the child welfare system to juvenile court are often referred to as "crossover youth." Dependent youth whose child welfare cases remain open simultaneously with delinquency court jurisdiction are frequently referred to as "dual-jurisdiction" or "dual-status" youth. Youth in the delinquency system who require services from multiple sources are often called "multisystem" youth.[3]

These Standards do not endorse any one definition of "crossover," "dual-jurisdiction," or "multisystem" youth. The Standards are intentionally broad to guide juvenile court and system professionals in addressing the needs and rights of these youth, however they are defined. Further, even when the Standards do not use the term

---

1. The Blume Professor of Law; Director, Juvenile Justice Clinic & Initiative, Georgetown Law.

2. Visiting Scholar, Temple University Beasley School of Law; Executive Director Emeritus, Juvenile Law Center.

3. The National Center for Juvenile Justice's JJGPS has a state-by-state "systems integration" section with information about different aspects of crossover or dual-jurisdiction youth. Unfortunately, states vary wildly in how they gather and report information about these youth. There are thus no consistent measures that allow for state comparisons. For example, some states keep records of youth served by child welfare and juvenile justice. Others only keep track of child welfare referrals to juvenile justice. Others have neither of those data sets but present different data. States are also inconsistent in the way they report their capacity for data sharing and formal or informal interagency agreements. Nevertheless, http://www.jjgps.org/ is regularly updated and is a useful source.

"crossover youth," they are written with this population in mind. (These Standards, which took ten years to develop, supplement excellent work done by others in the field. The Center for Juvenile Justice Reform (CJJR) at Georgetown University has created a Crossover Youth Practice Model (CYPM) that has shown promising results. CJJR has published rich, helpful literature on the topic.[4] Similarly, the RFK National Resource Center for Juvenile Justice has produced thoughtful resources for addressing dual-status youth.[5])

These youth have many challenges.[6] They have needs that public systems must address. Indeed, a credible body of research and an emerging body of data confirm that crossover, dual-jurisdiction, and multisystem youth have an increased need for behavioral health and educational services.[7] Youth who enter the juvenile justice system from the child welfare system are treated more harshly than their peers who are not in child welfare.[8] By promptly and accurately identifying crossover, dual-jurisdiction, and multisystem youth, and by creating appropriate protocols for handling these cases, professionals can more accurately assess cases, determine whether referral to the juvenile system is truly warranted, and identify and meet youths' needs.[9]

These Standards address the many issues that arise when youth with multiple problems and needs end up at the door of juvenile court. Under what circumstances should the juvenile justice system assume jurisdiction? How should youth who are appropriately in the

---

4. https://cjjr.georgetown.edu/resources/publications/. CJJR has significant experience involving policies and practices regarding crossover or dual-jurisdiction youth; in addition, the California Evidence-Based Clearinghouse for Child Welfare, has designated the CYPM as having Promising Research Evidence and High Relevance to Child Welfare Case Practice. *Crossover Youth Practice Model*, THE CALIFORNIA EVIDENCE-BASED CLEARINGHOUSE FOR CHILD WELFARE, https://www.cebc4cw.org/program/crossover-youth-practice-model-cypm/.

5. *Dual Status Youth Reform Resources*, ROBERT F. KENNEDY CHILDREN'S ACTION CORPS, https://rfknrcjj.org/resources/dual-status-youth/.

6. Mark E. Courtney et al., *Midwest Evaluation of the Adult Functioning of Former Foster Youth: Conditions of Youth Preparing to Leave State Care*, CHAPIN HALL CENTER FOR CHILDREN AT THE UNIVERSITY OF CHICAGO (2004), a product of Chapin Hall's three-state longitudinal study.

7. Denise C. Herz, Sharon Harada, Gregory Lecklitner, Michael Rauso & Joseph P. Ryan, *Identifying and Responding to Criminogenic Risk and Mental Health Treatment Needs of Crossover Youth*, in HANDBOOK OF VIOLENCE RISK ASSESSMENT AND TREATMENT 495–528 (Joel T. Andrade ed., New York: Springer Publishing Company 2009).

8. Joseph P. Ryan et al., *Maltreatment and Delinquency: Investigating Child Welfare Bias in Juvenile Justice Processing 29*, in CHILDREN & YOUTH SERVICES REVIEW 8 (2007).

9. The Crossover Youth Practice Model, Center for Juvenile Justice Reform, Georgetown University, 2015.

system be served? How should the juvenile justice system manage the re-entry into the community of youth with multiple needs? These Standards provide a guide to juvenile justice system professionals as they answer these questions.

School-based behavior has long been a source of referral of students to law enforcement and juvenile court. In Pennsylvania, for example, school-based arrests almost tripled from 1999 to 2007.[10] In Florida, in 2007–08, there were over 21,000 referrals from schools to the state's juvenile justice system—over two-thirds for misdemeanors.[11] In North Carolina, almost 16,500 students were referred to juvenile court by schools in 2008–09.[12] Other states have had similar histories.[13] As racial disparities in school discipline have increased as well, students of color disproportionately bear the burden of such disciplinary practices.[14]

The metaphor of "the school-to-prison pipeline" is apt. As we will see here, there is also a foster care-to-prison pipeline. These pipelines exacerbate racial disparities in the juvenile justice system, because each feeder system is itself beset by racial disparities. As I wrote many years ago:

> It is useful to think of the juvenile justice system as similar to a pipeline. . . . Along the pipeline are diversion valves, which are the decision points at which children are either diverted from the pipeline or continue

---

10. Test, Punish, and Push Out: How "Zero Tolerance" and High Stakes Testing Funnel Youth into the School-to-Prison Pipeline, Advancement Project 4 (March 2010).

11. *Id.*

12. *Id.* at 18.

13. *Id.* The only national database is the Department of Education's Civil Rights Data Collection, https://ocrdata.ed.gov/, which is spotty at best. CRDC data are only available through 2015–16. An example of underinclusive data collection is found in Lee V. Gaines, *Student Arrest Records a "Disturbing Mess" at Illinois School Districts*, Illinois Newsroom (Sept. 28, 2020), describing an Illinois school district that "has not accurately reported arrest and law enforcement referral data to the federal government for the 2013–14, 2015–16 and 2017–18 school years, . . ." with a local spokesperson attributing the problem "to the manner in which the data is stored." A 2019 ACLU report on police in schools shows that arrest levels remain high, with consistently high racial disparities. *See* "Cops and No Counselors How the Lack of School Mental Health Staff Is Harming Students," https://www.aclu.org/sites/default/files/field_document/030419-acluschooldisciplinereport.pdf.

14. Test, Punish, and Push Out, *supra* note 10, at 15, 18. In a U.S. Department of Education sample from 2009–10, over 70 percent of students involved in school-related arrests or referred to law enforcement were Hispanic or African American. Office for Civil Rights: The Transformed Civil Rights Data Collection (CRDC), https://www2.ed.gov/about/offices/list/ocr/docs/crdc-2012-data-summary.pdf. Black girls are subject to particularly high rates of school discipline and arrest. Erica L. Green, Mark Walker & Eliza Shapiro, *Racism in the Principal's Office: Seeking Justice for Black Girls*, N.Y. Times, Oct. 2, 2020, at 1.

through its various gates and locks—these are the points of arrest, detention, adjudication, disposition, and disposition review. . . . [A]t every point of the system "valves" are available to send some children home, some to other systems, and others to noninstitutional care.[15]

Adherence to these Standards will thus reduce racial disparities by affecting the pipeline in significant ways. It will reduce unnecessary referrals from systems that themselves disproportionately impact Black and Brown children, thereby reducing the number of Black and Brown children who are arrested. If they are arrested, adherence to these standards will increase diversion of Black and Brown children at every decision point in the system.

The American Bar Association, through the work of its Commission on Youth at Risk and through policies adopted by the Association, has recognized that teens who have been maltreated or who are in foster care are at high risk of being referred to the juvenile justice system:

> [T]he average juvenile delinquency rate for youth previously abused or neglected is 47% higher than for children with no abuse or neglect histories. Researchers have found children who had at least one foster care placement (many children have multiple placements) significantly more likely to find themselves subject to a delinquency court petition.[16]

In addition, recent studies have shown that more than 45 percent of youth referred to juvenile probation in some jurisdictions have a diagnosable mental health disorder.[17] That percentage is higher among youth held in juvenile detention, with one study finding roughly two-thirds of youth in detention with a diagnosable mental health

---

15. Laurence Steinberg & Robert G. Schwartz, *Developmental Psychology Goes to Court, in* YOUTH ON TRIAL: A DEVELOPMENT PERSPECTIVE ON JUVENILE JUSTICE 14 (Thomas Grisso & Robert G. Schwartz, eds., University of Chicago Press, 2000).

16. American Bar Association, ABA Policy And Report On Crossover And Dual Jurisdiction Youth (Feb. 2008), https://www.njjn.org/uploads/digital-library/resource_671.pdf. Reproduced here as Appendix I. *See also* G.R. CUSICK, M.E. COURTNEY, J. HAVLICEK & N. HESS, CRIME DURING THE TRANSITION TO ADULTHOOD: HOW YOUTH FARE AS THEY LEAVE OUT-OF-HOME CARE (Chapin Hall at the University of Chicago 2011).

17. *See, e.g.,* Gail A. Wasserman et al., *Gender Differences in Psychiatric Disorders at Juvenile Probation Intake*, 95(1) AM. J. PUB. HEALTH 131–47 (Jan. 2005). *See also* Larkin S. McReynolds et al., *Psychiatric Disorder in a Juvenile Assessment Center*, 54(2) CRIME & DELINQUENCY 313–34 (Apr. 2008) (finding 30 percent of youth referred to a juvenile assessment center in Florida had a diagnosable mental health disorder). ABA policy recognizes the high prevalence of trauma exposure suffered by youth in both the juvenile justice and child welfare systems, American Bar Association, https://www.ameri canbar.org/groups/public_interest/child_law/resources/attorneys/child-trauma/.

disorder.[18] That study also revealed that 60 percent of those with mental health disorders also meet criteria for a substance abuse disorder.

Every day, decision-makers refer some youth to the juvenile justice system, while directing others into different youth and family serving systems. Indeed, many youth in the four major youth-serving systems—education, juvenile justice, child welfare, and behavioral health (which includes mental health and drug and alcohol services)—are remarkably similar to one another, even though they may be assigned different labels. Youth can be referred to different systems based on their traits or conduct, or based on the traits or conduct of their parents, rather than by their needs or even the needs of society.

Unfortunately, this sorting process often reflects disparities in race and ethnicity.[19] Racial and ethnic disparities and disproportionality are the backdrop for these Standards. While there are references to these challenges scattered throughout this volume, readers should never overlook their insidious presence. Explicit and implicit bias leads to disproportionality and disparities in child welfare; in referrals of youth in foster care, and of students, to the juvenile justice system; and in the composition of youth in the juvenile justice system itself.[20] These Standards provide a structured approach to reducing bias's cumulative, corrosive impact.[21]

As the commentary that follows demonstrates, racism's impact is multifaceted. Involvement with the justice system is traumatic. It labels youth in ways that have lifetime consequences. Youth lose educational, employment, and housing opportunities. Fines can limit their opportunities years into adulthood. Youth lose significant opportunities for normative adolescent development. Adherence to these Standards will take some of the edge off racism's bite.

---

18. KATHLEEN R. SKOWYRA & JOSEPH J. COCOZZA, BLUEPRINT FOR CHANGE: A COMPREHENSIVE MODEL FOR THE IDENTIFICATION AND TREATMENT OF YOUTH WITH MENTAL HEALTH NEEDS IN CONTACT WITH THE JUVENILE JUSTICE SYSTEM, (National Center for Mental Health and Juvenile Justice & Policy Research Associates 2007).

19. Disproportionality occurs in both the child welfare and juvenile systems. *See* Dorothy E. Roberts, *Shattered Bonds: The Color of Child Welfare*, Civitas Books, 2002; W. Haywood Burns Institute, *Repairing the Breach: A Brief history of Youth of Color in the Justice System* (2015), at https://www.courts.ca.gov/documents/BTB24-4H-1.pdf.

20. References to disproportionality and disparities are scattered through the Commentary.

21. Georgetown Law's Juvenile Justice Initiative and the National Juvenile Defender Association have published a Racial Justice for Youth Toolkit for juvenile defenders, https://defendracialjustice.org/about-toolkit/. While access to most of the toolkit is limited to defenders, some materials are available to a larger public.

Although other systems are equipped—and even mandated—to respond to these youths' needs and to protect the public by addressing their behavior, too often youth find themselves in juvenile court. Of the dependency, education, behavioral health, and delinquency systems—the four suits in the service delivery deck—delinquency is always the trump suit. If there is any conduct that falls within the definition of a delinquent act, the juvenile court can assume jurisdiction if it chooses. Although the juvenile justice system is a service-delivery system, it is ultimately punitive as well as rehabilitative and thus should be used only when necessary. Although the juvenile justice system can help youth who are appropriately in its care, involvement in the juvenile justice system can be harmful, stigmatize the youth, and produce long-term consequences that may affect a youth for a lifetime.[22]

Although there are serious offenses for which referral to juvenile court is obviously appropriate, in many circumstances referrals are not the result of a thoughtful matching of a youth to the most appropriate system. Referral to the juvenile justice system should be carefully considered and not made for convenience or because services are not available in other systems.

These Standards give detailed implementation guidance to jurisdictions and professionals interested in implementing the American Bar Association's 2008 policy on crossover and dual-jurisdiction youth. That policy appears as Appendix I.

These Black Letter Standards also advance principles from the IJA-ABA Juvenile Justice Standards that the ABA adopted in 1980. The 1980 Standards had 20 volumes that were drafted by the best thinkers of their day. While some of those Standards have lost their potency, much is still vital. Indeed, the drafters were often prescient. The 1980 Standards anticipated these Dual-Status Standards by giving discretion to juvenile probation officers to divert cases, even when a complaint is legally sufficient.[23] Diversion is warranted in less serious cases, or when juvenile court involvement "would cause undue harm to the juvenile or exacerbate the problems that led to his or her

---

22. *See* Riya Saha Shah & Jean Strout, *Future Interrupted: the Collateral Damage Caused by Proliferation of Juvenile Records*, JUVENILE LAW CTR. (2016), https://jlc.org/resources/future-interrupted-collateral-damage-caused-proliferation-juvenile-records.

23. Juvenile Justice Standards, Standards Relating to the Juvenile Probation Function: Intake and Predisposition Investigative Services, 2.8A.

delinquent acts. . . ."[24] Diversion—decriminalizing adolescence—can and should be more routine. It is the first step in rejecting the long history of racial disproportionality in referrals to the juvenile justice system. Appendix II is a catalog of state laws on diversion—it is a tool that is routinely available to police, prosecutors, probation officers, and courts.

Events during the spring of 2020 have shown that it may be possible to reduce entry into all aspects of the juvenile justice pipeline without reducing public safety. The COVID-19 pandemic led police, juvenile probation departments, and juvenile courts to arrest fewer youth, detain fewer youth, and incarcerate fewer youth. A survey of 33 states found that detention admissions fell over 50 percent in March and April 2020, matching the decline of the prior 13 years.[25]

Public Safety and These Standards

These Standards take the lessons of the 2020 pandemic even further. They are meant to give youth opportunities to become productive adults while advancing public safety by holding youth accountable in developmentally appropriate ways. They build upon the growing body of literature, since the turn of the century, on how youth differences matter when it comes to the justice system.

These Standards recognize that most adolescent misbehavior is "normative." That is, risk-taking—such as driving too fast, underage drinking, underage sex, smoking—is genetically built into adolescence. Adolescence is a time of experimentation. Adolescents often fail

24. *Id.*

25. *Survey: 52% Drop in Admissions to Youth Detention in Two Months Matches Reduction over 13 Years*, ANNIE E. CASEY FOUND. (June 3, 2020), https://www.aecf.org/blog/survey-52-drop-in-admissions-to-youth-detention-in-two-months-matches-reduc/. As with any decline in juvenile justice numbers, there are multiple causes. For example, school closures undoubtedly led to fewer arrests; Standard 3.3 provides guidance on reducing school-based arrests when schools are open. Police may be exercising discretion differently. Youth may be staying indoors. The pandemic-related decline in arrests accelerates a 25-year trend that has been particularly pronounced in the last 15 years. Sarah Hockenberry & Charles Puzzanchera, *Juvenile Court Statistics, 2018*, NAT'L CTR. FOR STATE CTS. (Apr. 2020), https://ojjdp.ojp.gov/sites/g/files/xyckuh176/files/media/document/juvenile-court-statistics-2018.pdf?utm_source=govdelivery&utm_medium=email&utm_campaign=publications.

to see risks; and they are less able than adults to evaluate the severity of a risk or the probability of a risk occurring.[26]

Adolescent differences were at the core of the U.S. Supreme Court's *Roper v. Simmons*[27] holding that the death penalty is unconstitutional for crimes committed before a person's 18th birthday.

The *Roper* Court observed:

> First, as any parent knows and as the scientific and sociological studies respondent and his *amici* cite tend to confirm, "[a] lack of maturity and an underdeveloped sense of responsibility are found in youth more often than in adults and are more understandable among the young. These qualities often result in impetuous and ill-considered actions and decisions."[28]

The Court added that teens are more susceptible to peer pressure and negative influences than adults, pointing out that "the character of a juvenile is not as well formed as that of an adult. The personality traits of juveniles are more transitory, less fixed."[29]

Social science research has long confirmed that youth misbehavior is "transitory." A classic study of every boy born in Philadelphia in 1945 showed that a significant number of first-time offenders never offend again, and that a very small number of offenders count as chronic, serious offenders.[30] Later studies confirmed that a small percentage of youth continue to offend into their adult years.[31]

These Dual-Status Standards recognize that managing risk and addressing youths' behavior is not the province of the juvenile justice system alone. The Standards ask, and answer, questions such as:

---

26. *See, e.g.,* Laurence Steinberg, Age of Opportunity: Lessons from the New Science of Adolescence (Eamon Dolan/Houghton Mifflin Harcourt 2014); National Research Council, Reforming Juvenile Justice: A Developmental Approach (The National Academies Press 2013); David Dobbs, *The Teenage Brain,* Nat'l Geographic, Oct. 2011; Elizabeth Scott & Laurence Steinberg, Rethinking Juvenile Justice (Harvard University Press 2008); Thomas Grisso & Robert G. Schwartz, Eds., Youth on Trial: A Developmental Perspective on Juvenile Justice (University of Chicago Press 2000).

27. 543 U.S. 551 (2005).

28. *Id.* at 569 (citations omitted).

29. *Id.* at 569–70.

30. Marvin E. Wolfgang et al., Delinquency in a Birth Cohort (University of Chicago Press 1972).

31. Terrie E. Moffitt, *Adolescence-Limited and Life-Course-Persistent Antisocial Behavior: A Developmental Taxonomy,* 100(4) Psych. Rev. 674–701 (American Psychological Ass'n 1993); *See also* the comprehensive work of Edward P. Mulvey and Carol A. Schubert in the early 21st-century longitudinal Pathways to Desistance research, the products of which can be found at https://www.pathways study.pitt.edu/.

- What do we expect juvenile court to deliver in terms of services, risk management, or public policy that other systems cannot?
- When referrals are made to juvenile court, how should the juvenile justice professionals determine whether the referral is appropriate?
- When youth with multiple needs are appropriately under juvenile court jurisdiction, how can their needs be met so that society's interest in protection is satisfied while giving these youth the best opportunity to become productive citizens?

Referral to Juvenile Court

These Standards first address how the juvenile court, through judicial leadership, prudent prosecutorial discretion, thoughtful defense advocacy, and appropriate probation decisions, can control the entry of youth into the juvenile justice system. The Standards provide guidance to judges and juvenile court personnel on when and how youth who are referred by and would be better served by other systems should be diverted from the juvenile court.

Youth Who Are Appropriately in Juvenile Court

These Standards also address the court's obligation to ensure that youth who are appropriately before the juvenile court receive services from other systems, including, where appropriate, services that are normally provided by the child welfare system. The Standards address the juvenile court's continuing responsibility to determine whether, how, and for how long delinquent youth are served by more than one system.

Youth Returning to the Community from Placement and Exiting the Juvenile Justice System

Finally, these Standards address the responsibility of the juvenile justice system as a whole to plan and facilitate re-entry for youth who are dual status, regardless of who has responsibility for that function.

These Standards thus set forth a framework for how juvenile justice system professionals should make decisions about and serve youth who are referred by other systems, are involved with more than one system at a time, or have needs that should be met by more than one system.

The Standards begin in Part I with definitions of key terms and a statement of general principles.

Part II addresses structural issues that are important to system collaboration. These include the need for a sound legislative framework, cross-system protocols, and guidance on court docketing when youth and families must attend multiple hearings and administrative proceedings. Recognizing the inherent tension between a youth's right to privacy and confidentiality and the need for information sharing and data collection about youth who are involved in multiple systems, Part II also guides juvenile justice professionals in determining whether, when, and how to share and collect information.

Part III covers the many issues related to control of juvenile court jurisdiction. This part gives special attention to reducing unnecessary referrals from schools and child welfare agencies.

Part IV augments Part III by providing standards for juvenile court personnel to follow when they receive referrals of youth who are, or who are likely to become, involved with more than one system. The Standards discuss how court personnel can reject inappropriate referrals and encourage personnel to pay special attention to appropriate referrals of dual-status youth.

Part V guides court personnel in obtaining services from other systems to avoid juvenile court involvement, or to provide better treatment for youth who are appropriately in the juvenile justice system.

Parts VI and VII address adjudication and disposition of dual-status youth, paying particular attention to the guarantees of due process and the need for loyal and engaged defense attorneys.

Part VIII deals with the unique problems of re-entry, while Part IX examines appeals. Part X provides guidance on juvenile records and expungement. Parts XI and XII cover ethical obligations of prosecuting attorneys and defense counsel, respectively. Part XIII briefly touches on the special challenges of dual-status youth who are confined in detention centers.

BLACK LETTER

Part I: Definitions and General Principles

Standard 1.1   Definitions

(a) "Behavioral Health Services" are a continuum of services for individuals at risk of, or suffering from mental health or substance abuse conditions.

(b) "Best Interest Advocate" is an individual, not functioning or intending to function as a lawyer, appointed by the court to assist the court in determining the best interests of the youth.

(c) "Child Welfare System" is the legal structure including courts, residential facilities, foster care placements, and services designed to promote the well-being of youth alleged or found to be status offenders or to be abused, neglected, abandoned, homeless, or exploited, by ensuring safety, achieving permanency, improving well-being, and building the family's capacity to care for their youth successfully.

(d) "Collateral Consequences" are consequences flowing from arrest or adjudication, other than the direct dispositional order, that may impact opportunities for future education, financial aid, employment, housing, immigration status, public benefits, or other individual rights, services, or benefits.

(e) "Congregate Care Facility" is a housing facility in which each individual has a private or semi-private bedroom but shares with other residents a common dining room, recreational room, or other facilities.

(f) "Critical Youth Services" are services required for the well-being of youth, including supervision, housing, clothing, nutrition, education, recreation, and physical and behavioral healthcare.

(g) "Cultural Competence" is an ability to understand, communicate with, and effectively interact with people across different cultures and socio-economic backgrounds.

(h) "Data" is information that is captured for aggregate reporting purposes but does not identify individuals.

(i) "Delinquency" is any behavior that would be a crime if committed by an adult.

(j) "Defense Counsel" is a lawyer hired or appointed to represent a youth's expressed interest in a delinquency proceeding.

(k) "Dependency Case" is a legal proceeding involving youth and parents in the child welfare system.

(l) "Dependency Counsel" is a lawyer hired or appointed to represent a youth's expressed legal interests in a dependency case.

(m) "Diversion" is the referral of an accused youth, without adjudication of criminal or delinquency charges, to a youth service agency or other program, accompanied by a formal termination of all legal proceedings against the youth in the juvenile justice system upon successful completion of the program requirements.

(n) "Dual-Status Youth" are youth under the concurrent jurisdiction of the child welfare system and the juvenile justice system.

(o) "Dual-Status Docket" is a specialized docket within the Family Court that exercises jurisdiction over youth who are concurrently involved in the juvenile justice and child welfare systems.

(p) "Family Court" is a court with jurisdiction over one or more of the following cases involving: delinquency; abuse and neglect; status offenses; the need for emergency medical treatment or behavioral health crisis intervention; voluntary and involuntary termination of parental rights proceedings; adoption proceedings; appointments of legal guardians for juveniles; intrafamily criminal offenses; proceedings in regard to divorce, separation, annulment, alimony, custody, and support of juveniles; proceedings under the Uniform Interstate Family Support Act.

(q) "Information" is any communication—recorded or unre-corded—record, or material that may identify individuals.

(r) "Juvenile Justice System" is the legal structure including law enforcement agencies, courts, detention facilities, probationary and re-entry services for diverting, detaining, adjudicating, supervising and discharging youth alleged or found to be delinquent.

(s) "Juvenile Court" is the court and court personnel responsible for diverting, adjudicating, detaining, confining, and supervising youth alleged or found to be delinquent.

(t) "Minor Delinquent Behavior" is conduct that does not rise to the level of significant or repeated harm to others, significant or repeated property loss or damage, or a threat of significant harm to others.

(u) "Outcome" is a pre-defined, objective measure of change of limited scope.

(v) "Records" are all reports, pleadings, court orders, and other documents prepared or gathered in connection with Juvenile and Family Court proceedings.

(w) "School Resource Officer" is a certified, sworn police officer employed by a local police agency but assigned to work in a school.

(x) "Staff-secure facility" is a facility that houses a small number of residents who have the freedom to enter or leave the premises.

(y) "Status Offense" is conduct that is prohibited only for persons under the age of majority, such as truancy, curfew violations, or running away from home.

(z) "Youth" is a person who has not yet attained the age of majority or otherwise is not subject to the jurisdiction of the criminal court; or who, as a result of a delinquency petition, remains subject to the juvenile court's jurisdiction.

(aa) "Youth-Serving Agency or System" is an agency or system of agencies responsible for providing child welfare services, critical youth services, or behavioral health services.

Standard 1.2   General Principles

(a) All youth need and deserve adequate care, education, and physical and behavioral health services.

(b) Child welfare and other youth-serving agencies should not refer a youth for law enforcement intervention for minor delinquent behavior.

(c) Cooperation between the juvenile justice system and other youth-serving systems is essential in differentiating between conduct that warrants intervention by the juvenile justice system and conduct that does not warrant such intervention, developing protocols that discourage inappropriate referrals to juvenile court, and developing positive support systems and behavioral strategies that reduce referrals to juvenile court.

(d) Information-sharing between and among juvenile justice and other youth-serving agencies should be regulated to accommodate the youth's need for coordinated services, as well as the youth's need for privacy and protection against self-incrimination.

(e) Locked and staff-secure facilities should only be used after arrest, during the court process, or as a dispositional option when needed for the protection of the community or to reduce a risk of flight.

(f) Services provided to youth removed from their home or community should be provided in the least restrictive setting and a setting that is close to family, consistent with public safety and the safety of the youth.

(g) Youth receiving critical youth services, child welfare services, or behavioral health services should be entitled to continuity in those services in the least restrictive setting consistent with public safety when they are removed from their home to the custody of the juvenile or criminal justice systems.

(h) Services for youth involved in the juvenile or criminal justice systems should be provided by appropriate youth-serving agencies in the community. When a youth is in detention or custody, the youth should receive services comparable to those they would receive in the community, in a setting that is close to family.

(i)   Youth should have an opportunity to be heard, through the aid of counsel, regarding any decision that affects their physical placement, need for and selection of services, and general well-being.

(j)   The juvenile justice system should ensure that youth needing services from both the child welfare and juvenile justice systems receive the most appropriate services without adversely affecting the severity or duration of the youth's detention, placement, or probation supervision.

(k)   Arrangements for follow-up treatment, services, placement, and protection that the youth will need once released from custody should be made during the period of their confinement, be in place upon their release, and not delay release.

(l)   The child welfare system and agencies should not terminate services or close a youth's dependency case solely because the youth was arrested or adjudicated in the juvenile or criminal justice system.

(m)   Parents, guardians, and caretakers of youth involved in the juvenile justice system are entitled to respect and the opportunity to participate in decision-making involving the youth if appropriate for the youth's legal interests, safety, and well-being.

(n)   Youth released from custody should be reunited with their parents when in the youth's best interests; when reunification is not in the youth's best interest, the youth should be placed in the care of other appropriate relatives, the child welfare system, or other appropriate systems.

PART II: SYSTEMS COLLABORATION AND COORDINATION OF SERVICES FOR DUAL-STATUS YOUTH

A. STATE STRUCTURE AND LEGISLATION

Standard 2.1 Legislative Provisions for Effective Care of Dual-Status Youth

(a) State laws and policies should ensure that dual-status youth continue to receive critical youth services despite the youth's involvement in the juvenile justice system.

(b) State and federal laws should eliminate funding barriers and statutory restrictions that inhibit dual-status youth from accessing state and federal funding allocated for youth in the child welfare system.

(c) State laws should mandate and facilitate interagency planning, coordination and accountability between and among agencies that have a legal obligation to each youth.

(d) Mandatory arrest provisions in domestic violence and criminal justice statutes should not mandate arrests for youth who engage in minor delinquent behavior in congregate care facilities in the child welfare, juvenile justice, or other youth-serving systems.

Standard 2.2 Structure of State Juvenile Justice and Child Welfare Systems

(a) State systems should be structured so that:

    i. a single state agency is responsible for the licensing and regulation of programs for status offenders and delinquent and dependent youth and for ensuring that all residential facilities meet minimum licensing standards;

    ii. non-secure juvenile justice programs have access to and may utilize child welfare funding, partially covered by federal support, for family-based care and small group placements that will support youth in less restrictive, community-based settings while affording them additional protections under federal law;

iii. child welfare services are available to juvenile courts and the courts may at any appropriate stage of the juvenile court proceedings enter any order authorized for a dependent youth; and

iv. dependent youth who are not adjudicated delinquent should not be placed in residential facilities that are primarily for the care of delinquent youth.

(b) State systems should engage behavioral health, education, and child welfare agencies and ensure that crisis intervention and other services are implemented to avoid the need for arrest and referral to the juvenile justice system.

(c) States should ensure that congregate care facilities in the child welfare, juvenile justice, and other youth-serving systems are able to meet the needs of the youth they serve, including addressing minor delinquent behavior, without relying on law enforcement for discipline.

B. FAMILY COURT ORGANIZATION, POLICIES, AND PROCEDURES

Standard 2.3   Juvenile Court Policies, Protocols, and Rules

(a) Juvenile and Family Courts should establish policies and protocols that ensure the fair treatment of dual-status youth in diversion, detention, adjudication, and disposition decisions and eliminate practices that result in the unnecessary detention, adjudication, or prolonged incarceration of youth who are or should be served by the child welfare system.

(b) Juvenile and Family Courts should establish policies and protocols for delinquency complaints involving youth referred by or receiving services from the child welfare or other youth-serving systems. Such policies and protocols should:

i.   recognize the *in loco parentis* role of the child welfare agency and require the agency to fulfill the role a responsible parent would be expected to fulfill when a youth comes into contact with the juvenile justice system;

ii.   limit secure confinement to situations in which the youth meets detention criteria applied to other youth and ensure that a youth who does not have an intact home to which to return is not securely detained solely as a result of the youth's family status;

iii. set strict timelines for the completion of the juvenile intake process;

iv.   establish a process to determine whether a youth is better served in the juvenile justice system, the child welfare system, or by concurrent jurisdiction of the two;

v.   develop procedures for providing accommodations to youth with disabilities;

vi.   permit concurrent jurisdiction by the child welfare and juvenile justice systems when appropriate, and

vii. provide that a youth's arrest or adjudication of delinquency will not result in the closure of a child welfare case or the termination of services from other youth-serving agencies solely because of the youth's involvement in the juvenile justice system.

(c) Consistent with standards concerning information sharing and confidentiality in these standards and state and federal laws governing confidentiality and privilege, juvenile courts should develop policies and protocols for the prompt notification of a youth's caregiver, child welfare caseworker, and attorney, and for the involvement of other youth-serving agencies as appropriate when a youth is arrested or referred to the juvenile court.

Standard 2.4   Juvenile Court Leadership

Juvenile courts should exercise leadership in developing working relationships and protocols with community agencies serving youth and families with multiple legal issues and in need of services from multiple systems.

Standard 2.5   Juvenile and Criminal Court Jurisdiction

(a)   State laws governing the transfer of youth from juvenile court to adult court or from adult court to juvenile court should require probation officers, prosecutors, and juvenile court judges to consider the dual-status youth's need for services from the child welfare and other youth-serving agencies in determining whether transfer is appropriate. The attorney for the youth should have an opportunity to present evidence as to the youth's need for child welfare services.

(b)   Juvenile courts should consider whether the child welfare and other youth-serving systems have fulfilled their duties to a youth before considering whether to transfer the youth to criminal court and should establish protocols to ensure that youth who receive services from multiple systems are not disadvantaged in discretionary transfer decisions solely due to their involvement in other systems.

(c)   Consistent with public safety, state laws should permit transfer of youth from the criminal court to the juvenile court when the youth needs services from the child welfare, juvenile justice, or other youth-serving agencies.

(d)   If a youth is transferred or has a case originally filed in criminal court, the youth should still be eligible for child welfare services, including social service placements and programs.

Standard 2.6   Dependency Jurisdiction

(a)   Dependency courts should develop protocols that:

i.   acknowledge the *in loco parentis* role of the child welfare agency and require the agency to fulfill the role a responsible parent would be expected to fulfill when a youth comes into contact with the juvenile justice system;

ii.   ensure that a youth's arrest or adjudication of delinquency will not result in the closure of a child welfare case or the termination of services from other youth-serving agencies solely because of the youth's involvement in the juvenile justice system;

iii. prevent the use of civil and criminal contempt violations in the child welfare system as a basis for a delinquency petition;

iv.   facilitate coordination, planning and accountability when the child welfare and juvenile justice systems have concurrent jurisdiction over the youth;

v.   ensure that a youth's defense counsel receives notice when the youth becomes involved in the child welfare system; and

vi.   ensure that a youth's dependency counsel receives notice when the youth becomes involved in the juvenile justice system.

(b)   State laws should ensure that youth have a right to defense counsel and a court hearing at which they have the right to testify, present evidence, and cross-examine witnesses on the youth's need for child welfare services and whether their dependency case will be terminated after an arrest or referral to juvenile or criminal court.

Standard 2.7   Docketing Proceedings Involving Dual-Status Youth

(a)   In scheduling delinquency and other Family Court proceedings, clerks and other court personnel should be attentive to the youth's and family's obligation to appear in other legal proceedings. Court personnel should communicate with the youth and family to reduce multiple trips to court and court-related appointments and to avoid scheduling conflicts, school absences, and other avoidable inconveniences.

(b) Consistent with standards related to information sharing and confidentiality in these Standards and state and federal laws governing confidentiality and evidentiary privilege, juvenile court staff should have access to the docket of all Family Court cases so they can identify youth and families with multiple legal proceedings within the court.

(c) The same judge should consider all legal issues that involve the same family; however, to ensure fundamental fairness, each youth should have:

   i.   a lawyer at all stages of a delinquency and dependency case, including the intake, adjudicatory, disposition, post-disposition, and appellate stages;

   ii. an adjudicatory hearing at which each charge of delinquency will be considered by a neutral judicial officer as consistent with due process and fundamental fairness;

   iii. the right to notice of all hearings and case staffing or case management conferences related to the youth's cases; and

   iv. the right to attend all hearings and case conferences related to the youth's cases and a meaningful opportunity to be heard as to the youth's strengths, interests, disabilities, needs, and preferences regarding placement, services, and case outcomes.

(d) Juvenile and Family Courts should develop policies that allow for the consolidation of post-adjudication matters involving dual-status youth. The policies should be consistent with the following principles:

   i.   When feasible, a single judge should hear all dispositional and post-dispositional matters involving dual-status youth.

   ii. After a youth has been adjudicated delinquent, the youth's juvenile court dispositional proceedings should be consolidated with child welfare and other Family Court proceedings concerning the youth.

      iii. The court should ensure continuity of legal representation for the youth throughout all phases of the delinquency matter, including disposition.

      iv. The court should require that representatives responsible for case management and supervision of the youth in the child welfare and juvenile justice systems attend the consolidated proceeding.

      v. The court should ensure, to the extent consistent with the missions of the child welfare and juvenile justice systems, that youth and family case plans be aligned in terms of goals, permanency planning, services, and responsibility for implementation.

(e) To the extent possible, services and other legal proceedings in the child welfare system should not be delayed pending resolution of a delinquency case, unless the youth or the youth's defense counsel believes such a delay is necessary.

Standard 2.8   Designated Dual-Status Dockets

(a) A jurisdiction should have authority to create a specialized dual-status docket for youth involved in both the juvenile and the child welfare systems, if it finds that the traditional juvenile court cannot effectively address cases involving youth with particular needs or characteristics.

(b) Dual-status dockets should be developed and implemented by an interdisciplinary team that includes representatives from the judiciary, prosecution, defense bar, best interest advocates, families, and relevant service providers.

(c) Youth assigned to a dual-status docket should have access to services from all systems that have expertise related to the youth's needs.

(d) Dual-status dockets should provide an opportunity for youth to be diverted from the juvenile justice system or benefit from alternatives to detention at the pre-trial and disposition stage of the delinquency case.

(e) Judges presiding over dual-status dockets should utilize incentives for positive behavior, graduated responses to negative behavior, close judicial oversight, a team approach, coordination of services, and meaningful re-entry strategies.

(f) Judges presiding over dual-status dockets should ensure that any sanctions imposed serve a rehabilitative purpose.

(g) Courts with a dual-status docket should have rigorous intake and screening procedures to ensure the Court accepts only those youth who are appropriate for the dual-status docket.

(h) The interdisciplinary team responsible for developing a dual-status docket should adopt policies and protocols that ensure that:

   i.   the youth's due process rights are protected at all stages of the delinquency case, including the youth's right to a fair and impartial hearing at the adjudicatory and disposition stages of the case;

   ii. the parents' due process rights are protected at all stages of the dependency case, including the parents' right to a fair and impartial hearing to adjudicate any allegation of abuse or neglect;

   iii. the youth and the youth's defense counsel have a right to be heard and participate in all decisions regarding the youth's placement and service plan;

   iv. youth and parents with disabilities receive accommodations necessary to ensure meaningful participation at all stages of the case; and

   v.   when the youth is not diverted from the juvenile justice system before adjudication, the youth's dependency case should not be consolidated with a delinquency case on a dual-status docket unless and until there is an adjudication of delinquency.

(i) Dual-status dockets should be presided over by a judge instead of a referee, master, or magistrate.

(j) A judge presiding over a dual-status docket should have authority to dismiss the delinquency petition for a youth who has successfully completed the requirements set by the dual-status court.

C. INTERSTATE COOPERATION

Standard 2.9   Dual-Status Youth Crossing State and Local Jurisdictions

(a)   Courts and state legislatures, individually or with neighboring states, should develop policies and procedures consistent with the Interstate Compact for Juveniles, the Interstate Compact on the Placement of Children, and the Uniform Child Custody and Jurisdiction Act that will facilitate cooperation by justice system personnel and youth-serving agencies in addressing cross-jurisdictional issues.

(b)   Policies and procedures for cross-jurisdictional cooperation should focus on:

    i.   reducing delay, uncertainty, and unnecessary detention of youth,

    ii.   providing prompt resolution of legal matters involving dual-status youth,

    iii.   expediting the necessary transport of dual-status youth across jurisdictions, and

    iv.   avoiding scheduling conflicts for youth and families with legal obligations in multiple jurisdictions.

(c)   Policies and procedures should adopt a presumption that legal proceedings will take place in the jurisdiction where the youth has the most significant ties.

(d)   Policies and procedures to facilitate cross-jurisdictional cooperation should abide by principles of confidentiality and privacy.

D. INFORMATION SHARING AND DATA COLLECTION

Standard 2.10   Purposes of Information Sharing and Data Collection

(a)   Information sharing and data collection are necessary for any effective collaboration and coordination of services for dual-status youth.

(b) States should authorize and facilitate the sharing of information about individual youth between and among multiple systems and agencies to

    i. reduce duplication of assessments and services for the youth and the youth's family,

    ii. enhance understanding of the youth's strengths, interests, preferences, needs, and

    iii. improve individual case planning and decision-making for the youth.

(c) States should authorize and facilitate the collection of data for aggregate reporting on the characteristics of dual-status youth and the processes for handling those youth.

(d) States should use data:

    i. to improve the policies, practices, and coordinated responses of agencies responsible for the care of and provision of services to dual-status youth, and

    ii. to evaluate the need for and effectiveness of programs and practices designed to achieve improved outcomes for youth.

Standard 2.11   Policies and Procedures for Confidentiality during Information Sharing

(a) All states should develop and require the use of protocols for information sharing about individual dual-status youth from arrest to termination of jurisdiction.

(b) All agreements or protocols to share information between the juvenile justice system and other youth-serving systems and agencies should ensure that information-sharing protocols provide appropriate protection for the privacy of youth and their families and follow federal and state law and ethical requirements regarding confidentiality of privileged information.

(c) All agreements or protocols should specify the purposes of information sharing and limit the information shared to the specified purposes.

(d) States should limit the use of information about the youth's involvement in multiple systems to the coordination of case management and the continuity and integration of services and treatment. Protocols should:

   i.   prohibit the unauthorized disclosure of, or unauthorized access to, information relating to the dual-status youth, and

   ii. develop quality control measures that minimize the inadvertent disclosure of information relating to the youth.

(e) Absent an explicit exception under applicable state and federal law, juvenile justice agencies and professionals should always obtain informed written consent from the youth and the parent or guardian of the youth, before sharing personally identifiable information between agencies serving the youth. Youth, parents, or guardians with disabilities should receive accommodations necessary to provide informed consent.

(f) Any written consent for information sharing should state the purpose of sharing, the specific information to be shared, and the time frame within which the information will be shared.

(g) Information about dual-status youth should be shared with and used by youth-serving agencies in a manner that complies with state and federal laws governing confidentiality, including re-disclosure and privilege, and protects the youth's right against self-incrimination and right to due process as a respondent or defendant in any delinquency, criminal, summary offense, status offense, or child welfare case.

(h) Juvenile justice officials sharing information about dual-status youth should ensure that any youth-serving agency and system receiving that information is aware of and adheres to rules and standards governing confidentiality of Family Court records, including restrictions on the dissemination of physical and behavioral health records and limitations on the use of records for specified purposes.

(i) The juvenile court and other youth-serving agencies should develop docketing, filing, and records-disclosure systems that will allow court staff to redact and separate records and information that may be disclosed from those that may not be disclosed pursuant to state and federal confidentiality laws.

Standard 2.12   Data Collection for Law, Policy, and Program Development

(a) Courts, legislatures, and state agencies should develop a system for collecting, reporting, and sharing data regarding dual-status youth to achieve one or more of the purposes identified in Standard 2.10 of these standards.

(b) Courts, legislatures, and state agencies should use data collection to improve outcomes for dual-status youth and to reduce unnecessary referral to and penetration into the juvenile and criminal justice systems.

(c) Lawyers, judges, and other government agents should ensure that data collection protocols comply with applicable rules regarding confidentiality.

(d) Courts and state legislatures should periodically review the aggregate data collected to determine how to allocate resources to youth-serving agencies and systems within the jurisdiction, to improve procedures for handling youth who engage in delinquent behavior while in the care or custody of a youth-serving agency, and to improve the continuity of care for youth in multiple youth-serving systems.

Standard 2.13   Access to Court Records

(a) The use of and access to Family Court records should be strictly controlled to limit the risk of unnecessary and harmful disclosure.

(b) Court records involving youth alleged or adjudicated delinquent or dependent should normally be closed to the general public.

(c) Juvenile justice officials who disclose information about dual-status youth should ensure that all recipients of that information are informed of all rules and standards governing confidentiality of Family Court records.

(d) Courts and state legislatures should develop and enforce meaningful sanctions for the unlawful dissemination of Family Court records.

(e) Juvenile justice professionals who disclose information about dual-status youth should separate records that may be disclosed from those that may not be disclosed and redact disclosed records accordingly.

(f) Defense counsel in any juvenile or criminal case in which a youth is involved should normally have access to all Family Court records involving the youth.

(g) The Family Court should avoid standing orders or policies that grant the public, court staff, juvenile justice officials, or other youth-serving agencies broad access to any category of records generally found within a Family Court file. Instead, the Court should develop policies and protocols to grant access to such records only after a judicial officer or appropriate designate makes an individualized analysis of a records request.

Standard 2.14   Waivers of Confidentiality

(a) Juvenile justice or other youth-serving agency officials may ask a youth to waive confidentiality protections.

(b) A youth's waiver is valid only if it is made knowingly, intelligently, and voluntarily.

(c) If a youth has appointed or retained counsel, agency officials should permit the youth an opportunity to consult with counsel before waiving any confidentiality protections. Waivers obtained without such an opportunity should be considered presumptively invalid.

(d) In advising a youth regarding a possible waiver of confidentiality, the youth's lawyer should ensure the youth understands privilege, the youth's rights with respect to consent and confidentiality, and the potential consequences of waiving confidentiality or privilege in releasing information to others.

(e) Agency officials should allow a youth to consult with a parent or guardian before waiving any confidentiality protections; but a parent cannot waive the youth's rights or privileges. In a delinquency proceeding, the decision to waive should be the youth's.

(f) Any written waiver form should use youth-appropriate language and be written in a language the youth speaks or understands. If a youth has limited literacy, any waiver should be obtained and recorded in a manner that is understandable to the youth.

(g) A youth may negotiate the terms of the waiver to limit the time, scope or purpose of the waiver.

(h) A parent or guardian may waive confidentiality protections for records involving the parent.

E. CROSS-SYSTEM TRAINING

Standard 2.15   Need for Cross-System Training

(a) Family Courts and youth-serving agencies should promote training for all professionals in the juvenile justice and child welfare systems to reduce inappropriate referrals to the juvenile justice system.

(b) Training should include:

i. the scope and availability of services and means for accessing services from the child welfare, behavioral health, physical health, public benefits, Family Court, and education systems;

ii. information regarding any memoranda of understanding or other agreements between and among the various youth-serving agencies regarding the provision of services for youth;

iii. laws, rules, and procedures applicable to confidentiality and privilege;

iv. the role of the youth's defense counsel and best interest advocate for the youth;

v.   child and adolescent development, brain development, disabilities, trauma, and resiliency development;

vi.   sexual orientation and gender-identity;

vii.   cultural competence;

viii.   racial bias;

ix.   evidence-based research on the effectiveness of services and programs in achieving good outcomes for youth in the juvenile justice and child welfare systems;

x.   family and youth engagement; and

xi.   the immigration consequences of the youth's involvement in the child welfare or juvenile justice system.

PART III: ARREST AND REFERRALS TO THE JUVENILE JUSTICE SYSTEM

Standard 3.1   Guidelines for Child Welfare Agencies

(a) Child welfare agencies should adopt policies discouraging staff from referring youth to the juvenile justice system for minor delinquent behavior.

(b) Child welfare agencies should have protocols for responding to delinquent and status offense behavior by youth in their care. These protocols should:

    i.   be developed in consultation with representatives of other youth-serving agencies, including the juvenile court, probation, behavioral health, schools, law enforcement, prosecution, defense, best interest advocates, and community service providers;

    ii.   set forth the specific procedures to be followed when a youth violates rules of a program or placement or engages in behavior that poses a threat to others in a program or placement;

    iii.   specify behavioral support or staffing strategies that agencies should utilize instead of referral to law enforcement;

    iv.   be in writing, made available to agency staff and youth served by the agency, and be incorporated into any agency staff training; and

    v.   provide for periodic review and revision of the protocols.

(c) Staff in child welfare or other youth-serving agencies and facilities should be trained in crisis intervention techniques, including strategies to de-escalate youth behavior arising out of behavioral health or other disability-related needs, and such techniques should be employed first, before any law enforcement referral.

(d) Public child welfare agencies that contract with private service providers should, in the contracts, set forth the circumstances under which those agencies may refer youth to law enforcement and provide guidance on alternatives to law enforcement and juvenile court referrals in case of a behavioral crisis or placement concerns.

Standard 3.2   Responsibilities of Law Enforcement in Responding to Referrals Involving Dual-Status Youth

(a) In deciding whether to arrest, divert, warn, detain, or refer a youth to the juvenile court, law enforcement officers should:

   i.   have a presumption against arresting youth who have been referred from the child welfare system to the juvenile justice system for minor delinquent behavior; and

   ii. consider whether the youth is or can be engaged with other youth-serving systems or agencies that will work to ensure the youth's appearance in court, divert the youth from custody or supervision, and minimize the youth's risk to public safety.

(b) Law enforcement agencies should develop inter-agency crisis intervention strategies that discourage arrests of youth experiencing emergency behavioral health crises that do not create a serious risk to public safety.

(c) If a youth needs emergency psychiatric or other behavioral health intervention, law enforcement officers should contact a behavioral health mobile crisis team; if such a team is not available, the officers should take the youth into custody without arrest and transport them to an appropriate crisis intervention facility.

(d) When a youth appears to be homeless, a runaway, or declines to give home contact information, the law enforcement agency should determine whether the youth is under the care or supervision of the child welfare agency, and if not should determine whether the youth should be referred to an appropriate youth-serving agency.

(e) Law enforcement should notify the caregiver or welfare caseworker of any youth who is arrested while committed to a child welfare agency.

Standard 3.3   Responsibilities of Law Enforcement, Schools, and Juvenile Courts in Responding to School-Related Conduct

(a) The primary authority responsible for school climate, discipline, and school safety is the school principal. Police should not be deployed in schools absent a significant showing of a demonstrable, time-limited need to protect students. If police are to be deployed in schools, memoranda of understanding and guidelines regarding their interaction with school officials and the scope and parameters of their authority should be established consistent with the principles set forth in these standards.

(b) Law enforcement, including school resource officers (hereinafter SROs), should not arrest or refer youth to the juvenile justice system for minor delinquent conduct at school and should not have primary responsibility for the enforcement of school discipline.

(c) Law enforcement personnel interacting with youth in schools should interact with students in ways that foster positive relationships and promote a better understanding of each other and should not be limited to arrest and law enforcement.

(d) Schools should adopt written policies and establish protocols limiting the presence and use of SROs in accordance with the principles set forth in section (e) below. Law enforcement, including SROs, should not be assigned within schools on a permanent basis, and school and law enforcement officials should periodically reassess the need for law enforcement presence and use.

(e) Formal law enforcement intervention includes issuance of a citation, ticket, or summons, filing of a delinquency petition, referral to a probation office, searches, use of restraints, or actual arrest. Law enforcement officials should not initiate formal law enforcement intervention for school-related conduct except as permitted in written protocols developed in accord with principles set forth in section (f) below.

(f)   Law enforcement agencies should work with school officials to develop written protocols to ensure that referrals to the juvenile court from schools are not for behavior that is more appropriately handled by the school. Such protocols should:

　　i.   allow law enforcement officials, including SROs, to transport a truant youth back to school without an arrest or referral to the juvenile justice system, and encourage school officials to develop educational programs, social services, and public health responses to truancy in lieu of arrest;

　　ii.   promote programs that are preventive, educational, and recreational to guide young people away from negative behaviors;

　　iii.   develop guidelines that limit disruption in educational placement or receipt of educational services resulting from law enforcement intervention;

　　iv.   encourage schools to implement disciplinary practices that:

　　　　a.   are age and developmentally appropriate;

　　　　b.   are culturally competent;

　　　　c.   engage the youth and family; and

　　　　d.   take into account that a student's behavior may be related to a disability;

　　v.   reject zero tolerance policies and mandatory suspension, expulsion, arrest, or referrals of students to juvenile or criminal court without regard to the circumstances or nature of the offense or the student's disability or history.

(g)   Students should be involved in the development of school-law enforcement protocols and memoranda of understanding.

(h)   Law enforcement personnel, including SROs, who may have contact with students, especially those students who may be involved in the child welfare system, should receive extensive training that includes the following topics:

    i.   youth and adolescent development and psychology;

    ii.   the effects of neglect, abuse, and trauma, including the exposure to violence;

    iii. the effects of disabilities on behavior and the effects of medication taken to ameliorate the symptoms of disabilities;

    iv. common disabilities for youth and the protections afforded to youth under the Individuals with Disabilities Education Act (IDEA);

    v.   conflict resolution, peer mediation, and restorative justice techniques;

    vi. cultural competence and gender and sexuality sensitivity; and

    vii. research-based practices in de-escalation and alternative responses to the use of restraints against youth except in situations involving an arrest and serious and immediate threat to the physical safety or health of a member of the school community.

(i)   Both school districts and law enforcement should maintain data to assist in evaluating the presence and use of law enforcement, including SROs. Each data point should be disaggregated by offense, student's age, grade level, race, sex, disability status, eligibility for free or reduced lunch, English language proficiency, and disposition. Data collection should include the number of:

    i.   law enforcement personnel, including SROs, deployed to each school;

    ii.   school-based arrests (arrests of students that occur on school grounds during the school day or on school grounds during school-sponsored events) at each school;

    iii. referrals to the juvenile justice system for each school;

    iv. citations, summons or other actions taken by police personnel for each school; and

    v.   suspensions, in and out of school, and expulsions at each school.

(j)   Juvenile courts and law enforcement should not inform a school of a student's involvement in the court system for conduct which occurred off school grounds unless the conduct is likely to have an impact on school safety.

(k)   Juvenile courts should annually review all data collected on school-based referrals to identify high rates of referral from particular schools or for a particular youth demographic. If referrals are for a disproportionately high rate of referral for youth of color, the juvenile court and law enforcement officials should work with schools to develop protocols that will reduce unnecessary or inappropriate referrals from the schools and reduce disproportionality.

(l)   Legislatures should repeal or amend laws, including zero tolerance laws that require schools to refer youth to law enforcement agencies for minor delinquent behavior.

(m) Legislatures should protect the confidentiality of Family Court records by amending statutes that require courts and/ or law enforcement agencies to notify schools about arrests to prohibit such notification unless the student conduct is likely to have an impact on school safety.

Standard 3.4   Responsibilities of Child Welfare and Juvenile Justice Agencies in Addressing the Educational Needs of Dual-Status Youth

(a)   Child welfare and juvenile justice agencies should work with local school districts to develop inter-agency agreements that:

   i.   allow youth to remain in the same school, when practicable, even when the agency places a youth outside the school district area;

   ii. ensure the timely transfer of education records and credit information to whatever school a youth will attend; and

   iii. ensure a seamless re-entry of students discharged from a child welfare or juvenile justice placement back to the youth's home school.

(b) Child welfare and juvenile justice agencies should work with the relevant school district to ensure that every youth in out-of-home placement receives an education appropriate for the youth's grade level, special educational needs, and academic or career goals.

PART IV: JUVENILE INTAKE AND DETENTION

Standard 4.1 Responsibilities of Probation Offices at Intake

(a) Probation staff should develop written protocols to guide intake decisions and guard against the inappropriate processing of dual-status youth in the juvenile justice system. Protocols should:

    i. encourage the diversion of dual-status youth who engage in minor delinquent behavior from the juvenile justice system; and

    ii. encourage the delivery of services through youth-serving systems other than the juvenile justice system.

(b) Consistent with Standard 2.11 of these standards concerning Information Sharing, probation staff should examine relevant databases to determine whether a youth or a youth's family is or has been involved in other youth-serving systems.

(c) In deciding whether to recommend action or inaction by the juvenile court for a youth referred from the child welfare system, probation staff should consider:

    i. the seriousness of the offense;

    ii. any information about the youth's mental health status, treatment history, prescribed medications, educational status, and care and supervision by other youth-serving agencies and systems;

    iii. whether and to what extent the alleged behavior was related to the youth's disabilities, mental health issues, exposure to violence, prior placement deficiencies, substance abuse, or other identifiable factors;

    iv. whether the child welfare system made reasonable efforts to improve the youth's placement or services and prevent the referral to juvenile court;

      v.   whether services for the youth or family, such as crisis intervention or respite, could alleviate the need for a delinquency court referral; and

      vi.   whether the juvenile justice system has non-confinement placements that are appropriate for the youth.

(d) Probation staff should not recommend a delinquency petition if the youth's conduct is more appropriately addressed by another youth-serving agency or system. Probation staff should avoid:

      i.   duplication of services when the youth is already receiving or may receive similar services from a less restrictive, less coercive agency outside of the juvenile justice system; and

      ii.   processing the youth in the juvenile justice system when the juvenile justice system cannot effectively serve the youth because of the youth's developmental limitations, disabilities, or other cognitive or mental health impairments.

(e) Probation staff should refer dual-status youth for community-based services that are suitable for the youth's age, ethnicity, gender or sexual identity, cognitive disability, and developmental stage.

Standard 4.2   Responsibilities of Judges and Probation Offices in Recommending Detention or Release

(a) Probation offices should adopt written protocols and develop risk assessment instruments to guide detention and release decisions involving dual-status youth.

(b) In deciding whether to recommend detention or release for youth referred from the child welfare system, probation staff should use the same criteria applied to other youth. Those criteria should be objective and determine whether the youth poses a risk of danger to the community or failing to appear. Other criteria should include:

    i.   the existence of services available from other youth-serving agencies to address the youth's needs and reduce the youth's risk of flight or risk to public safety; and

    ii.   whether detention will jeopardize placement or services provided by other youth-serving agencies.

(c)   Probation staff should not recommend detention:

    i.   because the youth is awaiting suitable placement in the child welfare system;

    ii.   as a respite for caregivers in the child welfare system; or

    iii. when other youth-serving systems are providing or can provide placement and services that protect the court's and the public's interests.

(d)   The intake officer should not recommend detention in a facility that cannot adequately meet a youth's special, physical, or behavioral health needs.

(e)   If a youth is detained, probation staff should, consistent with Standard 2.11 of these standards concerning Information Sharing:

    i.   advise other agencies currently serving the youth that detention is temporary, and seek to preserve the placement and services the youth is receiving from those agencies;

    ii.   provide detention staff with information about the youth's strengths, interests, preference, educational needs, and physical or behavioral health needs; and

    iii. facilitate communication between the detention staff and other agencies serving the youth.

Standard 4.3 Diverting Delinquency to Dependency and Maintaining Dual jurisdiction

(a)   Juvenile court judges have authority to divert a delinquency petition to a child welfare or status offense petition.

(b)   The decision to dismiss or divert should be made as early as possible.

(c)   A judge presiding over child welfare proceedings should be authorized, when the youth is facing delinquency proceedings or has been adjudicated delinquent, to keep the child welfare matter open so the youth may receive necessary child welfare services.

Standard 4.4   Judicial Responsibilities Regarding Detention

(a)   In deciding whether to order detention or release for youth referred from the child welfare system, the juvenile court judge should use the same criteria applied to other youth. Those criteria should be objective and determine whether the youth poses a risk of danger to the community or failing to appear. Other criteria should include:

   i.   the existence of services available from other youth-serving agencies to address the youth's needs and reduce the youth's risk of flight or risk to public safety; and

   ii.   whether detention will jeopardize placement or services provided by other youth-serving agencies.

(b)   The juvenile court judge should not order detention:

   i.   because the youth is awaiting suitable placement in the child welfare system;

   ii.   as a respite for caregivers in the child welfare system; or

   iii. when other youth-serving systems are providing or can provide placement and services protect the court's and the public's interests.

(c)   The juvenile court judge should not order detention in a facility that cannot adequately meet a youth's physical or behavioral health needs.

(d)   A judge who has concurrent jurisdiction over delinquency and child welfare matters may order the appropriate child welfare agencies to:

   i.   arrange a suitable nonsecure placement for a youth as an alternative to detention in the juvenile justice system; or

   ii.   continue providing services for a youth in detention.

Standard 4.5   Intake and Detention of Pregnant or Parenting Youth

(a) Juvenile justice professionals should develop protocols to ensure that pregnant or parenting youth in the juvenile justice system have:

   i.   basic support and critical services to reduce the risk that they will engage in abusive or neglectful behavior toward their own children;

   ii. physical and behavioral health services commonly provided for high risk pregnancy and child-rearing;

   iii. alternatives to detention and pretrial release and disposition plans that address the youth's needs in caring for their own children;

   iv. opportunities for detained youth to visit with and engage their children; and

   v.   opportunities for parenting, financial management, and independent living skills training.

(b) When addressing alleged behavior by pregnant or parenting youth, juvenile justice professionals should seek to minimize harm to the health of the youth's child and minimize disruption in the child's living arrangements.

(c) Juvenile justice professionals should give special consideration to alternatives to detention during a youth's pregnancy and at least the first year of the newborn's life.

(d) When a judge detains a pregnant youth, juvenile justice professionals should address special prenatal needs of the youth by ensuring:

   i.   adequate prenatal care, including regular doctor visits, child-birth classes, and dietary supplements;

   ii. sanitary living conditions to reduce the risk of trauma and infection;

   iii. access to reproductive health counseling; and

   iv. no use of physical restraints during the term of pregnancy unless there are serious and immediate risks to the safety of the youth or others, in which case the least restrictive means of restraint should be used.

(e) During labor and delivery for detained youth, juvenile justice authorities should ensure that:

    i.   the detained youth is transported to an appropriate medical facility without delay, and

    ii.   shackles or other restraints are not used.

(f) After delivery, juvenile justice professionals should allow the mother and child to be together at least the first year, in the least restrictive placement possible. Professionals should:

    i.   develop re-entry plans that focus specifically on pregnant and parenting youth;

    ii.   ensure that parenting youth are provided appropriate postnatal care and services, including parenting classes, continued doctor visits, and behavioral health services as appropriate;

    iii. facilitating placements that permit the child to reside with a parent or, if not possible or in the best interests of the child, facilitate visits between the youthful parent and their child, including overnight and contact visits; and

    iv. facilitate visits with family or other caregivers providing care for the youth's child.

(g) Any diversion, disposition, and re-entry plan developed for pregnant or parenting youth should seek to reduce the chance that the youth's child will be placed in the child welfare system.

PART V: REFERRING YOUTH FOR SERVICES

Standard 5.1   Accessing Behavioral Health Services

(a)   To reduce the high rates of mental health and substance abuse conditions among dual-status youth, every jurisdiction should have a system that:

    i.   provides for early identification of youth in the child welfare and juvenile justice systems who have mental health or substance abuse conditions;

    ii.   seeks to prevent the unnecessary involvement in the juvenile justice system of children who need mental health or substance abuse services; and

    iii.   provides for timely access by youth in the child welfare system to appropriate mental health treatment by qualified professionals within the least restrictive setting that is consistent with public needs and reduces the risk of delinquent behavior by these youth.

(b)   A comprehensive system to address youth with mental health or substance abuse disorders should provide:

    i.   screening and assessment at entry and key points in the child welfare and juvenile justice processes;

    ii.   a continuum of evidence-based services at all stages of the youth's involvement in the child welfare and juvenile justice systems, including short-term interventions and crisis services, on-going supportive services, and continuity of care;

    iii.   family involvement in the least restrictive setting;

    iv.   protections against self-incrimination when youth participate in court-ordered mental health or substance abuse screening, assessment, and treatment; and

    v.   sustainable funding mechanisms to support the above.

(c) Juvenile justice authorities should have authority to obtain services from other youth-serving systems, including state and local child welfare, physical and behavioral health, physical health, educational, and alcohol and drug abuse treatment systems.

(d) Juvenile and child welfare courts should have authority to obtain services for youth with mental health and substance abuse conditions without having to alter the legal custody of the youth or transfer jurisdiction to another court or system.

PART VI: DELINQUENCY ADJUDICATION OF DUAL-STATUS YOUTH

Standard 6.1 Due Process at Adjudicatory Hearing

Charges of delinquency should be adjudicated at a full due process hearing by a judge who is a neutral fact-finder. The juvenile court judge should:

(a) not be influenced by knowledge of or prior interactions with the youth or the youth's family in a dependency case or other legal matters;

(b) make a determination of delinquency based on admissible evidence in the delinquency record; and

(c) not review information relating to the youth's involvement in a dependency case unless:

i. review is requested by a party to the delinquency case, and

ii. the information is relevant and appropriate for judicial review under applicable rules of evidence.

Standard 6.2 Legal Representation in a Delinquency Case

(a) Youth charged with delinquency are entitled to competent, loyal, and zealous representation by defense counsel. A "best interests" advocate for a child in a dependency proceeding should not also serve as the youth's defense counsel in a delinquency case.

(b) Incriminating statements made by a youth to a best interest advocate who is not bound by the rules of the attorney-client confidentiality should be inadmissible in a delinquency hearing absent a knowing, voluntary, and intelligent waiver.

PART VII: DISPOSITION OF DELINQUENCY CASES

Standard 7.1   Information Gathering and Information Sharing For Disposition

After adjudication, records relating to a youth's child welfare case may be reviewed by the juvenile court to:

(a) avoid conflicting court orders;

(b) ensure effective case management; and

(c) assist in the development of an effective disposition plan.

Standard 7.2   Disposition Process

(a) If a youth is adjudicated delinquent, the court should hold a full due process hearing to determine the youth's appropriate disposition. The youth's disposition hearing should be consolidated with child welfare proceedings involving the youth if the court determines that such proceedings will advance the best interests of the youth and promote efficient and effective coordination of services. Youth and family members with disabilities should receive accommodations necessary for meaningful participation in the proceedings.

(b) Risk or needs assessment tools used in disposition planning for dual-status youth should be validated and targeted to achieve the youth's best long-term interests in either the child welfare or delinquency system.

(c) Results of any risk or needs assessment tools should be in writing and provided to the parties, and any persons who administered the tool should be available for examination by the parties.

(d) Jurisdictions should develop protocols and teams to aid disposition planning for dual-status youth. Such teams should include representatives from youth-serving agencies necessary to address the youth's needs, as well as the youth, the youth's parents, guardian or caretaker, defense counsel, best interest advocate, service provider, and representatives from the state, such as a probation officer or prosecutor.

(e) When a youth participates in a disposition team meeting, the youth should be advised that the team will consider any information the youth provides in making placement decisions.

(f) The juvenile court judge should:

  i.   designate a lead agency responsible for coordinating services for the youth;

  ii. direct that disposition team meetings be completed before disposition, and expedited when a youth is detained pending disposition; and

  iii. order that the team prepare a written disposition report with a statement of reasons explaining how the recommendations will advance the best interests of the youth and the goals of the state's juvenile justice code. That report should be distributed to all parties including the youth and defense counsel in advance of the disposition hearing. The author of the report should be available for examination at or before the hearing.

(g) All parties should be permitted to review and respond to any information or testimony that will be or is presented to the court at the disposition hearing.

Standard 7.3   Postponement of Disposition

(a) The court may temporarily postpone disposition in a delinquency case and recommend referral to the appropriate child welfare agency that can serve the youth with minimal risk to public safety, when a delinquent youth is in immediate need of services from or awaiting placement by the child welfare system. Any such referral should be expedited if possible.

(b) The child welfare system should develop processes for expediting cases for delinquent youth who are pending disposition in a delinquency proceeding.

Standard 7.4   Disposition Options

(a) Courts ordering disposition for dual-status youth should be aware of and utilize all disposition options that are legislatively available for youth in the child welfare and delinquency systems.

(b) The juvenile court should order the least restrictive disposition that furthers the best interests of the youth and the goals of the juvenile justice system.

(c) Disposition options should include:

    i.   termination of the delinquency jurisdiction;

    ii. referral to other youth-serving systems;

    iii. maintaining dual jurisdiction; or

    iv. disposition within the delinquency system while providing access to other youth-serving services, systems or agencies.

(d) Juvenile courts should have authority to

    i.   review service, rehabilitative, and disposition plans developed in the child welfare system;

    ii. modify child welfare plans that are in conflict with the goals of the juvenile justice system; and

    iii. require child welfare and juvenile justice agencies to coordinate planning to satisfy their obligations to the youth.

(e) All youth who are adjudicated delinquent should have access to the same publicly funded services that are available to non-delinquent youth.

(f) Juvenile court judges and probation officers should assist youth in obtaining services from other youth-serving systems and develop protocols for expeditious service delivery from such systems and agencies.

Standard 7.5   Disposition Orders

(a) Disposition orders that place the youth out of the home should include:

    i.   a plan to maintain the youth's connection to parents, caregivers, or others who are important to the youth;

    ii.   a reunification or permanency plan that seeks to reunite the youth with family, caregivers or other significant supportive adult, to identify some other permanent stable living arrangement; and

    iii.   a re-entry and discharge plan that specifies where and how, after release from detention or residential placement, the youth will be educated, work, and receive appropriate services.

(b) Disposition orders should set forth the services expected from each agency and set regular status review hearings to assess compliance with the order.

Standard 7.6   Modification of Disposition Orders

(a) Juvenile courts should have authority to review and modify if necessary, any component of a disposition order for dual-status youth.

(b) Courts should not modify any disposition ordered until after notice to, and opportunity to be heard by, all parties.

(c) After disposition, any party in a delinquency case should have authority to petition the court, and the court should have authority to:

    i.   reduce the restrictiveness or duration of disposition when more appropriate and less restrictive options have become available; or

    ii.   increase the restrictiveness or duration of disposition only when the youth has violated the terms or conditions of disposition and the services being provided are not adequately addressing the youth's needs or ensuring public safety and no equally or less restrictive options are available.

(d) The court should not have authority to increase the restrictiveness or duration of disposition for a dual-status youth until after a full due process hearing, with counsel and an opportunity for the youth to be heard. Youth and family members with disabilities should receive accommodations necessary for meaningful participation in the proceedings.

(e) Absent informed consent by the youth, neither the restrictiveness nor the duration of disposition should be increased just to ensure the youth's access to funding.

PART VIII: POST-DISPOSITION AND RE-ENTRY

Standard 8.1 Key Principles Governing Re-entry and Discharge Planning

(a) Re-entry into the community and discharge from the juvenile justice system should be planned to include coordination with the child welfare system and ensure that dual-status youth receive all services they may need and all benefits to which they may be entitled.

(b) Re-entry and discharge planning should provide youth with a stable residential placement with appropriate services, support, and supervision from the child welfare and juvenile justice systems to promote their success in the community after discharge.

(c) Re-entry and discharge planning should:

    i. require the juvenile justice system to begin re-entry and discharge planning at or before disposition and complete it well in advance of the re-entry or discharge;

    ii. identify and implement services that, at a minimum, address continuity of education (including special education), housing, employment, and the need for physical and behavioral health services; and that are timely and coordinated across systems and agencies;

    iii. allow the filing of a petition for dependency, voluntary placement, or re-entry into foster care before a youth's 18th birthday, or whatever older age state law permits, if it appears the youth will need housing or other services when juvenile court jurisdiction terminates;

    iv. specify that delay in identifying, securing, or arranging appropriate post-discharge services may not be relied on to extend the duration of a residential placement; and

    v. allow the youth and the youth's family and counsel to participate fully in the development and periodic reviews of the re-entry plan.

Standard 8.2   Implementation of Re-Entry and Discharge Plan

(a) Youth discharged from residential placement but remaining under supervision of either the child welfare or delinquency system should have case managers assigned and trained to ensure timely and coordinated implementation of the youth's re-entry and discharge plan.

(b) Each agency with responsibility to the youth should:

   i.   participate in a discharge planning meeting with other service providers at least thirty (30) days in advance of the anticipated discharge date;

   ii.   ascertain, before discharge, the youth's strengths, interests, preferences and needs regarding services;

   iii. identify and secure, before discharge, a residence for the youth, to avoid delay in discharge; and

   iv.   assist youth in obtaining important documents (such as identification or driver's license and birth certificates) as well as coverage for essential services such as healthcare.

Part IX: Appeals

Standard 9.1   Right to Appeal

(a) Dual-status youth should have the same right to appeal any order of the Family Court as any other youth. The right to appeal should include a review of the facts, law, and disposition order. Procedural safeguards should exist to ensure that youth are not penalized due to delays and other consequences arising out the youth's involvement in multiple legal matters.

(b) A youth involved in multiple legal matters should be entitled to appellate review of, at a minimum:

    i. all orders of a juvenile or dependency court that dispose of any portion of any case or matter;

    ii. inconsistent orders in the youth's delinquency, dependency or other matters; and

    iii. orders that do not embody the least restrictive alternative to achieve the best interests of the youth and the goals of multiple systems.

Standard 9.2   Written Court Orders and Advice of Rights

(a) At the conclusion of any judicial proceeding involving dual-status youth and their families, the judge should:

    i. prepare a final written order delineating the court's rulings, the facts found, the law applied, the disposition ordered, and the reasons therefore;

    ii. advise the youth (and family) of the right to appeal;

    iii. advise the parent or guardian of the right to appeal in dependency proceedings; and

    iv. inquire of the youth's financial status, appoint appellate counsel if youth is indigent, or instruct defense counsel to secure the appointment of appellate counsel.

(b) At or before the conclusion of the matter, the youth and the youth's counsel should be entitled to a copy of any document in the court file, as well as a verbatim transcript or recording of any relevant hearing.

PART X: RECORDS EXPUNGEMENT

Standard 10.1 Expungement of Juvenile and Family Court Records

(a) Expungement of delinquency records should require the complete deletion of records from all files and databases in all courts as well as any agency that obtained the records from the juvenile justice system.

(b) Youth entitled to expungement of delinquency records should retain that right even when the youth is under the jurisdiction of other youth-serving agencies or systems.

(c) The juvenile court should establish procedures to ensure effective notification to other youth-serving agencies and systems that a youth's delinquency records should be expunged.

(d) In jurisdictions where the juvenile court or law enforcement agency is required to notify a youth's school of an arrest, adjudication, or disposition, the juvenile court should also be required to notify the school when any juvenile court record has been expunged, and the school should be required to destroy its records relating to any expunged matter.

PART XI: RESPONSIBILITIES OF PROSECUTING ATTORNEYS

Standard 11.1 Policies and Protocols

(a) Prosecutors should develop policies to guide intake decisions involving dual-status youth. Such policies should encourage diversion or non-intervention for youth who engage in minor delinquent behavior and who can obtain appropriate services from other youth-serving agencies and systems.

(b) Prosecutors should, in conjunction with state and local law enforcement officers and youth-serving agencies, develop policies governing referrals to the juvenile justice system from other youth-serving agencies and systems. Such policies should seek to reduce referrals to the juvenile justice system for minor delinquent behavior.

Standard 11.2 Training

Prosecutors should participate in cross-system training as set forth in Standard 2.15 of these standards concerning the Need for Cross-System Training.

Standard 11.3 Charging Decisions

(a) Consistent with Standard 2.11 of these standards concerning Information Sharing, when youth are referred to the juvenile justice system, prosecutors should review available Family Court records to determine whether the youth or the youth's family is or has been served by other youth-serving systems.

(b) The prosecutor should not file a delinquency petition:

    i.   when the alleged delinquent behavior is minor and the youth can obtain appropriate services from other agencies;

    ii.   when it is clear that the youth did not have the mental capacity, cognitive ability, or intent necessary to be held responsible for his behavior; or

      iii.   to secure services or placement for a youth when a delinquency charge would not otherwise be warranted.

(c)   The prosecutor should not prosecute delinquent behavior in juvenile or criminal court when the prosecutor determines that the purposes of the delinquency process can be accomplished outside of the juvenile or criminal justice system.

(d)   The prosecutor should make every effort to ensure that a delinquency petition will not result in the termination or disruption of appropriate services for the youth from other youth-serving systems. The prosecutor should discourage other government attorneys handling dependency cases from closing dependency proceedings just because a delinquency petition is filed.

Standard 11.4   Communicating with Victims

The prosecutor should advise victims, to the extent required by law or permitted under confidentiality laws or rules, of circumstances involving dual-status youth that lead to specific charging decisions and proposed resolutions. The prosecutor should advise victims of statutory, rule or other limitations on disclosure of information about the accused youth.

Standard 11.5   Diversion

(a)   The prosecutor should consider information regarding the youth's access to services from the child welfare system when deciding whether to divert a youth from the juvenile justice system.

(b)   If the prosecutor decides to divert a dual-status youth from the juvenile justice system, the prosecutor should:

      i.   refer the youth to a program suitable for the youth's age, ethnicity, culture, gender or sexual identification, disability, and developmental or cognitive ability; and

      ii.   consider diversion programs that allow the youth to participate in community service in lieu of a delinquency petition.

Standard 11.6   Detention

(a)   In deciding whether to request detention of an accused youth, the prosecutor should:

   i.   not seek detention for alleged minor delinquent behavior; and

   ii.   consider whether other youth-serving agencies outside the juvenile justice system can protect the youth and serve public safety.

(b)   The prosecutor should not seek detention just because no suitable child welfare placement has been identified.

(c)   The prosecutor should not seek detention when detention will likely cause the youth to lose placement or services from other youth-serving systems and public safety can be served without detention.

Standard 11.7   Communicating and Coordinating with Youth-Serving Agencies

(a)   If the prosecutor declines to file a delinquency petition, the prosecutor should communicate that decision to any referring agency.

(b)   The prosecutor should develop policies to govern the effective referral of youth to the child welfare system and other youth-serving agencies.

Standard 11.8   Disposition and Post-Disposition Planning

(a)   The prosecutor should participate in placement, re-entry, and disposition planning team meetings consistent with Standard 7.2 of these standards concerning the Disposition Process.

(b)   The prosecutor should not seek an out-of-home placement when the youth's supervision and service needs can be met in the community.

(c)   After disposition, the prosecutors should periodically review the case.

   i.   If it appears that additional or alternate services are needed to meet the needs of the youth or to ensure public safety, the prosecutor may seek to modify the dispositional plan as described above.

   ii.   If it appears that the youth no longer needs care and rehabilitation from the juvenile court and does not pose a risk to public safety, the prosecutor should file a request to terminate the delinquency disposition early.

PART XII: RESPONSIBILITIES OF DEFENSE COUNSEL

Standard 12.1   Ethical Obligations of Defense Counsel

Defense counsel representing dual-status youth should abide by all applicable professional and ethical obligations for defense counsel generally.

Standard 12.2   Training

Defense counsel should participate in cross-system training consistent with Standard 2.13 of these standards concerning Access to Court Records.

Standard 12.3   Investigation and Confidentiality Waivers

(a) Consistent with Standard 2.14 of these standards concerning Waivers of Confidentiality, defense counsel and dependency counsel should advise the youth in age-appropriate language, and when permitted and appropriate, inform the youth's parent or guardian, about the need for a signed waiver to allow counsel access to child welfare records and the implications of such waiver. Youth, parents, or guardians with disabilities should receive accommodations necessary to provide informed consent to the waiver.

   i.   The juvenile justice system should provide, and defense counsel should obtain, necessary interpretive services. Defense counsel should ensure that any written waiver form and other documents are appropriately translated.

   ii. When the youth is developmentally or cognitively limited or limited in his or her literacy skills, counsel should explain and obtain the waiver in a manner the youth can best understand.

(b) Defense counsel should gather and review all information that would likely affect the youth's custody, legal status, or services in the juvenile justice system.

Standard 12.4   Pre-Petition Advocacy by Delinquency Counsel

(a)   Defense counsel should advise the youth regarding the possibility of initiating a referral from the juvenile justice system to the child welfare system and the possible implications of such a referral.

(b)   Defense counsel should provide decision-makers all relevant information militating against, and advocate against, the filing of a delinquency petition and the inclusion of particular charges in a petition with the youth's voluntary and informed consent. Defense counsel should consider and recommend alternatives to provide needed services for the youth and, if necessary, to protect the public.

(c)   Defense counsel should communicate with the youth's dependency counsel and the youth's best interest advocate when the youth consents and such communication would not undermine the youth's rights in the delinquency case.

Standard 12.5   Advocacy at Detention Hearing

(a)   In and before a detention hearing, defense counsel should present facts and arguments to support placement in the community or in the custody of youth-serving agencies, if consistent with the youth's objectives. Facts and arguments should include evidence from youth-serving agencies regarding the availability of specific placements or services.

(b)   If the youth is detained or sent to another out-of-home placement, defense counsel should advocate for comparable or better education, physical or behavioral health, and other services than the youth had been receiving prior to the placement.

(c)   If the youth is ordered detained, defense counsel should, as soon as possible provide detention or shelter care staff with information about the youth's needs and advocate for the proper care and safety of the youth.

Standard 12.6   Disposition Advocacy

(a) Defense counsel representing dual-status youth should zealously advocate for the youth's stated objectives at all stages, including any multi-agency planning team meeting or disposition hearing.

(b) Counsel should protect the youth's due process interests, including in cases when the disposition hearing is consolidated with other Family Court proceedings.

(c) If necessary to advance the youth's objectives, counsel should challenge any evidence or reports submitted to the juvenile court at the disposition hearing, including items submitted by the multi-agency team.

Standard 12.7   Post-Disposition Advocacy

(a) Defense counsel's advocacy on behalf of dual-status youth should not end at the entry of a disposition order. Counsel should maintain contact with both the youth and the agency or agencies responsible for implementing the court's order, and:

    i. counsel the youth and inform the youth's family concerning the order and its implementation;

    ii. ensure the timely and appropriate implementation of the order; and

    iii. ensure the youth's rights are protected as the youth's disposition is implemented.

(b) Defense counsel should monitor the implementation of the youth's disposition order.

    i. If it appears that additional or different services are needed to meet the needs of the youth, counsel should seek to modify the dispositional plan or order, as consistent with the youth's stated interests.

    ii. If it appears the youth no longer needs rehabilitative services from the juvenile court and does not pose a risk to public safety, defense counsel should seek to modify or terminate disposition early.

(c) Relevant government jurisdictions should ensure that defense counsel have the authority and funding to continue representation after disposition consistent with these standards.

Standard 12.8   Appellate Advocacy

(a) After adjudication and disposition, defense counsel should

   i.   explain to the youth the meaning and consequences of the court's judgment and the youth's right to appeal any delinquency disposition or other court orders;

   ii. give the youth a professional judgment as to whether there are meritorious grounds for appeal and the probable results of an appeal; and

   iii. explain to the youth the advantages and disadvantages of an appeal.

(b) Defense counsel should take whatever steps are necessary to protect the youth's right to appeal any illegal disposition or other court order, as consistent with the youth's stated objectives.

Part XIII: Responsibilities of Detention and Residential Staff

Standard 13.1   Policies and Protocols

(a) Lawyers in the juvenile justice system should advocate for comparable or better treatment and services in juvenile detention settings than the youth would receive if allowed to remain in the community.

(b) Detention and residential facility staff should develop internal policies to eliminate barriers in detention to the provision of appropriate services to dual-status youth in detention. Such internal policies should, at a minimum:

   i.   ensure regular communication between detention and residential staff and child welfare and other youth-serving agencies and service providers with a legal obligation to the youth;

   ii. ensure that youth are transported to and from provider appointments, if safety and flight risks can be managed during transport;

   iii. develop or revise visitation policies to allow foster parents, guardians, family members, significant others, and representatives from the child welfare agencies and service providers to visit youth in detention; and

   iv. provide private and appropriate physical space for youth to meet with foster parents, guardians, family members, significant others, and representatives from the child welfare agencies and service providers.

BLACK LETTER AND COMMENTARY

PART I: DEFINITIONS AND GENERAL PRINCIPLES

Standard 1.1 Definitions

For the purpose of these Standards, the listed terms are defined as follows:

(a) "Behavioral Health Services" are a continuum of services for individuals at risk of, or suffering from mental health or substance abuse conditions.

(b) "Best Interest Advocate" is an individual, not functioning or intending to function as a lawyer, appointed by the court to assist the court in determining the best interests of the youth.

(c) "Child Welfare System" is the legal structure including courts, residential facilities, foster care placements, and services designed to promote the well-being of youth alleged or found to be status offenders or to be abused, neglected, abandoned, homeless, or exploited, by ensuring safety, achieving permanency, improving well-being, and building the family's capacity to care for their youth successfully.

(d) "Collateral Consequences" are consequences flowing from arrest or adjudication, other than the direct dispositional order, that may impact opportunities for future education, financial aid, employment, housing, immigration status, public benefits, or other individual rights, services, or benefits.

(e) "Congregate Care Facility" is a housing facility in which each individual has a private or semi-private bedroom but shares with other residents a common dining room, recreational room, or other facilities.

(f) "Critical Youth Services" are services required for the well-being of youth, including supervision, housing, clothing, nutrition, education, recreation, and physical and behavioral healthcare.

(g) "Cultural Competence" is an ability to understand, communicate with, and effectively interact with people across different cultures and socio-economic backgrounds.

(h) "Data" is information that is captured for aggregate reporting purposes but does not identify individuals.

(i) "Delinquency" is any behavior that would be a crime if committed by an adult.

(j) "Defense Counsel" is a lawyer hired or appointed to represent a youth's expressed interest in a delinquency proceeding.

(k) "Dependency Case" is a legal proceeding involving youth and parents in the child welfare system.

(l) "Dependency Counsel" is a lawyer hired or appointed to represent a youth's expressed legal interests in a dependency case.

(m) "Diversion" is the referral of an accused youth, without adjudication of criminal or delinquency charges, to a youth service agency or other program, accompanied by a formal termination of all legal proceedings against the youth in the juvenile justice system upon successful completion of the program requirements.

(n) "Dual-Status Youth" are youth under the concurrent jurisdiction of the child welfare system and the juvenile justice system.

(o) "Dual-Status Docket" is a specialized docket within the Family Court that exercises jurisdiction over youth who are concurrently involved in the juvenile justice and child welfare systems.

(p) "Family Court" is a court with jurisdiction over one or more of the following cases involving: delinquency; abuse and neglect; status offenses; the need for emergency medical treatment or behavioral health crisis intervention; voluntary and involuntary termination of parental rights proceedings; adoption proceedings; appointments of legal guardians for juveniles; intrafamily criminal offenses; proceedings in regard to divorce, separation, annulment, alimony, custody, and support of juveniles; proceedings under the Uniform Interstate Family Support Act.

(q) "Information" is any communication—recorded or unrecorded—record, or material that may identify individuals.

(r) "Juvenile Justice System" is the legal structure including law enforcement agencies, courts, detention facilities, probationary and re-entry services for diverting, detaining, adjudicating, supervising and discharging youth alleged or found to be delinquent.

(s) "Juvenile Court" is the court and court personnel responsible for diverting, adjudicating, detaining, confining, and supervising youth alleged or found to be delinquent.

(t) "Minor Delinquent Behavior" is conduct that does not rise to the level of significant or repeated harm to others, significant or repeated property loss or damage, or a threat of significant harm to others.

(u) "Outcome" is a predefined, objective measure of change of limited scope.

(v) "Records" are all reports, pleadings, court orders, and other documents prepared or gathered in connection with Juvenile and Family Court proceedings.

(w) "School Resource Officer" is a certified, sworn police officer employed by a local police agency but assigned to work in a school.

(x) "Staff-secure facility" is a facility that houses a small number of residents who have the freedom to enter or leave the premises.

(y) "Status Offense" is conduct that is prohibited only for persons under the age of majority, such as truancy, curfew violations, or running away from home.

(z) "Youth" is a person who has not yet attained the age of majority or otherwise is not subject to the jurisdiction of the criminal court; or who, as a result of a delinquency petition, remains subject to the juvenile court's jurisdiction.

(aa) "Youth-Serving Agency or System" is an agency or system of agencies responsible for providing child welfare services, critical youth services, or behavioral health services.

Standard 1.2   General Principles

(a) All youth need and deserve adequate care, education, and physical and behavioral health services.

(b) Child welfare and other youth-serving agencies should not refer a youth for law enforcement intervention for minor delinquent behavior.

(c) Cooperation between the juvenile justice system and other youth-serving systems is essential in differentiating between conduct that warrants intervention by the juvenile justice system and conduct that does not warrant such intervention, developing protocols that discourage inappropriate referrals to juvenile court, and developing positive support systems and behavioral strategies that reduce referrals to juvenile court.

(d) Information-sharing between and among juvenile justice and other youth-serving agencies should be regulated to accommodate the youth's need for coordinated services, as well as the youth's need for privacy and protection against self-incrimination.

(e) Locked and staff-secure facilities should only be used after arrest, during the court process, or as a dispositional option when needed for the protection of the community or to reduce a risk of flight.

(f) Services provided to youth removed from their home or community should be provided in the least restrictive setting and a setting that is close to family, consistent with public safety and the safety of the youth.

(g) Youth receiving critical youth services, child welfare services, or behavioral health services should be entitled to continuity in those services in the least restrictive setting consistent with public safety when they are removed from their home to the custody of the juvenile or criminal justice systems.

(h) Services for youth involved in the juvenile or criminal justice systems should be provided by appropriate youth-serving agencies in the community. When a youth is in detention or custody, the youth should receive services comparable to those they would receive in the community, in a setting that is close to family.

(i) Youth should have an opportunity to be heard, through the aid of counsel, regarding any decision that affects their physical placement, need for and selection of services, and general well-being.

(j) The juvenile justice system should ensure that youth needing services from both the child welfare and juvenile justice systems receive the most appropriate services without adversely affecting the severity or duration of the youth's detention, placement, or probation supervision.

(k) Arrangements for follow-up treatment, services, placement, and protection that the youth will need once released from custody should be made during the period of their confinement, be in place upon their release, and not delay release.

(l) The child welfare system and agencies should not terminate services or close a youth's dependency case solely because the youth was arrested or adjudicated in the juvenile or criminal justice system.

(m) Parents, guardians, and caretakers of youth involved in the juvenile justice system are entitled to respect and the opportunity to participate in decision-making involving the youth if appropriate for the youth's legal interests, safety, and well-being.

(n) Youth released from custody should be reunited with their parents when in the youth's best interests; when reunification is not in the youth's best interest, the youth should be placed in the care of other appropriate relatives, the child welfare system, or other appropriate systems.

Part I Commentary

1.1   Definitions

Family Court and **Juvenile Court.** Terminology varies from jurisdiction to jurisdiction. Terms like "Juvenile Court" and "Family Court" are defined differently in state statutes. In these Standards, "Family Court" is broadly defined to include a range of family-related matters, including child welfare cases; "Juvenile Court" is narrowly defined to address only delinquency matters.

Status offenses. State statutes often discuss "status offenses" with terminology such as Persons In Need of Supervision (PINS), Children in Need of Supervision (CHINS), Families in Need of Supervision (FINS), and Youth in Need of Supervision (YINS). These Standards refer to all of these designations as status offenders. Some states handle status offenses in the child welfare system and some in the delinquency system.

Dependency Counsel. In dependency cases, many states appoint a Guardian ad Litem (GAL) to advocate for "the best interest of the child"; the GAL may be an attorney or a trained volunteer/Court Appointed Special Advocate (CASA). Other states appoint legal counsel to protect the child's stated interests. ABA policy in dependency cases distinguishes between *lawyers* who represent children and others who may argue for a child's best interest.

In 2011, the ABA adopted a Model Act Governing the Representation of Children in Abuse, Neglect, and Dependency Proceedings.[1] The Model Act, which has been endorsed by the National Association of Counsel for Children,[2] says:

> (c) "Child's lawyer" (or "lawyer for children") means a lawyer who provides legal services for a child and who owes the same duties, including undivided loyalty, confidentiality and competent representation, to the child as is due an adult client . . .

---

    1. ABA, Model Act Governing the Representation of Children in Abuse, Neglect, and Dependency Proceedings (Aug. 2011), https://www.americanbar.org/content/dam/aba/administrative/child_law/aba_model_act_2011.pdf. The Model Act had broad support within the ABA and from bar associations across the country.

    2. *Child Law Standards of Practice*, Nat'l Ass'n of Couns. for Chil., https://www.naccchildlaw.org/page/StandardsOfPractice?&hhsearchterms=%22aba%22 (last visited Feb. 7, 2023).

(d) "Best interest advocate" means an individual, not functioning or intended to function as the child's lawyer, appointed by the court to assist the court in determining the best interests of the child.

It is essential that all professionals know the rules and standards governing dependency counsel and guardians ad litem in their jurisdictions. In jurisdictions where the child's attorney is bound by the stated interest of the child, the attorney must maintain the client's confidences and secrets and zealously advocate for the client's stated goals in the proceedings. In jurisdictions where attorney GALs advocate for the best interest of the child, they are rarely bound by rules of client confidentiality and privilege and routinely share information about the client with the court.

Youth. These Standards prefer to use "youth," rather than "juvenile," to describe children who are involved in multiple systems. This in part reflects a national trend to avoid calling children "juveniles," which seems to prejudge them through the use of a label. In addition, since these standards seek to keep youth *out* of the juvenile justice system, if possible, we use a more generic term. "Youth" is broad enough to include students, children in foster care, teens in mental health facilities, and adolescents in the justice system. At the same time, the Standards follow state laws and practices that continue to use the term "juvenile court," using that term when it is appropriate.

The court's jurisdiction over a youth, or the youth's ability to remain under court jurisdiction, will vary by the system that is involved and the age of the youth. The age of juvenile court jurisdiction varies from state to state. The Juvenile Justice and Delinquency Prevention Act of 1974, reauthorized as the Juvenile Justice Reform Act of 2018, defines a juvenile offender as "an individual subject to the exercise of juvenile court jurisdiction for purposes of adjudication and treatment based on age and offense limitations as defined by state law."[3]

Increasingly, 18-, 19-, and 20-year-olds are allowed (as ABA policy supports) to voluntarily remain in or return to the custody of a child welfare agency. These youth, for whom the state receives federal financial support, are deemed "youth" by these Standards. The Fostering Connections to Success and Increasing Adoptions Act of 2008,[4] provided financial incentives to states that enable youth to remain in

---

3. 60 Fed. Reg. 28450 (May 31, 1995).
4. Pub. L. No. 110-351.

foster care past their 18th birthday. Unlike extended juvenile court jurisdiction—in which states allow juvenile courts to *involuntarily* keep youth over age 18 in the juvenile justice system—extended foster care for dependent youth is voluntary.[5] Dependent youth may stay in or return to care if they are over age 18, with the state receiving federal reimbursement through Title IV-E of the Social Security Act, if they are completing secondary school (or the equivalent), enrolled in post-secondary or vocational school, participating in a program or activity that promotes or removes barriers to employment, employed 80 hours a month, or incapable of school and/or work requirements due to a documented medical condition.[6]

Diversion and 1.2 General Principles

See Appendix II for state laws allowing for diversion.

Reducing referrals to juvenile court has long been ABA policy. The 1980 IJA-ABA Juvenile Justice Standards recognized the importance of diversion, defining "diversion" similar to the definition in these Standards.[7] Public policy has long supported diverting youth who exhibit minor delinquent behavior. Such policy is supported by the 1980 IJA-ABA Juvenile Justice Standards,[8] the 2008 ABA resolution by the Commission on Youth at Risk,[9] and federal[10] and state statutes (listed in Appendix II). Some state statutes explicitly define who is eligible for diversion programs[11] or how juvenile diversion programs should be structured.[12] While the ABA Standards and every state allows for—and encourages—diversion in appropriate situations, there are few

---

5. An exception to the rule is Massachusetts, which permits youth under 22 in the custody of the Department of Youth Services to ask to remain in care "for the purposes of specific educational or rehabilitative programs, under conditions agreed upon by both the department and such persons and terminable by either." MASS. ANN. LAWS, pt. I, tit. XVII, ch. 120, § 16, Discharge—Upon Attaining Certain Age.

6. 42 U.S.C. § 675(8)(B)(iv) (2015). Older foster youth have access to additional benefits from the Foster Care Independence Act, Public Law 106-169, known as the Chafee Act.

7. *See* Standards Relating to Interim Status, 2.19 ("Diversion. The unconditional release of an accused juvenile, without adjudication of criminal charges, to a youth service agency or other program outside the juvenile justice system, accompanied by a formal termination of all legal proceedings against the juvenile and erasure of all records concerning the case.").

8. *Id.*

9. American Bar Association Recommendation Adopted by the House of Delegates on February 11, 2008 § (a). This policy is in Appendix I.

10. Juvenile Justice and Delinquency Prevention Act of 2018 § 205(a)(E)(iv).

11. *See, e.g.,* ARK. CODE ANN. § 9-27-323.

12. *See, e.g.,* ARIZ. REV. STAT. § 8-328.

guidelines on how discretion to divert cases should be exercised. The unanswered questions have been *which* youth should be referred, for *what* conduct, and under *what* conditions. An additional unanswered question is the timing of diversion, as diversion *before* charges are filed can mitigate collateral consequences. These Standards provide guidance for legislators, defense attorneys, judges, probation officers, prosecutors, service providers, and others who seek to answer these questions.

While there are more serious offenses that can and should be diverted from the juvenile justice system—state laws in Appendix II provide great flexibility to probation officers and prosecutors—these Standards focus on "minor delinquent behavior." The definition captures significant numbers of "offenses" that are now referred to juvenile court. "Minor delinquent behavior" is frequently typical adolescent risk-taking,[13] which accounts for significant numbers of referrals to juvenile court. "Minor delinquent behavior" also covers many of the "offenses" that schools refer to courts, using the juvenile court as the school disciplinarian. The ABA, since 2001, has adopted policies that frown on arresting youth for minor misbehavior.[14] Arrests of students with disabilities for minor misbehavior is also problematic—and particularly well-suited to be addressed by these Standards. "Not only [are] . . . students with disabilities more likely to be restrained or secluded than their able-bodied peers, they also [have] . . . higher rates of arrests and law-enforcement referrals."[15] Although schools are supposed to have behavior management plans, in Individual Education Programs, for students with disabilities,[16] nothing in federal law prohibits schools from seeking the arrest of special education students. These Standards discourage such behavior.

These Standards adopt a developmental approach to youth justice, recognizing that most youth "age out" of adolescent risk-taking that may lead to arrest. Most youth age out of antisocial behavior on their

---

13. *See, e.g.*, Laurence Steinberg, Age of Opportunity: Lessons from the New Science of Adolescence (2014); David Dobbs, *Beautiful Brains*, Nat'l Geographic, Oct. 2011.

14. *See* Rosa Hirji, *20 Years of Policy Advocacy against Zero Tolerance: A Critical Review*, ABA (Jan. 16, 2018), https://www.americanbar.org/groups/litigation/committees/childrens-rights/articles/2018/winter2018-20-years-policy-advocacy-against-zero-tolerance-critical-review/.

15. Elizabeth Cassidy, *Students with Disabilities Are More Likely to Be Restrained or Arrested at School*, The Mighty (Apr. 30, 2018), https://themighty.com/2018/04/students-with-disabilities-re strained-arrested/.

16. 34 C.F.R. § 300.324(a)(2)(i).

own.[17] While some individuals exhibit "life-course-persistent" antisocial behavior, this is rare.[18] By contrast, adolescence-limited individuals are so prevalent that their desistence from offending is typical rather than abnormal.[19] However, contact with the juvenile justice system can impede development and reduce the chance that youth will successfully age out of these negative behaviors.[20] The approach taken by these Standards advances the principle that public systems should do more good than harm, and give youth opportunities to develop into productive adults.

These Standards also provide support for the many juvenile court diversion programs that are growing around the country.[21]

17. Terrie E. Moffitt, *Life-Course-Persistent versus Adolescence-Limited Antisocial Behavior*, *in* DEVELOPMENTAL PSYCHOPATHOLOGY: RISK, DISORDER, AND ADAPTATION 570–98 (Dante Cicchetti & Donald J. Cohen eds., 2006).

18. *Id.*

19. *Id.*

20. *See* Laurence Steinberg et al., *Reentry of Young Offenders from the Justice System: A Developmental Perspective*, 2(1) YOUTH VIOLENCE & JUV. JUST. 21 (Jan. 2004).

21. Some of these are supported by the Annie E. Casey Foundation. *See Webinars Spotlight Juvenile Court Diversion Programs*, ANNIE E. CASEY FOUND. (Jan. 7, 2020), https://www.aecf.org/blog/webinars-spotlight-juvenile-court-diversion-programs/. Other examples include Duval County, Florida: Tessa Duvall, *Diversion Programs Help Kids Avoid Criminal Records While Saving Taxpayers Money*, THE FLA. TIMES UNION (MAR. 26, 2016), https://www.jacksonville.com/2016-05-02/stub-6; Delaware: Nick Ciolino, *Dept. of Justice Working to Resolve Misdemeanors Out of Court*, DEL. PUB. MEDIA (Sept. 12, 2018), https://www.delawarepublic.org/post/dept-justice-working-resolve-juvenile-misdemeanors-out-court; and Toledo, Ohio: *Ohio Country Expands Diversion for Youth with Misdemeanor Charges*, ANNIE E. CASEY FOUND. (Feb. 6, 2017), https://www.aecf.org/blog/ohio-county-expands-diversion-for-youth-with-misdemeanor-charges/.

PART II: SYSTEMS COLLABORATION AND COORDINATION OF SERVICES FOR DUAL-STATUS YOUTH

A. STATE STRUCTURE AND LEGISLATION

Standard 2.1 Legislative Provisions for Effective Care of Dual-Status Youth

(a) State laws and policies should ensure that dual-status youth continue to receive critical youth services despite the youth's involvement in the juvenile justice system.

(b) State and federal laws should eliminate funding barriers and statutory restrictions that inhibit dual-status youth from accessing state and federal funding allocated for youth in the child welfare system.

(c) State laws should mandate and facilitate interagency planning, coordination and accountability between and among agencies that have a legal obligation to each youth.

(d) Mandatory arrest provisions in domestic violence and criminal justice statutes should not mandate arrests for youth who engage in minor delinquent behavior in congregate care facilities in the child welfare, juvenile justice, or other youth-serving systems.

Standard 2.2 Structure of State Juvenile Justice and Child Welfare Systems

(a) State systems should be structured so that:

    i. a single state agency is responsible for the licensing and regulation of programs for status offenders and delinquent and dependent youth and for ensuring that all residential facilities meet minimum licensing standards;

    ii. non-secure juvenile justice programs have access to and may utilize child welfare funding, partially covered by federal support, for family-based care and small group placements that will support youth in less restrictive, community-based settings while affording them additional protections under federal law;

iii. child welfare services are available to juvenile courts and the courts may at any appropriate stage of the juvenile court proceedings enter any order authorized for a dependent youth; and

iv. dependent youth who are not adjudicated delinquent should not be placed in residential facilities that are primarily for the care of delinquent youth.

(b) State systems should engage behavioral health, education, and child welfare agencies and ensure that crisis intervention and other services are implemented to avoid the need for arrest and referral to the juvenile justice system.

(c) States should ensure that congregate care facilities in the child welfare, juvenile justice, and other youth-serving systems are able to meet the needs of the youth they serve, including addressing minor delinquent behavior, without relying on law enforcement for discipline.

B. FAMILY COURT ORGANIZATION, POLICIES, AND PROCEDURES

Standard 2.3   Juvenile Court Policies, Protocols, and Rules

(a) Juvenile and Family Courts should establish policies and protocols that ensure the fair treatment of dual-status youth in diversion, detention, adjudication, and disposition decisions and eliminate practices that result in the unnecessary detention, adjudication, or prolonged incarceration of youth who are or should be served by the child welfare system.

(b) Juvenile and Family Courts should establish policies and protocols for delinquency complaints involving youth referred by or receiving services from the child welfare or other youth-serving systems. Such policies and protocols should:

i.   recognize the *in loco parentis* role of the child welfare agency and require the agency to fulfill the role a responsible parent would be expected to fulfill when a youth comes into contact with the juvenile justice system;

ii.   limit secure confinement to situations in which the youth meets detention criteria applied to other youth and ensure that a youth who does not have an in-tact home to which to return is not securely detained solely as a result of the youth's family status;

iii.   set strict timelines for the completion of the juvenile intake process;

iv.   establish a process to determine whether a youth is better served in the juvenile justice system, the child welfare system, or by concurrent jurisdiction of the two;

v.   develop procedures for providing accommodations to youth with disabilities;

vi.   permit concurrent jurisdiction by the child welfare and juvenile justice systems when appropriate, and

vii.   provide that a youth's arrest or adjudication of delinquency will not result in the closure of a child welfare case or the termination of services from other youth-serving agencies solely because of the youth's involvement in the juvenile justice system.

(c)   Consistent with standards concerning information sharing and confidentiality in these standards and state and federal laws governing confidentiality and privilege, juvenile courts should develop policies and protocols for the prompt notification of a youth's caregiver, child welfare caseworker, and attorney, and for the involvement of other youth-serving agencies as appropriate when a youth is arrested or referred to the juvenile court.

Standard 2.4   Juvenile Court Leadership

Juvenile courts should exercise leadership in developing working relationships and protocols with community agencies
serving youth and families with multiple legal issues and in
need of services from multiple systems.

Standard 2.5   Juvenile and Criminal Court Jurisdiction

(a)   State laws governing the transfer of youth from juvenile
court to adult court or from adult court to juvenile court
should require probation officers, prosecutors, and juvenile
court judges to consider the dual-status youth's need for services from the child welfare and other youth-serving agencies in determining whether transfer is appropriate. The
attorney for the youth should have an opportunity to present
evidence as to the youth's need for child welfare services.

(b)   Juvenile courts should consider whether the child welfare
and other youth-serving systems have fulfilled their duties
to a youth before considering whether to transfer the youth
to criminal court and should establish protocols to ensure
that youth who receive services from multiple systems are
not disadvantaged in discretionary transfer decisions solely
due to their involvement in other systems.

(c)   Consistent with public safety, state laws should permit
transfer of youth from the criminal court to the juvenile
court when the youth needs services from the child welfare,
juvenile justice, or other youth-serving agencies.

(d)   If a youth is transferred or has a case originally filed in criminal court, the youth should still be eligible for child welfare
services, including social service placements and programs.

Standard 2.6   Dependency Jurisdiction

(a)   Dependency courts should develop protocols that:

i.   acknowledge the *in loco parentis* role of the child welfare agency and require the agency to fulfill the role a
responsible parent would be expected to fulfill when

a youth comes into contact with the juvenile justice system;

ii.   ensure that a youth's arrest or adjudication of delinquency will not result in the closure of a child welfare case or the termination of services from other youth-serving agencies solely because of the youth's involvement in the juvenile justice system;

iii.   prevent the use of civil and criminal contempt violations in the child welfare system as a basis for a delinquency petition;

iv.   facilitate coordination, planning and accountability when the child welfare and juvenile justice systems have concurrent jurisdiction over the youth;

v.   ensure that a youth's defense counsel receives notice when the youth becomes involved in the child welfare system; and

vi.   ensure that a youth's dependency counsel receives notice when the youth becomes involved in the juvenile justice system.

(b)   State laws should ensure that youth have a right to defense counsel and a court hearing at which they have the right to testify, present evidence, and cross-examine witnesses on the youth's need for child welfare services and whether their dependency case will be terminated after an arrest or referral to juvenile or criminal court.

Standard 2.7   Docketing Proceedings Involving Dual-Status Youth

(a)   In scheduling delinquency and other Family Court proceedings, clerks and other court personnel should be attentive to the youth's and family's obligation to appear in other legal proceedings. Court personnel should communicate with the youth and family to reduce multiple trips to court and court-related appointments and to avoid scheduling conflicts, school absences, and other avoidable inconveniences.

(b) Consistent with standards related to information sharing and confidentiality in these Standards and state and federal laws governing confidentiality and evidentiary privilege, juvenile court staff should have access to the docket of all Family Court cases so they can identify youth and families with multiple legal proceedings within the court.

(c) The same judge should consider all legal issues that involve the same family; however, to ensure fundamental fairness, each youth should have:

    i.   a lawyer at all stages of a delinquency and dependency case, including the intake, adjudicatory, disposition, post-disposition, and appellate stages;

    ii.   an adjudicatory hearing at which each charge of delinquency will be considered by a neutral judicial officer as consistent with due process and fundamental fairness;

    iii.   the right to notice of all hearings and case staffing or case management conferences related to the youth's cases; and

    iv.   the right to attend all hearings and case conferences related to the youth's cases and a meaningful opportunity to be heard as to the youth's strengths, interests, disabilities, needs, and preferences regarding placement, services, and case outcomes.

(d) Juvenile and Family Courts should develop policies that allow for the consolidation of post-adjudication matters involving dual-status youth. The policies should be consistent with the following principles:

    i.   When feasible, a single judge should hear all dispositional and post-dispositional matters involving dual-status youth.

    ii.   After a youth has been adjudicated delinquent, the youth's juvenile court dispositional proceedings should be consolidated with child welfare and other Family Court proceedings concerning the youth.

iii. The court should ensure continuity of legal representation for the youth throughout all phases of the delinquency matter, including disposition.

iv. The court should require that representatives responsible for case management and supervision of the youth in the child welfare and juvenile justice systems attend the consolidated proceeding.

v. The court should ensure, to the extent consistent with the missions of the child welfare and juvenile justice systems, that youth and family case plans be aligned in terms of goals, permanency planning, services, and responsibility for implementation.

(e) To the extent possible, services and other legal proceedings in the child welfare system should not be delayed pending resolution of a delinquency case, unless the youth or the youth's defense counsel believes such a delay is necessary.

Standard 2.8   Designated Dual-Status Dockets

(a) A jurisdiction should have authority to create a specialized dual-status docket for youth involved in both the juvenile and the child welfare systems, if it finds that the traditional juvenile court cannot effectively address cases involving youth with particular needs or characteristics.

(b) Dual-status dockets should be developed and implemented by an interdisciplinary team that includes representatives from the judiciary, prosecution, defense bar, best interest advocates, families, and relevant service providers.

(c) Youth assigned to a dual-status docket should have access to services from all systems that have expertise related to the youth's needs.

(d) Dual-status dockets should provide an opportunity for youth to be diverted from the juvenile justice system or benefit from alternatives to detention at the pre-trial and disposition stage of the delinquency case.

(e) Judges presiding over dual-status dockets should utilize incentives for positive behavior, graduated responses to negative behavior, close judicial oversight, a team approach, coordination of services, and meaningful re-entry strategies.

(f) Judges presiding over dual-status dockets should ensure that any sanctions imposed serve a rehabilitative purpose.

(g) Courts with a dual-status docket should have rigorous intake and screening procedures to ensure the Court accepts only those youth who are appropriate for the dual-status docket.

(h) The interdisciplinary team responsible for developing a dual-status docket should adopt policies and protocols that ensure that:

    i. the youth's due process rights are protected at all stages of the delinquency case, including the youth's right to a fair and impartial hearing at the adjudicatory and disposition stages of the case;

    ii. the parents' due process rights are protected at all stages of the dependency case, including the parents' right to a fair and impartial hearing to adjudicate any allegation of abuse or neglect;

    iii. the youth and the youth's defense counsel have a right to be heard and participate in all decisions regarding the youth's placement and service plan;

    iv. youth and parents with disabilities receive accommodations necessary to ensure meaningful participation at all stages of the case; and

    v. when the youth is not diverted from the juvenile justice system before adjudication, the youth's dependency case should not be consolidated with a delinquency case on a dual-status docket unless and until there is an adjudication of delinquency.

(i) Dual-status dockets should be presided over by a judge instead of a referee, master, or magistrate.

(j) A judge presiding over a dual-status docket should have authority to dismiss the delinquency petition for a youth who has successfully completed the requirements set by the dual-status court.

C. INTERSTATE COOPERATION

Standard 2.9   Dual-Status Youth Crossing State and Local Jurisdictions

(a) Courts and state legislatures, individually or with neighboring states, should develop policies and procedures consistent with the Interstate Compact for Juveniles, the Interstate Compact on the Placement of Children, and the Uniform Child Custody and Jurisdiction Act that will facilitate cooperation by justice system personnel and youth-serving agencies in addressing cross-jurisdictional issues.

(b) Policies and procedures for cross-jurisdictional cooperation should focus on:

   i.   reducing delay, uncertainty, and unnecessary detention of youth,

   ii. providing prompt resolution of legal matters involving dual-status youth,

   iii. expediting the necessary transport of dual-status youth across jurisdictions, and

   iv. avoiding scheduling conflicts for youth and families with legal obligations in multiple jurisdictions.

(c) Policies and procedures should adopt a presumption that legal proceedings will take place in the jurisdiction where the youth has the most significant ties.

(d) Policies and procedures to facilitate cross-jurisdictional cooperation should abide by principles of confidentiality and privacy.

D. INFORMATION SHARING AND DATA COLLECTION

Standard 2.10   Purposes of Information Sharing and Data Collection

(a) Information sharing and data collection are necessary for any effective collaboration and coordination of services for dual-status youth.

(b) States should authorize and facilitate the sharing of information about individual youth between and among multiple systems and agencies to

    i.   reduce duplication of assessments and services for the youth and the youth's family,

    ii.   enhance understanding of the youth's strengths, interests, preferences, needs, and

    iii. improve individual case planning and decision-making for the youth.

(c) States should authorize and facilitate the collection of data for aggregate reporting on the characteristics of dual-status youth and the processes for handling those youth.

(d) States should use data:

    i.   to improve the policies, practices, and coordinated responses of agencies responsible for the care of and provision of services to dual-status youth, and

    ii.   to evaluate the need for and effectiveness of programs and practices designed to achieve improved outcomes for youth.

Standard 2.11   Policies and Procedures for Confidentiality During Information Sharing

(a) All states should develop and require the use of protocols for information sharing about individual dual-status youth from arrest to termination of jurisdiction.

(b) All agreements or protocols to share information between the juvenile justice system and other youth-serving systems and agencies should ensure that information-sharing protocols provide appropriate protection for the privacy of youth and their families and follow federal and state law and ethical requirements regarding confidentiality of privileged information.

(c) All agreements or protocols should specify the purposes of information sharing and limit the information shared to the specified purposes.

(d) States should limit the use of information about the youth's involvement in multiple systems to the coordination of case management and the continuity and integration of services and treatment. Protocols should:

　　i.　prohibit the unauthorized disclosure of, or unauthorized access to, information relating to the dual-status youth, and

　　ii.　develop quality control measures that minimize the inadvertent disclosure of information relating to the youth.

(e) Absent an explicit exception under applicable state and federal law, juvenile justice agencies and professionals should always obtain informed written consent from the youth and the parent or guardian of the youth, before sharing personally identifiable information between agencies serving the youth. Youth, parents, or guardians with disabilities should receive accommodations necessary to provide informed consent.

(f) Any written consent for information sharing should state the purpose of sharing, the specific information to be shared, and the time frame within which the information will be shared.

(g) Information about dual-status youth should be shared with and used by youth-serving agencies in a manner that complies with state and federal laws governing confidentiality, including re-disclosure and privilege, and protects the youth's right against self-incrimination and right to due process as a respondent or defendant in any delinquency, criminal, summary offense, status offense, or child welfare case.

(h) Juvenile justice officials sharing information about dual-status youth should ensure that any youth-serving agency and system receiving that information is aware of and adheres to rules and standards governing confidentiality of Family Court records, including restrictions on the dissemination of physical and behavioral health records and limitations on the use of records for specified purposes.

(i) The juvenile court and other youth-serving agencies should develop docketing, filing, and records-disclosure systems that will allow court staff to redact and separate records and

information that may be disclosed from those that may not
be disclosed pursuant to state and federal confidentiality
laws.

Standard 2.12   Data Collection for Law, Policy, and Program Development

(a) Courts, legislatures, and state agencies should develop a
     system for collecting, reporting, and sharing data regarding
     dual-status youth to achieve one or more of the purposes
     identified in Standard 2.10 of these standards.

(b) Courts, legislatures, and state agencies should use data col-
     lection to improve outcomes for dual-status youth and to
     reduce unnecessary referral to and penetration into the juve-
     nile and criminal justice systems.

(c) Lawyers, judges, and other government agents should ensure
     that data collection protocols comply with applicable rules
     regarding confidentiality.

(d) Courts and state legislatures should periodically review
     the aggregate data collected to determine how to allocate
     resources to youth-serving agencies and systems within the
     jurisdiction, to improve procedures for handling youth who
     engage in delinquent behavior while in the care or custody
     of a youth-serving agency, and to improve the continuity of
     care for youth in multiple youth-serving systems.

Standard 2.13   Access to Court Records

(a) The use of and access to Family Court records should be
     strictly controlled to limit the risk of unnecessary and harm-
     ful disclosure.

(b) Court records involving youth alleged or adjudicated delin-
     quent or dependent should normally be closed to the general
     public.

(c) Juvenile justice officials who disclose information about
     dual-status youth should ensure that all recipients of that
     information are informed of all rules and standards govern-
     ing confidentiality of Family Court records.

(d) Courts and state legislatures should develop and enforce meaningful sanctions for the unlawful dissemination of Family Court records.

(e) Juvenile justice professionals who disclose information about dual-status youth should separate records that may be disclosed from those that may not be disclosed and redact disclosed records accordingly.

(f) Defense counsel in any juvenile or criminal case in which a youth is involved should normally have access to all Family Court records involving the youth.

(g) The Family Court should avoid standing orders or policies that grant the public, court staff, juvenile justice officials, or other youth-serving agencies broad access to any category of records generally found within a Family Court file. Instead, the Court should develop policies and protocols to grant access to such records only after a judicial officer or appropriate designate makes an individualized analysis of a records request.

Standard 2.14   Waivers of Confidentiality

(a) Juvenile justice or other youth-serving agency officials may ask a youth to waive confidentiality protections.

(b) A youth's waiver is valid only if it is made knowingly, intelligently, and voluntarily.

(c) If a youth has appointed or retained counsel, agency officials should permit the youth an opportunity to consult with counsel before waiving any confidentiality protections. Waivers obtained without such an opportunity should be considered presumptively invalid.

(d) In advising a youth regarding a possible waiver of confidentiality, the youth's lawyer should ensure the youth understands privilege, the youth's rights with respect to consent and confidentiality, and the potential consequences of waiving confidentiality or privilege in releasing information to others.

(e) Agency officials should allow a youth to consult with a parent or guardian before waiving any confidentiality protections; but a parent cannot waive the youth's rights or privileges. In a delinquency proceeding, the decision to waive should be the youth's.

(f) Any written waiver form should use youth-appropriate language and be written in a language the youth speaks or understands. If a youth has limited literacy, any waiver should be obtained and recorded in a manner that is understandable to the youth.

(g) A youth may negotiate the terms of the waiver to limit the time, scope or purpose of the waiver.

(h) A parent or guardian may waive confidentiality protections for records involving the parent.

E. CROSS-SYSTEM TRAINING

Standard 2.15   Need for Cross-System Training

(a) Family Courts and youth-serving agencies should promote training for all professionals in the juvenile justice and child welfare systems to reduce inappropriate referrals to the juvenile justice system.

(b) Training should include:

    i. the scope and availability of services and means for accessing services from the child welfare, behavioral health, physical health, public benefits, Family Court, and education systems;

    ii. information regarding any memoranda of understanding or other agreements between and among the various youth-serving agencies regarding the provision of services for youth;

    iii. laws, rules, and procedures applicable to confidentiality and privilege;

    iv. the role of the youth's defense counsel and best interest advocate for the youth;

v. child and adolescent development, brain development, disabilities, trauma, and resiliency development;

vi. sexual orientation and gender-identity;

vii. cultural competence;

viii. racial bias;

ix. evidence-based research on the effectiveness of services and programs in achieving good outcomes for youth in the juvenile justice and child welfare systems;

x. family and youth engagement; and

xi. the immigration consequences of the youth's involvement in the child welfare or juvenile justice system.

PART II COMMENTARY

2.1 Systems Collaboration

Youth are sometimes referred to the juvenile justice system on the premise that there is "no other place" to send them, even though they are eligible for and entitled to receive services in other systems. Often this happens during a behavioral crisis or deteriorating situation in a child welfare placement that may or may not be qualified to address the youth's needs. State systems should provide crisis intervention services that may address the presenting issues, as well as support and respite services for caregivers that could preserve existing placements and prevent unnecessary referral to the justice system.

There are many examples of local agencies working together since the late 1980s, when "coordination, cooperation, and collaboration" became bywords for agencies that serve children.[22] Often sister agencies may be able to provide behavioral supports, such as drug and alcohol treatment, addiction prevention and recovery services, mental health counseling, and other services that appropriately address the issues that prompted referral to the delinquency system. Local

---

22. *See, e.g.*, SHARON LYNN KAGAN, ET AL., COLLABORATIONS IN ACTION: RESHAPING SERVICES FOR YOUNG CHILDREN AND THEIR FAMILIES (1990).

collaborations have worked to prevent avoidable out-of-home place-ment of youth with serious emotional, behavioral, or mental health issues.[23]

These Standards go further. They assert that state law should *require* various agencies with legal obligations to the youth to work together. This is because, as noted earlier, youth are often referred to the juvenile justice system for behavior that would be within the expected range of misbehavior for adolescents. Fist fights, vandalism, minor drug use, conflict with authority figures, and even minor theft are behaviors that parents across America deal with on a regular basis without involving the court system. Foster care providers and biologi-cal parents may sometimes need help addressing these issues; states should implement crisis services and provide other support to care-givers when problems arise. The Standards call for state systems to provide alternative means of addressing such misbehavior before call-ing law enforcement or referring youth to the delinquency system. At the same time, nothing in Part II prohibits the discretionary referral of youth who engage in serious delinquent behavior.

These Standards recommend that state laws mandate and facilitate coordination between and among agencies that have a legal obligation to children. California, for example, has long required the child wel-fare and juvenile justice systems to develop a "written protocol" . . . to "initially determine which status will serve the best interests of the minor and the protection of society."[24] In some states, such as Califor-nia, the juvenile court has authority, in either delinquency or depen-dency proceedings, to join all agencies with a legal obligation to serve the youth in juvenile court proceedings.[25] Joinder provisions facilitate interagency coordination, planning, and accountability.

In some states, as in South Carolina, the juvenile court has authority to designate a "lead agency" to conduct a family assessment that iden-tifies the strengths and weaknesses of the family, problems interfering with the functioning of the family or the best interest of the child, and recommendations for a comprehensive service plan to strengthen the

---

23. The most widely cited of these programs is Wraparound Milwaukee. *See* WRAPAROUND MIL-WAUKEE, http://wraparoundmke.com/.

24. CAL. WELF. & INST. CODE ANN. § 241.1 (Deering 2020). Determination of minor's status. While section (a) of this statute prevents a youth from becoming dual status, section (e) allows the court to designate a youth as "dual status," to be served concurrently by both systems.

25. CAL. WELF. & INST. CODE §§ 362(a), 727 (Deering 2020); CAL. CT. r. 5.575(a).

family and assist in resolving issues. The lead agency is also responsible for monitoring compliance with any court-ordered plan developed after the family assessment.[26]

Part (d) of this Standard recognizes that broad definitions in contemporary domestic violence statutes define "domestic violence" to include any criminal or delinquent behavior that is alleged to have been perpetrated against a co-inhabitant of any residence, including congregate care facilities.[27] In contrast, this Standard encourages discretion in the arrest and referral of youth to the juvenile justice system, especially youth referred by or receiving services from a child welfare or other youth-serving agency or facility.

2.2 Structure of State Juvenile Justice and Child Welfare Systems

Too often foster or dependent youth who are transferred to the juvenile justice system are deprived of placements, services, funding, and protections they would otherwise receive in the foster care or child welfare systems. However, crossover youth and dual jurisdiction youth by virtue of their "crossover" characteristics need access to services and placements from both systems. Statutes and practices that attempt to maintain a purity of placements between the child-welfare and delinquency population ignore the fact that many youth do not fit neatly into one category or the other. It is essential that crossover and dual jurisdiction youth have access to all of the services and placements that are appropriate to meet their needs.[28] Even more important,

---

26. S.C. CHILD. CODE § 63-19-1410(A)(2).

27. Of course, apart from domestic violence, youth in congregate care can be, and are, arrested for a broad range of offenses.

28. Following the Supreme Court's 1967 *Gault* decision, states scrambled to enact new juvenile codes. In 1968, the National Conference of Commissioners on Uniform State Laws promulgated the Uniform Juvenile Court Act. This act, which was adopted by some states, recognized that a juvenile court should be able to order for delinquent youth any of the services that the court could order for dependent (called, in 1968, "deprived") youth. Uniform Juvenile Court Act § 31 [Disposition of Delinquent Child]. The ABA approved the Uniform Juvenile Court Act at its 1968 Annual Meeting. Increasing access to services is easy to legislate. For example, Pennsylvania, which adopted the Uniform Juvenile Court Act in 1972, gives judges in delinquency cases authority to issue "Any order authorized by section 6351 (relating to disposition of dependent child)." 42 PA. C.S. § 6352(a)(1). The 1980 IJA-ABA Juvenile Justice Standards go further, saying that at disposition "All publicly funded services to which nonadjudicated juveniles have access should be made available to adjudicated delinquents. In addition, juveniles adjudicated delinquent should have access to all services necessary for their normal growth and development." Standards Related to Disposition 4.1.

dependent youth in appropriate child welfare placements should not be removed from existing placements after an arrest, unless detention is otherwise warranted in the juvenile justice system due to the severity of the youth's delinquent offense. Such movement can be traumatic and creates instability for a youth, including disruption of positive relationships with program staff and in school (when they change schools, youth may lose positive role models, extracurricular activities, and supportive programs).

These Standards encourage states to ensure that any youth sent to non-secure residential care as a result of a delinquency or status offense petition receive the same protections and access to resources that other youth in foster care receive under Title IV-E of the Social Security Act.

The Social Security Act has long been a source of funding for children's services, primarily through Titles IV-B[29] and IV-E.[30] They were first enacted as part of the Adoption Assistance and Child Welfare Act of 1980.[31] That law, which has been amended several times (most recently as the Family First Prevention Services Act,[32] hereafter "Family First"), provides for federal financial participation to state child welfare systems if certain conditions are met. Title IV-B provides funds to state child welfare agencies that manage the foster care system, among other duties. Foster care—broadly defined as all out-of-home care that is not a public secure (locked) residential facility—is funded by Title IV-E. If youth are eligible—and if those out-of-home juvenile justice services are managed by the IV-B agency—delinquent services may be eligible as well for IV-E reimbursement.

Put another way, under Title IV-E of the Social Security Act, federal dollars can be used for a delinquent or status offender's placement in a "foster family home." Such a home is a setting for youth that is licensed or approved by the state in which it is situated. It can also be a "child care institution," which means a private child care institution, or a public child care institution, which accommodates no more than 25 young people, and which is licensed or approved by the state. However, an eligible "child care institution" does not include detention centers, forestry camps, training schools, or any other facility

---

29. 42 U.S.C. §§ 620 *et seq.*
30. *Id.* §§ 670 *et seq.*
31. Pub. L. No. 96-272.
32. Pub. L. No. 115-123, §§ 50731 *et seq.*, at 42 U.S.C §§ 670 *et seq.*

operated primarily for the detention of delinquent youth. Youth in foster care may lose considerable benefits if they leave the child welfare system for the delinquency system, especially if they end up in placements that are ineligible for IV-E reimbursements.[33]

For a youth to qualify for these federal subsidies, in addition to a court making the findings required by Family First, discussed later, a court must make findings that "reasonable efforts" were made to avoid the need for placement and later to provide legal permanency for the youth. The court must also find that placement is in the youth's best interests. These findings must be made in the first court order authorizing the youth's removal from home, but no later than 60 days after removal. The youth must also receive a written "case plan" no later than 60 days after removal.

Such "IV-E placements" give states not only a way of obtaining federal subsidies for youth placement (saving considerable state funds) but also trigger a range of procedural protections that delinquent or status offender youth might otherwise not receive through the juvenile justice system. They are also beneficial because the status of the placed youth must be frequently reviewed by a court. Other IV-E benefits include the fact that the youth's parents must be parties to the permanency hearing (so that there is a focus on improving the care and supervision of the youth if they are to return home), that the youth's foster parents, relatives, and others must have advance notice of court hearings and the opportunity to be heard at them, and that children and youth eligible for IV-E funding are automatically entitled to Medicaid coverage. The Affordable Care Act provides an additional benefit: youth who were in foster care and enrolled in Medicaid at their 18th birthday are entitled to Medicaid coverage until their 26th birthday.[34]

The use of Title IV-E funding for youth in, and transitioning from, the juvenile justice system has become even more important since federal law in 2008[35] authorized states to use IV-E funding for youth in foster care through their 21st birthdays. Since this law was enacted, most states, through law, policy, or practice, permit 18-, 19-, and 20-year-old youth to voluntarily remain in foster care (or to re-enter

---

33. Lauren Wylie, *Closing the Crossover Gap: Amending Fostering Connections to Provide Independent Living Services for Foster Youth Who Crossover to the Justice System*, 52 FAM. CT. REV. 298 (Apr. 2014).

34. Patient Protection and Affordable Care Act, Pub. L. No. 111–148, § 2004.

35. Fostering Connections to Success and Increasing Adoptions Act, Pub. L. No. 110-351.

after they earlier left care) or to reside in independent living settings with IV-E financial support. Many dependency courts have had their jurisdictional age increased beyond 18 in order to review the cases of these older youth periodically and monitor child welfare agency efforts to prepare youth adequately for a successful transition to adulthood.

Child welfare agencies can also use a separate pot of federal money, known as "Chafee Act" funds,[36] to pay for a youth's independent living services, as well as for room or board for children who left foster care at age 18. There is also funding under this program for education and training vouchers that can financially support older youths' college and vocational education costs. It is therefore important that older youth still in the juvenile justice system have access to these post-age 18 Title IV-E and Chafee Act funds.

Enacted in 2018, Family First is the latest iteration of Title IV-E. Family First dollars are available for foster care. As with earlier versions of the Social Security Act, those dollars can also be used for delinquent youth, if those youth are included in a state's Title IV-B plan. Under Family First, there are many benefits to a system that claims Title IV-E dollars for both dependent and delinquent youth.

First, states will be able to use IV-E dollars to pay for prevention services upon implementation of Family First. IV-E dollars can then be used for youth who are "candidates" for foster care, meaning they are identified in a prevention plan as being at imminent risk of entering care but can safely remain at home or in a kinship placement if provided services that prevent entry into foster care, such as substance abuse treatment. Counties can provide preventive services for up to 12 months and there are no income eligibility requirements for families. Such services must be trauma-informed, and they must be evidence-based.[37]

Second, Family First has the potential to transform residential programs into short-term, trauma-informed programs that have better health care and do much more to engage families than current juvenile justice programs. Eligible programs are called Qualified Residential

---

36. This law, named after a former senator, is known as the John H. Chafee Foster Care Independence Program, but the formal title of the law is the Foster Care Independence Act, Pub. L. No. 106-169.

37. See 42 U.S.C. § 671 for the elements of a state's plan that are required to claim federal IV-E dollars. Evidence-based programs must be reviewed and approved by the Title IV-E Prevention Services Clearinghouse, https://preventionservices.abtsites.com/.

Treatment Programs (QRTP); alongside family foster homes, QRTPs will be the only residential programs that qualify for IV-E reimbursement for youth in care for more than two weeks.[38]

Family First also requires an assessment that a QRTP is necessary before IV-E dollars can flow to the state. The person doing the assessment must address the youth's strengths and needs using an age-appropriate, evidence-based, validated, functional assessment tool. Although the HHS Secretary can waive this requirement, Family First calls for the administration of an assessment tool by an independent professional who cannot be the juvenile probation officer. The assessment must be done within 30 days of placement, in order for IV-E to pay for residential care. Family First has additional requirements, including timely juvenile court review of placements.

States also receive federal funds through the Juvenile Justice and Delinquency Prevention Act (JJDPA) formula grant program. JJDPA conditions federal funds on states meeting a number of requirements. One such requirement—which has been included in all recent JJDPA reauthorizations, says that state JJDPA plans must

> provide assurances that juvenile offenders whose placement is funded through [Title IV-E] section 472 of the Social Security Act (42 U.S.C. 672) receive the protections specified in section 471 of such Act (42 U.S.C. 671), including a case plan and case plan review as defined in section 475 of such Act (42 U.S.C. 675).[39]

There are thus "crossover" prescriptions in the two major federal funding laws governing juvenile justice and child welfare.

2.3   Juvenile Court Policies, Protocols, and Rules

Delinquency cases involving youth coming from the child welfare system are more likely to involve treatment that is harsher than that applied to other youth. Indeed, decades of research has shown that there is a "child welfare system bias" in favor of processing misbehaving youth through the juvenile justice system.[40]

---

38. *See* 42 U.S.C. § 672 for the various prerequisites to a state claiming IV-E dollars for a QRTP.
39. 34 U.S.C. § 11133(a)(27).
40. This leads to the overuse of detention, and the underuse of diversion, that brings dependent youth unnecessarily deeper into the juvenile justice system. *See generally* Joseph P. Ryan, et al., *Maltreatment and Delinquency: Investigating Child Welfare Bias in Juvenile Justice Processing*, 29 CHILD. & YOUTH SERVICES REV. (Aug. 2007).

To respond to this bias, many courts have developed Memoran-
dums of Understanding (MOU) or policies to address dual status
youth. The National Council of Juvenile and Family Court Judges'
National Center for State Courts describes three such efforts in "When
Systems Collaborate: How Three Jurisdictions Improved Their Handling of Dual-Status Cases."[41]

2.4 Juvenile Court Leadership

Judicial leadership is crucial to successful juvenile court reforms. That
has been particularly true of recent efforts to reduce the unnecessary
use of juvenile detention,[42] to keeping status offenders out of the delinquency system,[43] and to reducing school referrals to juvenile court.[44]

Research on Georgetown's Crossover Youth Practice Model has
demonstrated the importance of juvenile court leadership to achieving
reforms that benefit youth:

> Engaged and active leadership is a pillar in any change process—it
> makes a meaningful difference in every aspect of an organization's work.
> This support is ever more critical when multiple agencies and organiza-
> tions are working together collaboratively. In working with dual system
> youth, leadership from child welfare, the courts, and juvenile justice are
> essential to achieving success. Because of the authority and high regard
> that the courts have over not only these two systems but many others,
> judicial leadership can be used to set the tone for the change process and
> ensure cross-systems work is a priority to the stakeholders involved.
> Effective judicial leaders can leverage their authority to identify and con-
> vene important stakeholders, determine areas in need of improvement,

41. Douglas Thomas et al., *When Systems Collaborate: How Three Jurisdictions Improved Their Handling of Dual-Status Cases, Juvenile Justice Geography Policy, Practice & Statistics*, Nat'l Ctr. for Juv.
Just. (Apr. 2015), http://www.ncjj.org/pdf/Juvenile%20Justice%20Geography,%20Policy,%20Prac
tice%20and%20Statistics%202015/WhenSystemsCollaborateJJGPSCaseStudyFinal042015.pdf.
42. *See* JDAI, *Illinois Symposium Focuses on Rural Judicial Leadership*, JDAI News, (June 2004),
http://www.aecf.org/upload/publicationfiles/june2004.pdf; Bart Lubow, *Safely Reducing Reliance
on Juvenile Detention: A Report from the Field*, 67.5 Corrections Today (Aug. 2005); and Richard A.
Mendel, Two Decades of JDAI: From Demonstration Project to National Standard (Annie
E. Casey Foundation 2009), http://www.aecf.org/~/media/Pubs/Initiatives/Juvenile%20Deten
tion%20Alternatives%20Initiative/TwoDecadesofJDAIFromDemonstrationProjecttoNat/JDAI
_National_final_10_07_09.pdf.
43. Steven C. Teske & J. Brian Huff, *The Dichotomy of Judicial Leadership: Working with the Community to Improve Outcomes for Status Youth*, 61(2) Juv. & Fam. Ct. J. 54 (2010), https://www.njjn
.org/uploads/digital-library/resource_1680.pdf.
44. *See* NCJFCJ's School Justice Partnership, https://schooljusticepartnership.org/, which
has relied on juvenile court leadership. This is discussed more in Part III.

and implement solutions to address challenges. Given the positioning of judges they are also able to institute measures of accountability to demand collaboration for the wellbeing of youth.[45]

2.5   Juvenile and Criminal Court Jurisdiction

Youth may be "transferred" or "waived" to adult court through a number of statutory frameworks, including direct filing by prosecuting attorneys, age and offense exclusions from juvenile court jurisdiction, and transfer hearings before a juvenile court judge. "Waiver" was the term used in the 1980 IJA-ABA Standards.[46] These Standards apply across the range of terminology and transfer mechanisms.

Despite states in the early 1990s making it easier to transfer youth to criminal court,[47] the 1980 Standards disfavor transfer,[48] putting the burden on prosecutors to convince a court that a youth is "not a proper person to be handled by the juvenile court."[49] In making a transfer decision under the 1980 Standards, the juvenile court must include a determination, by clear and convincing evidence, supported by expert opinion, of "the likely efficacy of the dispositions available to the juvenile court."[50]

---

45. Denise C. Herz & Carly B. Dierkhising, OJJDP Dual System Youth Design Study: Summary of Findings and Recommendations for Pursuing a National Estimate of Dual System Youth Final Technical Report, Nat'l Crim. Just. Reference Serv. 24 (2018), https://www.ncjrs.gov/pdffiles1/ojjdp/grants/252717.pdf.

46. Robert E. Shepherd, Jr. et al., *Standards Relating to Transfer between Courts*, 2.1, in IJA-ABA Juvenile Justice Standards Annotated: A Balanced Approach (1996).

47. *See Jurisdictional Boundaries*, Juv. Just. Geography, Pol'y, Prac. & Stat., http://www.jjgps.org/jurisdictional-boundaries (last visited Feb. 7, 2023).

48. Studies have shown that transferring youth to criminal court increases recidivism, in particular among violent offenders, does not increase public safety, and has little general deterrent effect in the juvenile population. *See* the overview of research in Richard E. Redding, *Juvenile Transfer Laws: An Effective Deterrent to Delinquency?* Office of Juvenile Justice & Delinquency Prevention, Juvenile Justice Bulletin (June 2010), https://www.ncjrs.gov/pdffiles1/ojjdp/220595.pdf. Numerous national organizations have addressed the harm that transfer does to youth; they have also documented racial and ethnic disparities in transfer. *See, e.g.*, The W. Haywood Burns Institute for Justice Fairness & Equity, Burnsinstitute.org; Campaign for Youth Justice, campaignforyouthjustice.org; The Campaign for the Fair Sentencing of Youth, fairsentencingofyouth.org; No Kids in Prison, nokidsinprison.org; and The Sentencing Project, sentencingproject.org.

49. JJGPS, note 73, *supra* note 46, 2.2C.

50. *Id.* at 2.2C.4. While disfavoring transfer, these Standards do not address how dependent children should be treated if they are transferred. Guidance may be found, however, in *Youth in the Criminal Justice System: Guidelines for Policymakers and Practitioners*, ABA (2001), the seven guiding principles of which were adopted as ABA policy in 2002.

These Standards go further, requiring juvenile courts that make the transfer decision to consider how services from the child welfare system can assist youth and promote public safety.

2.6   Dependency Jurisdiction

Dependency court protocols are particularly important to address the arrest of youth in the child welfare system. These standards address two discrete circumstances: (1) youth who are arrested for conduct that is not connected to their status as a dependent child; and (2) youth who are charged with crimes and referred to juvenile court by representatives of the child welfare system, such as foster parents or group home staff.

In the former instance, when the child welfare system acts as the child's parent, it is imperative that social workers, foster parents, or institution staff take the child home from the police station; prevent interrogation or questioning of the youth without counsel;[51] supervise the child to avoid the use of secure detention; and support the child before, during, and after juvenile court hearings. This is what any "responsible parent" would do. In New York City, for example, when a foster youth has been arrested, child welfare agencies are required to communicate to ensure that a responsible guardian is present to take custody of the child and reduce the need for secure detention.[52]

In either instance, these Standards require juvenile courts to make sure that children don't unnecessarily lose the benefits of their "dependent child" status. These benefits include the Title IV-E and health care benefits discussed earlier in commentary to Standard 2.2.

The federal government since 1974, with the adoption of the Juvenile Justice and Delinquency Prevention Act (JJDPA),[53] has used the leverage of funding to decriminalize and deincarcerate "status offenders," that is, children whose behavior would not be criminal if committed by an adult. These provisions were strengthened in 2018, when the JJDPA was reauthorized through the Juvenile Justice Reform Act, although the 2018 act continues to permit detention of status

---

51. Youth are vulnerable to police questioning. *J.D.B. v. North Carolina*, 546 U.S. 261 (2011). Foster youth, many of whom have a history of trauma, are likely to be particularly vulnerable.

52. Dylan Conger & Timothy Ross, *Project Confirm: An Outcome Evaluation of a Program for Children in the Child Welfare and Juvenile Justice Systems*, 4(1) YOUTH VIOLENCE & JUV. JUST. (2006).

53. Pub. L. No. 93-415.

offenders for violation of valid court orders, with restrictions.[54] The original IJA-ABA Standards included a volume, Standards Relating to Noncriminal Misbehavior, that was tabled by the House of Delegates as too controversial."[55] Other national organizations have opposed criminalization of status offenders and rejected the valid court order exception.[56] These Standards effectively reject the valid court order exception by requiring courts to avoid using civil or criminal contempt citations to "bootstrap" youth into the delinquency system.[57]

One cannot assume that youth in the child welfare system already have legal representation. As noted earlier (see definition of "dependency counsel"), the American Bar Association in 2011 adopted as policy *The Model Act Governing the Representation of Children in Abuse, Neglect, and Dependency Proceedings.*[58] The ABA Model Act, in general, calls for client-directed lawyers to represent children in all child welfare cases.[59] Nevertheless, as of 2019, only two-thirds of the states require counsel for children in abuse and neglect proceedings; of those 34 jurisdictions, "only 15 of the 34 require client-directed counsel under all reasonable circumstances."[60]

---

54. Pub. L. No. 115-385, § 223(a)23), at 34 USCS § 11133(a)(23).

55. Barbara Flicker, *Introduction, in,* IJA-ABA JUVENILE JUSTICE STANDARDS: A BALANCED APPROACH xviii (Robert E. Shepherd, Jr., ed., 1996).

56. Jessica Kendall et al., *National Standards for the Care of Youth Charged with Status Offenses,* COAL. FOR JUV. JUST. (2014).

57. The use of contempt to turn a status offender into a delinquent youth has been a subject of contention for decades. *See, e.g., Interest of Taessing H.*, 281 Pa. Super. 400, 422 A.2d 530 (1980), rejecting "bootstrapping"; *but see* In Interest of J.E.S., 817 P.2d 508 (Colo. S. Ct. 1991).

58. For a summary, *see* Andrea Khoury, *ABA Adopts Model Act on Child Representation,* ABA (Sept. 1, 2011), https://www.americanbar.org/groups/public_interest/child_law/resources/child_law_practiceonline/child_law_practice/vol30/september_2011/aba_adopts_modelactonchildrepresentation/. For a link to the Model Act, go to http://nfpcar.org/Legislation/ABA/index.htm.

59. The U.S. Supreme Court has not addressed children's right to counsel in dependency cases. The Washington State Supreme Court rejected a constitutional right to counsel in all cases. *See In re Dependency of E.H.*, 191 Wn. 2d 872 (2018). *See also In the Interest of D. B. and D. S.*, 385 So. 2d 83, Supreme Court of Florida (1980). On the other hand, an intermediate appellate court in New York found both a constitutional and statutory right to counsel in dependency cases. *In the Matter of Jamie TT*, 191 A.D.2d 132, 136, 599 N.Y.S.2d 892 (1993). State supreme courts have usually treated this as a statutory issue, upholding a right to counsel when it is authorized by the legislature. *See, e.g.,* Stapleton v. Dauphin County Child Care Services, 228 Pa. Super, 371, 324 A.2d. 562 (1974). In some states, appointing a guardian ad litem does not satisfy the state's statutory requirement that children have lawyers in dependency proceedings. *See, e.g., In re Stacey S.*, 737 N.E.2d 92 (Ohio Ct. App. 1999).

60. *A Child's Right to Counsel: A National Report Card on Legal Representation for Abused & Neglected Children,* FIRST STAR INST. & THE CHILDREN'S ADVOCACY INST., 4th ed. (2019), http://www.caichildlaw.org/Misc/RTC4.pdf.

However, all youth charged in a delinquency case have a constitutional right to counsel.[61] Given the stakes involved, these Standards require that crossover and dual jurisdiction youth should have the assistance of defense counsel in navigating and expressing their views in the dependency system as well as in the delinquency system. Specifically, crossover youth should have the aid of counsel in expressing their views on whether their dependency case should be terminated after an arrest or referral to juvenile court, after considering all of the economic benefits of extended foster care jurisdiction and transition funding. This is particularly important given the rights that dependent children have after their 18th birthday, described in the commentary to Standard 2.2.

2.7   Docketing Proceedings Involving Dual-Status Youth

At any given time, children and families may be involved in multiple legal proceedings within the juvenile court or Family Court. As a result, family members will need to appear in court on multiple occasions across systems, causing them to miss work, school, treatment, and other important obligations. The Family Court, in tandem with the juvenile court, should make every effort to reduce the number of days a family will need to appear in court and minimize the disruption the proceedings cause to the family and child. The Family Court and juvenile court clerk's offices should play an important role in ensuring that court hearings are scheduled at times that are most convenient for the family.

IJA/ABA Standards say that "the same judge should consider the different legal issues that relate to all members of the same family."[62] Further, the same Standard says that a "judge who presides at an adjudicatory hearing should conduct the disposition hearing of the case."[63]

> There are various benefits to using a coordinated approach to serving dual status youth. First, having one judge familiar with the family can encourage a more holistic approach in both the child welfare and juvenile justice cases. With comprehensive information about a youth's family,

---

61. *In re* Gault, 387 U.S. 1 (1967).
62. Standards Relating to Court Organization and Administration, 1.1B.
63. The ABA in 1994 adopted policy calling for Unified Juvenile and Family Courts, at the same time confirming the Association's support for the 1980 Standards Relating to Court Organization and Administration 1.1. The 1994 policy can be found at *Index to ABA Criminal Justice Policies*, ABA (Nov. 11, 2019).

behavior, and detention history as well as education, mental health, and other needs, judges can make better decisions about what services and support are needed to meet the child's best interests while protecting the community against future delinquent conduct. Regular collaboration and communication among professionals serving dual status youth fosters more efficient use of staff resources, helps avoid unnecessary delay in court proceedings, and maximizes the potential for positive outcomes. From the youth or family perspective, a coordinated approach can mean less missed days from work or school; fewer requests to repeat the same, often emotionally complex, information; and more consistent support and interventions.[64]

These Standards recognize that there are times when a judge who presides over dual-jurisdiction and crossover youth may become so engaged in the family that it becomes difficult for the judge at trial to fairly adjudicate the youth's involvement or non-involvement in delinquency. The appearance of impropriety in certain cases may also dictate assignment of the youth's adjudicatory hearing to a neutral fact-finder.[65] Thereafter, cases should be consolidated for dispositional and post-dispositional proceedings.[66]

Dispositions and post-disposition planning of dual status youth should account for permanency planning. Whether held in the child welfare case or in the delinquency case (for states receiving Title IV-E funding for delinquents), permanency hearings are required under the Family First Act discussed earlier in commentary to Section 2.2. Having a single judge issue orders to juvenile probation and child welfare social workers will, perforce, create a single permanency goal for the youth to which all systems subscribe. Permanency planning should be a core component of the delinquency system as well as the dependency system: youth in the justice system should receive help

---

64. Gary Coley & Lisa Jarrett, *Two Doors to the Courthouse: A Judicial Perspective on Dual Status Youth*, STATE BAR OF TEXAS (Oct. 2019), https://lsc-pagepro.mydigitalpublication.com/publication/?m=21412&i=620101&view=articleBrowser&article_id=3482608&ver=html5.

65. Although small or rural jurisdictions may have difficulty assigning judges who have never presided over a particular child's case, states should make efforts so that each jurisdiction has enough judges to ensure due process protections. The greatest need will likely arise in contested delinquency adjudicatory hearings.

66. *See* Gene Siegel & Rachael Lord, *When Systems Collide: Improving Court Practices and Programs in Dual Jurisdiction Cases*, 56 JUV. & FAM. CT. J., 39–59 (2005); and a case study of Cook County, Illinois's juvenile court initiative in JANET K. WIIG ET AL., GUIDEBOOK FOR JUVENILE JUSTICE & CHILD WELFARE SYSTEM COORDINATION AND INTEGRATION: A FRAMEWORK FOR IMPROVED OUTCOMES 75 (Robert F. Kennedy Children's Action Corps, 3d ed. 2013). For additional discussion, *see* Part VII, *infra*.

planning for and developing sustained relationships with a caring adult. Permanency planning is a core component of aftercare ("re-entry") planning for delinquent youth as well as dependent youth.[67] It is an important vehicle for engaging youth in their cases and planning their futures as they make a transition to adulthood. Client-directed counsel, as required by these standards, are ideally positioned to assist youth to whom federal law gives a right to actively participate in planning their transitions.[68]

2.8   Designated Dual-Status Dockets

These Standards encourage juvenile courts to serve as gatekeepers, to reject entry into the juvenile justice system of youth whose behavior can easily be managed by other systems. Minor misbehavior—defined earlier as "minor delinquent behavior"—should be managed when possible by schools, mental health providers, and child welfare agencies. At the same time, some youth are appropriately referred to juvenile court because of the seriousness of their misbehavior. When that happens, it is important that court systems avoid sending inconsistent messages to children and families. When the dependency court issues orders that conflict with the delinquency court, it is like a mother and father giving different instructions to their children.

Thus, a single dual status docket is particularly important for youth who are in both the delinquency and child welfare systems. A single judge, at the disposition or disposition review hearing, can make sure that a juvenile probation's plans are consistent with those of the child welfare case manager. A single judge will understand a youth's exposure to trauma and make sure that both systems consider that exposure when developing case plans. A single judge will make sure that a child's lawyers—with different legal responsibilities to the child welfare and juvenile justice system—don't confuse their roles or their clients, but deliver a consistent message to them.

A single judge with a dual status docket is the engine that drives these Standards for youth who end up in both systems.

---

67. *See* Part VIII., *infra.*

68. *See generally* Adrienne L. Fernandes-Alcantara, *Youth Transitioning from Foster Care: Background and Federal Programs,* https://fas.org/sgp/crs/misc/RL34499.pdf (last updated May 29, 2019).

Special docketing systems for crossover youth may be beneficial for systems integration, coordinating multiple agencies involved, reducing the complication of getting all of the agencies involved, helping courts allocate enough time to hear all of the matters and issues raised, ensuring effective delivery of services, and avoiding inconsistent or duplicative orders or services. The RFK National Resource Center has worked with many jurisdictions to help them fashion dual jurisdiction dockets.[69] RFK has prepared numerous other materials to assist practitioners, including a bench card for judges who manage these dockets.[70] The Center for Juvenile Justice Reform (CJJR) at Georgetown University categorizes court approaches as: dedicated dockets, one judge/one family approaches, and pre-court coordination.[71] CJJR developed a Crossover Youth Practice Model that involves judges in leadership roles, as jurisdictions rethink the way they address crossover and potentially crossover youth.[72]

2.9   Dual-Status Youth Crossing State and Local Jurisdictions

The Interstate Compact for Juveniles is implemented and interpreted by the Interstate Commission for Juveniles.[73] The Interstate Compact for Juveniles addresses delinquent youth and status offenders who,

---

69. These include Clark County, Ohio; Knox County, Ohio; Lancaster County, Pennsylvania; Santa Clara County, California; State of Delaware, with a special focus on Commercial Sexual Exploitation of Children. The Center has also provided technical assistance to other jurisdictions that are now operating dual jurisdiction dockets. These include Marion County, Indiana; Hampden County, Massachusetts; and Los Angeles County, California. See *Dual Status Youth Reform*, ROBERT F. KENNEDY CHILDREN'S ACTION CORPS, https://rfknrcjj.org/our-work/dual-status-youth-reform/. There are other dual docket jurisdictions, such as Philadelphia and Allegheny County, in Pennsylvania, but there is no single list that includes them all.

70. *See Dual Status Youth Bench Card*, ROBERT F. KENNEDY CHILDREN'S ACTION CORPS, https://rfknrcjj.org/wp-content/uploads/2016/06/Dual-Status-Youth-Bench-Card.pdf (last visited Feb. 7, 2023).

71. *See* Elizabeth Barnett et al., *Consolidated Court Proceedings for Crossover Youth*, CTR. FOR JUV. JUST. REFORM, CROSSOVER YOUTH PRACTICE MODEL BULLETIN SERIES (June 2018), https://cjjr.georgetown.edu/resources/publications/. CJJR has assisted with dedicated dockets in Prince George's County, Maryland; Travis County, Texas; and Sacramento County, California.

72. *See generally Crossover Youth Practice Model*, CTR. FOR JUV. JUST. REFORM, https://cjjr.georgetown.edu/our-work/crossover-youth-practice-model/#practicemodel (last visited Feb. 7, 2023).

73. *About the Interstate Compact for Juveniles*, INTERSTATE COMMISSION FOR JUVENILES, https://www.juvenilecompact.org/about (last visited Feb. 7, 2023).

in some states, are treated as dependent children.[74] The American Public Human Services Association (APHSA) administers the Interstate Compact on the Placement of Children (ICPC), which covers movement of dependent children, including foster youth.[75] The Uniform Child Custody Jurisdiction and Enforcement Act (the UCCJEA) governs state courts' jurisdiction to make and modify "child-custody determinations," a term that expressly includes custody and visitation orders (but not child support cases).[76] These statutes have gaps, but give direction to jurisdictions to ensure that the appropriate court assumes jurisdiction over dual status youth.

This Standard has particular importance *within* a state. The simple crossing of county lines can throw the management of dual status cases into chaos. For example, a youth in the child welfare system in County A is arrested in County B, raising issues of whether the youth is returned to County A for probation supervision and whether the conditions of probation and case plan are developed in concert with the case worker in County A. States generally allow for venue in the delinquency court to occur either where the delinquent act allegedly occurred or in the youth's county of residence.[77] There is a general lack of in-state guidance for determining venue when the arrested youth is residing in County A as a dependent child. This Standard prompts state legislatures—or Supreme Courts, through rule-making—to include the youth's dependency status in County B's determination of venue.

2.10–2.12   Information Sharing and Data Collection

These Standards build on existing IJA/ABA Standards Relating to Juvenile Records and Information Services, and draw on a large volume of literature in this area.[78]

---

74. *The Interstate Compact for Juveniles*, https://www.juvenilecompact.org/sites/default/files/IC JRevisedLanguage.pdf (last visited Feb. 7, 2023).

75. *Interstate Compact for Placement of Children*, NCSC, https://www.ncsc.org/Services-and-Exp erts/Government-Relations/Child-Welfare/Interstate-Compact-for-Placement-of-Children.aspx.

76. *See generally, Uniform Child Custody Jurisdiction and Enforcement Act: Guide for Court Personnel and Judges*, NCJFCJ, https://www.ncjfcj.org/publications/uniform-child-custody-jurisdiction-and -enforcement-act-guide-for-court-personnel-and-judges/.

77. Georgia's statute is a typical example of this venue provision. GA CODE §15-11-490 (2014).

78. *See* Standards 15.1 (A) and (B), which call for the strict control of access to and use of juvenile records.

These Standards address *information sharing* and *data sharing*, as well as access to court records. The substance of these Standards has been drawn from the MacArthur Foundation-supported "Models for Change Information Sharing Tool Kit, Second Edition."[79]

Information sharing involves information about an identified youth that is used for case planning and court decisions.

Recognizing the inherent tension between the youth's right to privacy and confidentiality and the need for information sharing and data collection about youth who are involved in multiple systems, these Standards attempt to guide juvenile justice professionals in determining whether, when, and how to share and collect information.

Too often, information-sharing protocols involving youth in multiple systems do not adequately protect against the possible *harms* of information sharing. Professionals often presume that with more information, decision-makers will make better and more appropriate decisions for a youth. While this may sometimes be true, it is not always true. Information can be harmful due to bias generated by increased knowledge about the youth or because the decision-maker simply does not know how to interpret or use the information. Sometimes a surfeit of information leads professionals to intervene with the best of intentions, causing them to ignore the most important injunction: "Do no harm." These Standards offer guidance on how information should and should not be used.

Information sharing, and prohibition on sharing, is governed by a host of federal and state laws. Sometimes these laws mandate collecting non-identifying data so policy makers can understand the impact of federal law. The Child Abuse Prevention and Treatment and Adoption Reform Act of 1978 requires grants to states to support and enhance "interagency collaboration between the child protection system and the juvenile justice system for improved delivery of services and treatment, including methods for continuity of treatment plan and services as children transition between systems."[80] The Juvenile Justice and Delinquency Prevention Act, reauthorized in 2018, requires research on a wide range of delinquency prevention topics, including

---

79. Published in 2015, the Toolkit is a joint product of Juvenile Law Center and the RFK National Resource Center for Juvenile Justice with contributions by Stephanie Rondenell, an independent consultant. It is available at http://www.modelsforchange.net/publications/759.

80. 42 U.S.C. § 5106(a)(12).

its connection to domestic violence, mental health, status offending, and other related areas.[81]

Other federal laws place restrictions on information sharing, in particular around individual identifying information related to health care[82] and education records.[83]

With respect to *Information Sharing*, these Standards are meant to supplement, and not override, the many state and federal legal, constitutional, and ethical principles regarding the confidentiality of personally identifiable information. Because these laws and provisions change often, juvenile justice professionals should remain familiar with current law and guidelines regarding confidentiality. These provisions include but are not limited to the Family Education Rights and Privacy Act (FERPA); Health Insurance Portability and Accountability Act (HIPAA); state and federal drug and alcohol laws; and state law protecting juvenile justice records, mental health records, and physical and behavioral health information. Jurisdictions developing information-sharing agreements should be clear that they are consistent with these Standards; that information might be permissibly shared does not mean that it should be. Special attention should be given to obtaining informed consent of the youth per Standards 2.11 and 2.14.

With respect to *Data Sharing*, these Standards supplement existing IJA-ABA Standards Relating to Monitoring, and IJA-ABA Standards Relating to Planning for Juvenile Justice.

It is important to track the source of referral to the juvenile justice system of dual-jurisdiction, crossover, or other youth with multisystem needs. Data regarding the source of referral can be used to identify possible gaps in services, sources of inappropriate referral, and priorities for funding. Referral sources may include schools, special

---

81. 34 U.S.C. § 11161(a).

82. Health Insurance Portability and Accountability Act of 1996 (HIPAA), Pub. L. No. 104-191. The act has five titles that are distributed throughout the U.S. Code.

83. The Family Educational Rights and Privacy Act (FERPA), 20 U.S.C. § 1232g. FERPA gives parents certain rights with respect to their children's education records. These rights transfer to the student when he or she reaches the age of 18 or attends a school beyond the high school level. Students to whom the rights have transferred are "eligible students." Generally, schools must have written permission from the parent or eligible student in order to release any information from a student's education record. However, FERPA allows schools to disclose those records, without consent, to State and local authorities, within a juvenile justice system, pursuant to specific state law. 34 C.F.R. § 99.31.

education programs, child welfare systems, drug or alcohol treatment programs, and mental health facilities.

Data tracking may inform resource allocation and aid in the development of policy and practice. Data should be collected with an eye toward reducing the number of inappropriate referrals to, and preventing unnecessary penetration deeper into, the juvenile justice system of youth with multisystem needs. In addition, data collection should be used to improve *services* for crossover and dual-jurisdiction youth in the juvenile justice system. Data collection may help intake officials in the juvenile justice system determine whether to accept jurisdiction of youth with multisystem needs and ensure that youth with multisystem needs are getting discharged into appropriate systems.

Data collection protocols may also track the following:

- The number of youth involved in the juvenile justice system who are also being served by or have previously been served by other youth-serving systems;
- The number of youth in the juvenile justice system in need of mental health intervention, substance abuse, or special education services;
- The number of youth referred by the juvenile justice system to other youth-serving agencies or systems, but who were ultimately rejected by or denied services, treatment, or care from the latter;
- The number of crossover and dual-jurisdiction youth referred to the juvenile justice system by race, gender, ethnicity, and LGBTQ status;
- The number of youth referred to the juvenile justice system who are pregnant or have children of their own; and
- Patterns and trends of delinquent behavior.

2.13 Access to Court Records

These Standards endorse a preference against unfettered public access to Family Court records, following the Model Act that the ABA adopted as policy in 2015.[84]

---

84. *Model Act Governing the Confidentiality and Expungement of Juvenile Delinquency Records*, ABA (Aug. 2015), https://www.americanbar.org/content/dam/aba/images/abanews/2015annualresolutions/103a.pdf.

Notwithstanding that preference, the Standards recognize that some jurisdictions have adopted narrow exceptions to confidentiality. For example, some jurisdictions allow victims of juvenile delinquency to get limited information from a juvenile record. Other jurisdictions allow the media to obtain limited information when a youth has been charged or adjudicated of some serious delinquent behavior. In states where such exceptions are made, procedures should be established to ensure that the recipient understands the limitations on the use and re-dissemination of that information.

Procedures should be established to enforce confidentiality provisions. In several jurisdictions, it is a criminal offense to unlawfully disseminate confidential information about a youth involved in a delinquency or depending proceeding.[85]

State laws should rarely make an entire file available to the public but should carefully delineate the types of information and portions of files that may be made public. Public access should be narrowly circumscribed for crossover and dual-jurisdiction youth. For example, many states allow the public to access records of certain serious offenses in the juvenile delinquency system. If youth are also involved in the dependency system, their dependency records should not be publicly available.

The court should rarely if ever issue a standing order granting access to any class of Family Court records or any type of record generally found within a Family Court file. Standing orders prevent judges from making the type of careful and individualized determinations about access to records that is necessary to ensure that records are maintained with the strictest of confidentiality.

2.14   Waivers of Confidentiality

As noted earlier, *information sharing*—which relates to individual-specific information that is used for planning, service delivery, and judicial decisions—can be both helpful and harmful. Systems should avoid pressuring youth to give broad waivers to confidentiality protections. Youth and their counsel must be clear about how information

---

85. *See, e.g.,* D.C. Code § 16-2336 ("Whoever willfully discloses, receives, makes use of, or knowingly permits the use of information concerning a child or other person in violation of these confidentiality provisions, shall be guilty of a misdemeanor and, upon conviction thereof, shall be fined not more than $250 or imprisoned not more than ninety days, or both.").

might help or hurt the youth. This is similar to informed consent in medicine, where patients are advised of an intervention's benefits and risks.

Juvenile justice officials routinely ask youth to waive confidentiality protections orally or by written waiver forms. Research in adolescent development and neuroscience has revealed limits on youths' abilities to resist adult appeals to relinquish rights.[86] These Standards are grounded in the developmental literature.[87] They stress the importance of having counsel for any child who is being asked to waive confidentiality rights.[88]

2.15   Need for Cross-System Training[89]

Juvenile courts should be familiar with evidence-based practices regarding the care and rehabilitation of youth in need of services from multiple agencies and systems. Judges should know the rudiments of adolescent development and positive youth development.[90] Indeed, all

---

86. *See, e.g.*, J. D. B. v. North Carolina, 564 U.S. 261 (2011).

87. *See, e.g.*, Kate Lodge, *Youth Engagement: Nothing About Us Without Us*, THE IMPRINT (Sept. 4, 2014), https://chronicleofsocialchange.org/opinion/youth-engagement-nothing-about-us-without -us/8042.

88. There has been a large literature on the perils of permitting youth to waive constitutional rights. *See, e.g.*, Naomi E.S. Goldstein et al., *Waving Good-Bye to Waiver: A Developmental Argument Against Youths'* Waiver of Miranda Rights, 21 N.Y.U. J. LEGIS. & PUB. POL'Y 1 (2018), https://www .nyujlpp.org/wp-content/uploads/2018/06/Legis-21-1-Article-Goldstein-WavingGoodbyeto Waiver.pdf; Barry C. Feld, *Juveniles' Competence to Exercise Miranda Rights: An Empirical Study of Policy and Practice*, 91 MINN. L. REV. 26 (2006).

89. There is a large literature on cross system training. Examples include Atelia I. Melaville & Martin J. Blank, *What It Takes: Structuring Interagency Partnerships to Connect Children and Families with Comprehensive Services*, U.S. DEP'T OF JUSTICE NATIONAL INSTITUTE OF JUSTICE (Jan. 1991), https:// www.ncjrs.gov/pdffiles1/Photocopy/151326NCJRS.pdf; ANDREW MOORE, BEYOND CITY LIMITS: CROSS-SYSTEM COLLABORATION TO REENGAGE DISCONNECTED YOUTH (National League of Cities Institute for Youth, Education, and Families, 2007); Pauline Jivanjee, et al., *Achieving Cross-System Collaboration to Support Young People in the Transition Years: A Tip Sheet for Service Providers*, RESEARCH AND TRAINING CENTER FOR PATHWAYS TO POSITIVE FUTURES (2016), https://www.pathwaysrtc.pdx .edu/pdf/projPTTP-cross-system-collaboration-tip-sheet.pdf.

90. *See, e.g.*, Jeffrey A. Butts, et al., *Positive Outcomes: Strategies for Assessing the Progress of Youth Involved in the Justice System*, JOHN JAY COLLEGE OF CRIMINAL JUSTICE RESEARCH AND EVALUATION CENTER (2018), https://johnjayrec.nyc/2018/02/01/positiveoutcomes2018/; Robert G. Schwartz, "Juvenile Justice and Positive Youth Development," in *Handbook of Applied Developmental Sciences* (Vol. 2), F. Jacobs, et al. eds., (2003). *See also*, Jonathan F. Zaff & Max Margolius, *Positive Youth Development Holds Promise for States Working With Transitioning Youth*, JUVENILE JUSTICE INFORMATION EXCHANGE, (Nov. 4, 2019), https://jjie.org/2019/11/04/positive-youth-development-holds -promise-for-states-working-with-transitioning-youth/.

professionals in the juvenile justice and child welfare systems should be thoroughly trained in the areas covered by this Standard.[91]

Juvenile justice and child welfare systems should also hear from youth and families in training sessions *and* when developing policies and practices. "Youth and family" voices "are critical to a well-functioning child welfare system."[92] Foster youth, like persons with disabilities, have proclaimed "Nothing about us without us." The Children's Bureau reminds child welfare agencies of the legal requirement that youth 14 or older must be involved in their case planning, while providing guidance to child welfare agencies on how to build upon youth and family strengths.[93]

The Pierce County (Tacoma) juvenile court in Washington state launched a Family Council that "is an advisory group of parents and young adults who . . . guide program and policy changes" in the

---

91. The field is replete with training on issues affecting youth. The incomplete list below names national organizations that have a long history of addressing these issues and providing training about them; most of these organizations focus on multiple issues addressed by these Standards. They bring a youth-oriented, youth-informed, and youth-led perspective. For information on racial justice and bias, *see* W. Haywood Burns Institute for Justice Fairness & Equity, https://www.burnsinstitute.org/; Center for Children's Law and Policy, https://www.cclp.org/; and National Juvenile Defender Center, https://njdc.info/; for information on sexual orientation, *see* Lambda Legal, https://www.lambdalegal.org/; National Center for Lesbian Rights, http://www.nclrights.org/; for information on homeless youth and related issues, *see* Covenant House, https://www.covenanthouse.org/; National Association for the Education of Homeless Children and Youth, https://naehcy.org/; for information on education of youth in foster care and youth in the justice system, *see* Legal Center for Foster Care and Education, http://www.fostercareandeducation.org/; Legal Center for Youth Justice and Education, https://jjeducationblueprint.org/; for information on the role of lawyers for children and youth, *see* National Juvenile Defender Center, https://njdc.info/; National Association of Counsel for Children, http://naccchildlaw.org/; for information on youth aging out of foster care, *see* Juvenile Law Center, https://jlc.org/; Youth Law Center, https://ylc.org/; for information on immigration and juvenile justice, *see* National Center for Youth Law, https://youthlaw.org/; for information on school-to-prison pipeline, *see* The Advancement Project, https://advancementproject.org/; *The Center for Civil Rights Remedies*, at The Civil Rights Project at UCLA, https://civilrightsproject.ucla.edu/resources/projects/center-for-civil-rights-remedies#:~:text=What%20we%20do%3A,local%2C%20state%20and%20federal%20levels.

92. *Engaging, Empowering, and Utilizing Family and Youth Voice in All Aspects of Child Welfare to Drive Case Planning and System Improvement*, U.S. Department of Health and Human Services Administration of Children and Families (Aug. 1, 2019), https://www.acf.hhs.gov/sites/default/files/cb/im1903.pdf.

93. *Id.*

county's juvenile justice system.[94] Youth and families involved with both systems have experience and opinions that should be heeded.[95]

Professionals in other systems often have unrealistic perceptions about what will happen to youth in the juvenile justice system. It is important for educated and thoughtful professionals to understand that the juvenile justice system faces immense challenges in serving youth with serious mental health needs. For example, it is difficult to provide comprehensive educational services in an institutional setting.[96] In deciding whether to refer a child to the delinquency system, or when developing service plans for youth who have "crossed over," it is also important for professionals to be aware of the research showing that crossover youth have worse outcomes than youth who remain in the child welfare system.[97]

Professionals from other youth-serving systems should be aware of the stigma and the collateral consequences associated with involvement in the juvenile justice system.

It is also important that juvenile justice professionals be trained in the operation of other systems—myth busting goes in many directions. A better understanding of why the child welfare, behavioral health, or education systems operate the way they do, what they have to offer, and what they are legally obligated to provide will help juvenile justice professionals reject unnecessary referrals, ensure that other systems cooperate with the justice system for the well-being of dual jurisdiction youth, and promote youths' smooth exit from the juvenile justice system. For example, during the time that the MacArthur Foundation supported Pennsylvania juvenile justice reform through Models for Change, the Foundation made grants to Education Law

---

94. *Probation Transformation Year in Review,* PIERCE COUNTY JUVENILE COURT (2015), https://www.piercecountywa.gov/DocumentCenter/View/40413/Probation-Transformation-2015-Year-In-Review?bidId=.

95. The 2007 Hofstra conference that launched the ABA Commission on Youth at Risk called for meaningful involvement of teenagers in all hearings affecting them. "Recommendations from the ABA Youth at Risk Initiative Planning Conference," 45 FAM. CT. REV. 3, 366–89 (2007).

96. *See, e.g.,* David Domenici & James Forman, Jr., *What It Takes to Transform a School Inside a Juvenile Facility: The Story of the Maya Angelou Academy, in* JUSTICE FOR KIDS: KEEPING KIDS OUT OF THE JUVENILE JUSTICE SYSTEM (Nancy Dowd, ed., NYU Press 2011).

97. *See generally* resources of the Center for Juvenile Justice Reform, at https://cjjr.georgetown.edu/; and *Building a Brighter Future for Youth with Dual Status: A Policy Roadmap Forward* (The Children's Partnership and RFK Children's Action Corps, Nov. 2018).

Center-PA (ELC-PA) to educate juvenile probation officers about the public education system. ELC-PA's training and publications helped juvenile probation officers become effective education advocates.[98]

98. *See* ROBERT G. SCHWARTZ, PENNSYLVANIA AND MACARTHUR'S MODELS FOR CHANGE: A SUCCESSFUL PUBLIC-PRIVATE PARTNERSHIP (Juvenile Law Center, 2013); and JENNIFER LOWMAN, EDUCATIONAL AFTERCARE & REINTEGRATION TOOLKIT FOR JUVENILE JUSTICE PROFESSIONALS (Education Law Center-PA, June 2009).

PART III: ARREST AND REFERRALS TO THE JUVENILE JUSTICE SYSTEM

Standard 3.1 Guidelines for Child Welfare Agencies

(a) Child welfare agencies should adopt policies discouraging staff from referring youth to the juvenile justice system for minor delinquent behavior.

(b) Child welfare agencies should have protocols for responding to delinquent and status offense behavior by youth in their care. These protocols should:

  i. be developed in consultation with representatives of other youth-serving agencies, including the juvenile court, probation, behavioral health, schools, law enforcement, prosecution, defense, best interest advocates, and community service providers;

  ii. set forth the specific procedures to be followed when a youth violates rules of a program or placement or engages in behavior that poses a threat to others in a program or placement;

  iii. specify behavioral support or staffing strategies that agencies should utilize instead of referral to law enforcement;

  iv. be in writing, made available to agency staff and youth served by the agency, and be incorporated into any agency staff training; and

  v. provide for periodic review and revision of the protocols.

(c) Staff in child welfare or other youth-serving agencies and facilities should be trained in crisis intervention techniques, including strategies to de-escalate youth behavior arising out of behavioral health or other disability-related needs, and such techniques should be employed first, before any law enforcement referral.

(d) Public child welfare agencies that contract with private service providers should, in the contracts, set forth the circumstances under which those agencies may refer youth to law enforcement and provide guidance on alternatives to law enforcement and juvenile court referrals in case of a behavioral crisis or placement concerns.

Standard 3.2   Responsibilities of Law Enforcement in Responding to Referrals Involving Dual-Status Youth

(a)   In deciding whether to arrest, divert, warn, detain, or refer a youth to the juvenile court, law enforcement officers should:

    i.   have a presumption against arresting youth who have been referred from the child welfare system to the juvenile justice system for minor delinquent behavior; and

    ii.   consider whether the youth is or can be engaged with other youth-serving systems or agencies that will work to ensure the youth's appearance in court, divert the youth from custody or supervision, and minimize the youth's risk to public safety.

(b)   Law enforcement agencies should develop interagency crisis intervention strategies that discourage arrests of youth experiencing emergency behavioral health crises that do not create a serious risk to public safety.

(c)   If a youth needs emergency psychiatric or other behavioral health intervention, law enforcement officers should contact a behavioral health mobile crisis team; if such a team is not available, the officers should take the youth into custody without arrest and transport them to an appropriate crisis intervention facility.

(d)   When a youth appears to be homeless, a runaway, or declines to give home contact information, the law enforcement agency should determine whether the youth is under the care or supervision of the child welfare agency, and if not should determine whether the youth should be referred to an appropriate youth-serving agency.

(e)   Law enforcement should notify the caregiver or welfare caseworker of any youth who is arrested while committed to a child welfare agency.

Standard 3.3   Responsibilities of Law Enforcement, Schools, and Juvenile Courts in Responding to School-Related Conduct

(a) The primary authority responsible for school climate, discipline, and school safety is the school principal. Police should not be deployed in schools absent a significant showing of a demonstrable, time-limited need to protect students. If police are to be deployed in schools, memoranda of understanding and guidelines regarding their interaction with school officials and the scope and parameters of their authority should be established consistent with the principles set forth in these standards.

(b) Law enforcement, including school resource officers (hereinafter SROs), should not arrest or refer youth to the juvenile justice system for minor delinquent conduct at school and should not have primary responsibility for the enforcement of school discipline.

(c) Law enforcement personnel interacting with youth in schools should interact with students in ways that foster positive relationships and promote a better understanding of each other and should not be limited to arrest and law enforcement.

(d) Schools should adopt written policies and establish protocols limiting the presence and use of SROs in accordance with the principles set forth in section (e) below. Law enforcement, including SROs, should not be assigned within schools on a permanent basis, and school and law enforcement officials should periodically reassess the need for law enforcement presence and use.

(e) Formal law enforcement intervention includes issuance of a citation, ticket, or summons, filing of a delinquency petition, referral to a probation office, searches, use of restraints, or actual arrest. Law enforcement officials should not initiate formal law enforcement intervention for school-related conduct except as permitted in written protocols developed in accord with principles set forth in section (f) below.

(f) Law enforcement agencies should work with school officials to develop written protocols to ensure that referrals to the juvenile court from schools are not for behavior that is more appropriately handled by the school. Such protocols should:

    i. allow law enforcement officials, including SROs, to transport a truant youth back to school without an arrest or referral to the juvenile justice system, and encourage school officials to develop educational programs, social services, and public health responses to truancy in lieu of arrest;

    ii. promote programs that are preventive, educational, and recreational to guide young people away from negative behaviors;

    iii. develop guidelines that limit disruption in educational placement or receipt of educational services resulting from law enforcement intervention;

    iv. encourage schools to implement disciplinary practices that:

        a. are age and developmentally appropriate;

        b. are culturally competent;

        c. engage the youth and family; and

        d. take into account that a student's behavior may be related to a disability;

    v. reject zero tolerance policies and mandatory suspension, expulsion, arrest, or referrals of students to juvenile or criminal court without regard to the circumstances or nature of the offense or the student's disability or history.

(g) Students should be involved in the development of school-law enforcement protocols and memoranda of understanding.

(h) Law enforcement personnel, including SROs, who may have contact with students, especially those students who may be involved in the child welfare system, should receive extensive training that includes the following topics:

i.   youth and adolescent development and psychology;

ii.   the effects of neglect, abuse, and trauma, including the exposure to violence;

iii. the effects of disabilities on behavior and the effects of medication taken to ameliorate the symptoms of disabilities;

iv.   common disabilities for youth and the protections afforded to youth under the Individuals with Disabilities Education Act (IDEA);

v.   conflict resolution, peer mediation, and restorative justice techniques;

vi.   cultural competence and gender and sexuality sensitivity; and

vii. research-based practices in de-escalation and alternative responses to the use of restraints against youth except in situations involving an arrest and serious and immediate threat to the physical safety or health of a member of the school community.

(i)   Both school districts and law enforcement should maintain data to assist in evaluating the presence and use of law enforcement, including SROs. Each data point should be disaggregated by offense, student's age, grade level, race, sex, disability status, eligibility for free or reduced lunch, English language proficiency, and disposition. Data collection should include the number of:

i.   law enforcement personnel, including SROs, deployed to each school;

ii.   school-based arrests (arrests of students that occur on school grounds during the school day or on school grounds during school-sponsored events) at each school;

iii. referrals to the juvenile justice system for each school;

iv.   citations, summons or other actions taken by police personnel for each school; and

v.   suspensions, in and out of school, and expulsions at each school.

(j) Juvenile courts and law enforcement should not inform a school of a student's involvement in the court system for conduct which occurred off school grounds unless the conduct is likely to have an impact on school safety.

(k) Juvenile courts should annually review all data collected on school-based referrals to identify high rates of referral from particular schools or for a particular youth demographic. If referrals are for a disproportionately high rate of referral for youth of color, the juvenile court and law enforcement officials should work with schools to develop protocols that will reduce unnecessary or inappropriate referrals from the schools and reduce disproportionality.

(l) Legislatures should repeal or amend laws, including zero tolerance laws that require schools to refer youth to law enforcement agencies for minor delinquent behavior.

(m) Legislatures should protect the confidentiality of Family Court records by amending statutes that require courts and/ or law enforcement agencies to notify schools about arrests to prohibit such notification unless the student conduct is likely to have an impact on school safety.

Standard 3.4   Responsibilities of Child Welfare and Juvenile Justice Agencies in Addressing the Educational Needs of Dual-Status Youth

(a) Child welfare and juvenile justice agencies should work with local school districts to develop interagency agreements that:

   i. allow youth to remain in the same school, when practicable, even when the agency places a youth outside the school district area;

   ii. ensure the timely transfer of education records and credit information to whatever school a youth will attend; and

   iii. ensure a seamless re-entry of students discharged from a child welfare or juvenile justice placement back to the youth's home school.

(b) **Child welfare and juvenile justice agencies should work with the relevant school district to ensure that every youth in out-of-home placement receives an education appropriate for the youth's grade level, special educational needs, and academic or career goals.**

Part III Commentary

3.1   Guidelines for Child Welfare Agencies

Child welfare referrals to the juvenile justice system fall into different types. Some referrals are from foster parents or kin; others are from congregate care programs, such as group homes or residential treatment facilities. Many child welfare referrals involve youth with behavioral health needs that were supposed to be addressed by child welfare.

Studies have raised "serious questions about the use of group homes for victims of physical abuse and neglect."[99] Youth in group homes, where staff such as those on overnight shifts are more likely to escalate conflict, are much more likely to be arrested than youth in foster care.[100] Such youth often have challenges that make them harder to place in traditional family foster care. They are disproportionately African American and female. Many have mental health conditions.[101]

> Although child welfare studies suggest that half to two-thirds of children entering foster care have behavior problems warranting mental health services, little is known about how the child welfare system identifies child delinquents or potential child delinquents and refers them to mental health services. . . . Yet this is a critical population for intervention because of the trauma many of these children have experienced from

---

99. Joseph P. Ryan et al., *Juvenile Delinquency in Child Welfare: Investigating Group Home Effects*, *Children and Youth Services Review*, 30 Child. & Youth Services Rev. 1088–99 (2008).

100. *Id.*

101. *See* Carrie Wang & Rachel Kohn, *Why Are LA's Foster Kids More Likely to Be Charged with Crimes?*, Ctr for Sustainable Journalism (Feb. 2016), https://fostercare.youthtoday.org/why-are-las-foster-kids-more-likely-to-be-charged-with-crimes/.

abuse and neglect, other risk factors for future delinquency, and the children's acting-out behavior.[102]

To the extent that youth in the child welfare system—in any setting—have mental health disorders, it is incumbent upon that system to train providers in addressing those needs. Too many youth are referred to juvenile justice to "treat" behavioral health conditions or respond to behavior arising from those problems.

> Multiple systems bear responsibility for these youth. While at different times, a single agency may have primary responsibility, these youth are the community's responsibility and all responses developed for these youth should be collaborative in nature. . . .[103]

Placement instability is not uncommon for youth in foster care. Fewer than 20 states are able to achieve a goal of fewer than two placements for youth in care; frequent placements have a negative impact on children's safety, their ability to achieve permanence, and their long-term well-being.[104] The likelihood of placement instability increases when youth are arrested.

Child welfare systems that reduce referrals to juvenile justice will contribute to reducing racial disparities in juvenile justice. The child welfare system has a history of racial disproportionality and disparities,[105] which in turn has an impact on youth in the justice system, including dual status youth.[106]

The negative effects of group home and residential care led Congress to limit federal financial support for their use. The Family First Prevention Services Act of 2018 prohibits federal reimbursement to states under Title IV-E[107] unless a youth is in a court-approved Qualified Residential Treatment Program (QRTP).[108] States may use group

---

102. Janet K. Wiig et al., Guidebook for Juvenile Justice & Child Welfare System Coordination and Integration: A Framework for Improved Outcomes xvii (Robert F. Kennedy Children's Action Corps, 3d ed. 2013).

103. *Supra* note 17.

104. *What Impacts Placement Stability?*, Casey Family Programs (Oct. 3, 2018), https://www.casey.org/placement-stability-impacts/.

105. *Child Welfare Practice to Address Racial Disproportionality and Disparity*, Bulletins for Professionals (Apr. 2021), https://www.childwelfare.gov/pubpdfs/racial_disproportionality.pdf.

106. *Disparities and Disproportionality in Child Welfare: Analysis of the Research*, The Annie E. Casey Found. (Dec. 2011), https://repositories.lib.utexas.edu/bitstream/handle/2152/15376/casey_disparities_childwelfare.pdf?sequence=5.

107. *See* commentary to Section 2.2.

108. 42 U.S.C. § 672(k).

homes and residential treatment facilities, but the federal government will not contribute funds to them unless they are a QRTP and other criteria are met.

For these reasons, the Standards encourage training of child welfare staff to reduce referrals to the juvenile justice system by creating a culture of care, understanding adolescent development, building relationships, and teaching discipline—all to promote child well-being and to de-escalate conflict.[109]

3.2 Responsibilities of Law Enforcement in Responding to Referrals Involving Dual-Status Youth

The International Association of Chiefs of Police has been a leader in calling for diversion of youth from the juvenile justice system. A national leadership summit of police leaders and other child-serving professionals led, in 2014, to a call for increased diversion. That call was based on several key findings:

Overarching Principles Identified by Summit Participants

Ineffective strategies: Large numbers of youth are arrested, referred to juvenile court, and detained for minor offenses—even as a growing body of evidence suggests these practices fuel recidivism rather than reducing the likelihood that youth reoffend.

Lack of alternatives: In some communities, law enforcement officers have few options for responding to youth in crisis and have to make a decision between arresting a young person and doing nothing. Law enforcement leaders can be powerful advocates for the development of effective services for youth and families focused on addressing the underlying causes of criminal behavior.

Need for referral and assessment systems: Even in communities where resources such as community-based diversion programs are available, law enforcement officers are sometimes unfamiliar with these resources or there are no systems in place to support officers in making assessments and subsequent referral decisions.[110]

---

109. *See* National Resource Center for Youth Services, Residential Child and Youth Care Professional Curriculum (2004).

110. MacArthur Foundation, *Law Enforcement's Leadership Role in Juvenile Justice Reform Actionable Recommendations for Practice & Policy*, Models for Change (July 2014), http://www.modelsfor change.net/publications/642.

In line with these concerns, these Standards supplement current ABA juvenile justice standards,[111] which provide extensive guidance to police officers in deciding how to respond to youth behavior. These Standards go a bit further. Law enforcement should not refer youth in the child welfare system to juvenile court for minor delinquent behavior, but may, if necessary and appropriate, refer the youth to a diversion program suitable for the youth's age, mental capacity, and developmental stage.

This Standard recognizes that child welfare and other youth-serving agencies, providers, and facilities will on occasion call police (1) to assist in responding to a mental health or behavioral crisis involving youth in their care and (2) to ensure the safety of other youth within its care. When this happens, youths' conduct arising from mental health disorders can too easily be redefined as criminal behavior. To address this concern, some communities have introduced police-based crisis intervention teams so that officers trained in mental illness management have the skills to divert persons suspected of having serious mental illness by bringing them to special mental health assessment centers rather than jail.[112] Police who are knowledgeable about adolescent behavioral health have an opportunity to assist providers and child welfare staff in de-escalating situations, obviate the need for arrest, and increase the likelihood that youth will receive appropriate services.

ABA policy also recognizes the importance of police notifying child welfare agencies promptly when they take into custody youth who are supervised by the child welfare system. Early notification is necessary to "promote the prompt post-arrest involvement of providers, caseworkers, or advocates acting on the youth's behalf; ensure fair treatment of foster youth in juvenile detention, incarceration, or probation decisions; and eliminate practices that result in detention or prolonged incarceration of youth due to foster care status or an

---

111. *See* IJA-ABA Juvenile Justice Standards Relating to Police Handling of Juvenile Problems; and IJA-ABA Standards Relating to Interim Status: The Release, Control and Detention of Accused Juvenile Offenders Between Arrest and Disposition, Part V, Standards for the Police, §§ 5.1–5.7.

112. Jeffrey Fagan et al., *New Models of Collaboration between Criminal Justice and Mental Health Systems*, MacArthur Found. on Mental Health Pol'y Rsch., https://www.macfound.org/media/files/CRIMINALJUSTICE.PDF.

absence of suitable placement options."[113] Youth in the child welfare system should have access to an attorney before police questioning; parental notification requirements are not satisfied merely by obtaining permission from the child welfare agency, whose interests may not be aligned with the youth.

3.3 Responsibilities of Law Enforcement, Schools, and Juvenile Courts in Responding to School-Related Conduct

Ending Zero Tolerance Policies

In the late 1980s, some school districts began to implement zero tolerance policies to address problems of drug abuse and gang violence in the schools.[114] In 1994, Congress passed the Gun Free Schools Act, which required that states adopt mandatory harsh penalties for students found with firearms and other weapons on school campuses. Although the act required that state laws authorize the head of each local educational agency to modify the expulsion mandate on a case-by-case basis,[115] most if not all states or schools ignored this additional mandate.[116] Zero tolerance policies began to proliferate to address not only gun violence and drug abuse but also general misbehavior in the schools.

Inappropriate zero tolerance policies led to "school pushout." School pushout refers to factors that prevent or discourage young people from remaining on track to complete their educations; it has severe and lasting consequences for students, parents, schools, and communities.[117] These factors include the failure to provide a high

---

113. *Policy on Dual Jurisdiction/Crossover Youth*, ABA (Aug. 2008), https://www.americanbar.org/groups/public_interest/child_law/resources/attorneys/dual_jurisdictioncrossoveryouth/. This is also found as Appendix I in this book.

114. Russell Skiba et al., Are Zero Tolerance Policies Effective in the Schools? An Evidentiary Review and Recommendations (American Psychological Association Zero Tolerance Task Force, Dec. 2008).

115. 20 U.S.C.A. § 7151(b)(1).

116. For example, the California Department of Education states on its website that the Gun Free Schools Act of 1994 "requires" school districts to adopt "zero tolerance" in regard to firearms in order remain eligible for funding. "Zero Tolerance: Information regarding zero tolerance policies for firearms in schools," https://ed100.org/lessons/discipline#:~:text=California%20law%20establishes%20that%20schools,offense%2C%20you're%20done.

117. Dignity in Schools, https://dignityinschools.org/about-us/mission/.

quality education; overreliance on zero tolerance practices and punitive measures such as suspensions and expulsions; overreliance on
law enforcement; and unnecessarily ceding disciplinary authority to
law enforcement personnel.[118] Excessive reliance on law enforcement
can discourage young people from staying in school; it makes it more
difficult for students to complete their educations.[119]

Zero tolerance policies proved to have an unfortunate and unnecessary disproportionate impact on youth of color.[120] An American Bar
Association Task Force recently found:

> These negative disproportionalities might be understood if removals
> from school were in fact making schools safer or if confinement in juve
> nile detention or other facilities led to improved outcomes. This does not
> appear to be the case in practice or in theory. Nor can the disproportion
> ate treatment of certain students and their overrepresentation in the neg
> atives of our education and juvenile justice systems be explained away
> because certain groups are more likely to be engaged in bad or delin
> quent behavior.[121]

As recently as 2019, the United States Commission on Civil Rights
declared that available literature suggests "that students of color with
disabilities face exclusionary discipline pushing them into the school-
to-prison pipeline at much higher rates than their peers without
disabilities."[122] The Commission added,

---

118. *Id.*

119. *See Juveniles for Justice and Youth Fostering Change, Operation: Education—An Action Kit to Achieve Positive Educational Outcomes for Youth in the Child Welfare and Juvenile Justice Systems*, Juvenile Law Ctr. (2019), https://jlc.org/sites/default/files/attachments/2019-06/Operation-Educa tion-FINAL-DIGITAL-FULL.pdf.

120. In 2014, the Offices of Civil Rights in the U.S. Department of Justice and the Department of Education issued a joint "Dear Colleague" letter of guidance "to assist public elementary and secondary schools in meeting their obligations under Federal law to administer student discipline without discriminating on the basis of race, color, or national origin." *Joint "Dear Colleague" Letter*, U.S. Dep't of Educ. (2014), https://www2.ed.gov/about/offices/list/ocr/letters/colleague-201401-title -vi.html. The guidance was rescinded by the next administration. *DeVos and DOJ Repeal Discipline Guidance that Clarifies Children's Civil Rights*, The Leadership Converence on Civil & Human Rights (2018), https://civilrights.org/2018/12/21/devos-and-doj-repeal-discipline-guidance-that -clarifies-childrens-civil-rights/.

121. https://scholarship.law.ufl.edu/cgi/viewcontent.cgi?article=1765&context=facultypub.

122. Letter of Transmittal (July 23, 2019), *in* Beyond Suspensions: Examining School Discipline Policies and Connections to the School-to-Prison Pipeline for Students of Color with Disabilities (U.S. Comm'n on Civil Rights, 2019).

Students of color as a whole, as well as by individual racial group, do not commit more disciplinable offenses than their white peers—but black students, Latino students, and Native American students in the aggregate receive substantially more school discipline than their white peers and receive harsher and longer punishments than their white peers receive for like offenses. Students with disabilities are approximately twice as likely to be suspended throughout each school level compared to students without disabilities.[123]

As zero tolerance policies spread, so did the related consequences of referring schoolchildren to the juvenile and criminal justice systems. In too many school districts throughout the nation, police personnel assumed the role of school disciplinarian, utilizing law enforcement approaches such as searches, handcuffing, and arrests to address minor disciplinary problems.[124] These zero tolerance policies increased after the 1999 Columbine school shootings.[125]

For decades, the ABA has opposed mandatory zero tolerance policies.[126] In 2001, the ABA adopted policy opposing zero tolerance policies that mandate either expulsion or referral of students to court without regard to the circumstances, nature of the offense, or student's history.[127] Later ABA resolutions and public statements expanded upon this policy by discouraging the criminalization of school-related conduct and encouraging procedural protections for students in disciplinary hearings. Particularly eloquent and comprehensive was ABA President Laurel Bellows 2012 testimony before the U.S. Senate Judiciary Committee's Subcommittee on Constitution, Civil Rights and Human Rights Hearing on "Ending the School-to-Prison Pipeline."[128]

---

123. *Id.*

124. Advancement Project, *Education on Lockdown: The Schoolhouse to Jailhouse Track* (Mar. 2005), https://www.njjn.org/uploads/digital-library/Education-on-Lockdown_Advancement-Project_2005.pdf. Johanna Wald & Dan Losen, *Defining and Re-directing a School-to-Prison Pipeline*, 99 NEW DIRECTIONS FOR YOUTH DEV. 9 (2003); Elora Mukherjee, *Criminalizing the Classroom: The Over-Policing of New York City Schools*, ACLU & NYCLU (2007), https://www.nyclu.org/sites/default/files/publications/nyclu_pub_criminalizing_the_classroom.pdf.

125. John Cloud, *The Columbine Effect*, TIME MAG., Nov. 28, 1999.

126. Rosa K. Kirji, *Advocacy against Zero Tolerance: A Critical Review*, Jan. 16, 2018, at https://www.americanbar.org/groups/litigation/committees/childrens-rights/articles/2018/winter2018-20-years-policy-advocacy-against-zero-tolerance-critical-review/.

127. A.B.A. Res.103B, 2001, https://www.americanbar.org/groups/public_interest/child_law/resources/attorneys/school_disciplinezerotolerancepolicies/.

128. https://www.govinfo.gov/content/pkg/CHRG-112shrg86166/pdf/CHRG-112shrg86166.pdf.

Thus, these Standards build on two decades of ABA policy. At their core, these policies declare that the juvenile court should not be a school disciplinarian. For minor misbehavior, risk can be managed at the family, school, and community levels.[129]

Reducing Police Presence While Promoting School Safety

In the years following Columbine, many school districts introduced a permanent presence for law enforcement officers, sometimes referred to as School Resource Officers (SROs), School Liaison Officers (SLOs), or School Safety Officers (SSOs). The status of these officers is often unclear, creating problems because of a lack of (1) clearly articulated roles and responsibilities of police officers who are called to or assigned to schools, and (2) an adequate governance structure to regulate police activities in the schools. These Standards oppose a permanent placement of police in schools. There is evidence that, **"Safety does not exist when Black and Brown young people are forced to interact with a system of policing that views them as a threat and not as students."**[130]

While some national groups have called for ending a regular police presence in schools,[131] these Standards recognize that the practice is common today. They therefore attempt to define and limit the role of law enforcement in schools while listing the special considerations that should inform the way law enforcement interacts with students.

The National Association of School Resource Officers (NASRO) has provided policies, training, and materials that seek to "bridge the gap" between law enforcement and students.[132] NASRO has sought to soften police presence by encouraging a "TRIAD Model" in which school police serve three roles: law enforcement, teacher (guest speaker), and informal counselor (mentor).[133] Standard 3.3, at bottom,

---

129. "Minor misbehavior" covers a wide range of adolescent conduct. Perhaps no arrest was more absurd than that of a 13-year-old for refusing to stop making "fake burps." The SRO arrested the boy "for interfering with the educational process." A.M. ex rel. F.M. v. Holmes, 830 F.3d 1123 (10th Cir. 2016).

130. *We Came to Learn*, THE ADVANCEMENT PROJECT 2 (2018), https://advancementproject.org /wp-content/uploads/WCTLweb/docs/We-Came-to-Learn-9-13-18.pdf?reload=1536822360635.

131. *See, e.g., id.*; *Counselors Not Cops*, DIGNITY IN SCHOOLS CAMPAIGN (Oct. 2018), https://dignity inschools.org/take-action/counselors-not-cops/.

132. *See generally* NATIONAL ASSOCIATION OF SCHOOL RESOURCE OFFICERS, https://www.nasro.org/.

133. *Id.*

strikes a different balance. While the Standard supports police building positive relationships with students when it is necessary to have
police in schools—and sets forth guidelines on how those positive
relationships are more likely to be achieved—the Standard has a preference for communities increasing funding for teachers and school
counselors rather than police.[134]

Progressive jurisdictions have linked juvenile courts and SROs
through a Memorandum of Understanding (MOU).[135] However, while
such MOUs address matters such as compensation structure, hiring,
termination, and the sharing of information and resources, many
MOUs do not adequately address the most controversial concerns
raised by the police presence in the schools: the details of the police
officer's responsibilities in the schools and how decisions involving
searches and arrests should be made.[136] Such MOUs do not address
the nuances of many school interactions that could technically be considered a violation of the penal law but that may not require a law
enforcement response—for example, should a minor hallway distur-
bance be considered disorderly conduct leading to an arrest, or should
it be considered childish behavior resulting in school-based detention?
Many MOU's do not address the need to develop a range of responses

---

134. The Dignity in Schools campaign, which opposes a "regular" police presence in schools, is
an example of a coalition promoting increased funding for school counselors. DIGNITY IN SCHOOLS,
supra note 117.

135. See Judge Steve C. Teske, *Testimony before the Senate Subcommittee on The Constitution, Civil
Rights, and Human Rights Subcommittee Hearing on "Ending the School to Prison Pipeline,"* CLAYTON
COUNTY JUVENILE COURT (Dec. 12, 2012), https://www.judiciary.senate.gov/imo/media/doc/12-12
-12TeskeTestimony.pdf. Teske began his work with schools in 2004; his efforts became a model for
the country—*see School Justice Partnership, Developing a Memorandum of Understanding (MOU) for
School-Justice Partnerships: Technical Assistance Tools,* NCJFCJ (2017), https://www.schooljusticepart
nership.org/component/mtree/resource-library/role-of-schools/318-developing-a-memorandum
-of-understanding-mou-for-school-justice-partnerships-technical-assistance-tools.html?Itemid=, and
much of the text of this Standard.

136. *See, e.g., Memorandum of Understanding,* MA PUBLIC SCHOOLS & DUXBURY POLICE DEP'T,
https://www.duxbury.k12.ma.us/cms/lib/MA01001583/Centricity/Domain/79/State%20Agen
cies%20Model%20Memorandum%20of%20Understanding%20for%20Massachusetts%20School%20
Resource%20Officers.pdf. *Memorandum of Understanding,* WESTFIELD WASHINGTON SCHOOL CORPO-
RATION & WESTFIELD POLICE DEPARTMENT, www.westfield.in.gov/egov/docs/1186157545_384521
.pdf; *Model Memorandum of Understanding,* U.S. DEP'T OF JUST., https://www.westfield.in.gov/egov
/docs/1186157545_384521.pdf. Philissa Cramer, *City Secretly Renewed Police Control over School Safety
in 2003,* CHALKBEAT NEW YORK, (June 26, 2009), https://ny.chalkbeat.org/2009/6/26/21085510/city
-secretly-renewed-police-control-over-school-safety-in-2003.

that take into consideration the youth's age and developmental capacity.[137] Moreover, many MOU's do not address situations where school officials request intervention from law enforcement agencies outside of school. Finally, too often parents and students are unaware of the MOUs and there is no system of accountability to oversee even the best of them.

Progressive law enforcement partnerships can reduce referrals to the juvenile justice system. There are examples in which strong leaders, with authority, have over time reduced school referrals by changing the SRO culture.

Philadelphia provides a striking example of how thoughtful limitations on law enforcement can contribute to reducing unnecessary referrals to juvenile court.[138] Philadelphia Deputy Police Commissioner Kevin Bethel launched a citywide school-based diversion program with the goal of reducing school arrests. Before the program was implemented in 2014, there were approximately 1,600 school-based arrests across the city each year.[139] By adopting a policy to divert youth who commit a first-time low-level offense on school property, school arrests dropped 54 percent in the first year.[140] The program required SROs and responding police to follow a checklist to determine which youth are or are not eligible. The checklist removed ambiguity and potential bias of police labeling students as "good" or "bad."[141] Rather than arresting students, officers refer families to a community-based prevention program where youth can receive voluntary individual and group counseling, academic support, life skills development, and

---

137. NASRO recognizes the importance of MOUs, but reminds its members in a mandatory (rather than "recommended") NASRO standard that "The SRO's continual collaboration with school personnel and his or her understanding of each student's needs may impact the decision to arrest but the responsibility is that of the SRO alone." Mo Canady, *Standards and Best Practices for School Resource Officer Programs*, NASRO (2018), https://www.nasro.org/clientuploads/About-Mission/NASRO-Standards-and-Best-Practices.pdf.

138. Naomi E.S. Goldstein et al., *Dismantling the School-to-Prison Pipeline: The Philadelphia Police School Diversion Program*, 101 CHILD. & YOUTH SERV. REV. (Feb. 2019).

139. Molly McCluskey, *This Former Philadelphia Cop Had an Incredibly Simple Plan to Keep Kids Out of Prison. Don't Arrest Them.*, WASH. POST (Mar. 30, 2017), https://www.washingtonpost.com/news/inspired-life/wp/2017/03/30/this-former-philadelphia-cop-had-an-incredibly-simple-plan-to-keep-kids-out-of-prison-dont-arrest-them/?noredirect=on.

140. Cherri Gregg, *Praise for New Diversionary Program for Phila. Schoolkids*, CBS PHILLY (June 4, 2015), https://philadelphia.cbslocal.com/2015/06/04/first-year-of-diversionary-program-for-phila-schoolkids-showing-exceptional-results/.

141. McCluskey, *supra* note 139.

community engagement.[142] In the first two years of the program, more than 1,000 arrests were averted, while the number of serious incidents in Philadelphia schools declined.[143] (At the end of 2019, Bethel became head of school safety. In the spring of 2020, school police were renamed "school safety officers"; they do not carry guns and do not have the power of arrest.[144])

The Clayton County, Georgia, model referenced in note 135, is another example of schools reducing referrals to juvenile court while improving student outcomes. While Philadelphia's effort was begun by police, Clayton County's was a judge-led initiative. Schools in Clayton County use SROs. Judge Steven C. Teske used the bully-pulpit of his bench to reduce unnecessary court referrals from schools. Zero tolerance policies coincided with higher drop-out rates, lower graduation rates, increased contact with the juvenile justice system, and lower test scores.[145] After noticing these trends, Judge Teske convened a partnership between system stakeholders to reduce school arrests in Clayton County, Georgia.[146] The MOU developed by the court with county school districts was a negotiated agreement, not one imposed by the court on the schools. Judge Teske, a national leader, has inspired judges across the country who have followed versions of Clayton County's model. Collaborative approaches in Georgia, Alabama, Kansas, and Connecticut have all reduced suspensions, expulsions, school arrests, referrals to the juvenile justice system, and weapons on school

142. *DHS Intensive Prevention Services*, CITY OF PHILADELPHIA, https://www.phila.gov/programs/intensive-prevention-services-ips/,

143. Samantha Melamed, *How a Philly Cop Broke the School-to-Prison Pipeline*, PHILADELPHIA INQUIRER (Sept. 26, 2016), https://www.inquirer.com/philly/news/394757641.html.

144. Kristin A. Graham, *No More 'Police' in Philly Schools; 'Safety Officers' in New Uniforms Coming this Fall*, PHILADELPHIA INQUIRER (June 25, 2020), https://www.inquirer.com/news/school-police-philadelphia-safety-officers-district-kevin-bethel-hite-20200625.html.

145. Russell J. Skiba, *Reaching a Critical Juncture for Our Kids: The Need to Reassess School-Justice Practices*, 51 FAM. CT. REV. 3, at 380–87 (2013); Russell Skiba et al., *Are Zero Tolerance Policies Effective in the Schools? An Evidentiary Review and Recommendations*, AM. PSYCH. ASS'N ZERO TOLERANCE TASK FORCE (Aug. 9, 2006); Tony Fabelo et al., *Breaking Schools' Rules: A Statewide Study of How School Discipline Relates to Students' Success and Juvenile Justice Involvement*, COUNCIL OF STATE GOV'TS JUST. CTR., THE PUB. POL'Y RSCH. INST., TEX. A&M UNIV. (July 2011); and James Earl Davis & Will J. Jordan, *The Effects of School Context, Structure, and Experiences on African American Males in Middle and High School*, 63 J. NEGRO EDUC., 570–87 (1994).

146. School-Justice Partnership, *Spotlight on Clayton County School-Justice Collaboration*, NCJFCJ, https://schooljusticepartnership.org/clayton-county-collaboration.html.

property, while increasing graduation rates.[147] The Clayton County blueprint—identifying stakeholders and a neutral moderator, collecting and providing data, establishing written protocols, appointing someone to monitor that the protocol is being followed, and providing cross training[148]—forms the skeleton of these Standards.

These Standards are consistent with recent reforms. Schools throughout the country have successfully implemented policies and practices that (1) reject or limit the reliance on SROs and SLOs as the way to secure safety, (2) respond to misbehavior through a process that embraces the educational process, and (3) focus on preventing misbehavior from occurring in the first place. For example, both the Denver Public Schools and San Francisco Unified School District prohibits school staff from requesting police intervention in offenses that are deemed not serious.[149] The Los Angeles Unified Schools District, Minneapolis Public Schools, and the New Orleans Recovery School District embrace school discipline policies that use a non-punitive approach that emphasizes prevention and effective intervention.[150]

There are other examples.[151] One study examined six New York City public schools that successfully maintained school safety while simultaneously promoting a nurturing school environment and limiting the

147. Jeana R. Bracey et al., *Connecticut's Comprehensive Approach to Reducing In-school Arrests: Changes in Statewide Policy, Systems Coordination and School Practices*, 51 FAM. CT. REV. 427–34 (July 2013); Steven C. Teske et al., *Collaborative Role of Courts in Promoting Outcomes for Students: The Relationship between Arrests, Graduation Rates, and School Safety*, 51 FAM. CT. REV. 418–26 (July 2013).

148. Steven C. Teske, *The Court's Role in Dismantling the School-to-Prison Pipeline*, JUVENILE & FAM. JUST. TODAY 14–17 (2011), http://www.ncjfcj.org/sites/default/files/Today%20Winter%202011 Feature%20(2).pdf. Clayton County's written protocol can be found at *Collective Agreement Between . . .* STRATEGIES FOR YOUTH, http://strategiesforyouth.org/sfysite/wp-content/uploads/2012/11 /School_Resource_Officer_Collab_Agreement.pdf.

149. Denver Public Schools Matrix Attachment B, http://webdata.dpsk12.org/policy/pdf/Pol icy_JK-R_Attachment_B.pdf; *Student and Parent/Guardian Handbook* 67, SFUSD, http://portal.sfusd .edu/data/pupil/SFUSD_StudentHandbook_2008-2009_ENGLISH.pdf.

150. Los Angeles Unified School District, Discipline Policy Bulletin, https://achieve.lausd.net /site/handlers/filedownload.ashx?moduleinstanceid=34064&dataid=42289&FileName= BUL-133307%20-%20Discipline%20Foundation%20Policy.pdf; LAUSD Policy Bulletin Attachment G, https://achieve.lausd.net/cms/lib/CA01000043/Centricity/Domain/383/BUL%205212.3%20Bully ing%20and%20Hazing.pdf; Minneapolis Public Schools Policy 5200, https://equalitycivilrights .mpls.k12.mn.us/uploads/policy_5200_2014.pdf; Louisiana Recovery School District Code of Conduct, at 13, https://www.njjn.org/uploads/digital-library/resource_1006.pdf.

151. Schools that have embraced Positive Behavioral Interventions and Supports have reduced referrals to juvenile court. *See* CENTER ON POSITIVE BEHAVIORAL INTERVENTIONS & SUPPORTS, https://www.pbis.org/.

role of police in the schools.[152] The schools highlighted in the report serve at-risk student populations similar to schools that employ some of the most draconian discipline policies. Yet none of the schools currently have metal detectors, although some once did. These schools now emphasize alternatives to harsh discipline and have higher graduation and attendance rates and lower incident and suspension rates than schools that serve similar populations and that employ metal detectors and zero tolerance policies.

These Standards thus reinforce ABA policy on ending zero tolerance policies, on limiting police presence in schools while clarifying their role, and on calling for transparent data so that the public can monitor progress in implementing these reforms.

3.4 Responsibilities of Child Welfare and Juvenile Justice Agencies in Addressing the Educational Needs of Dual-Status Youth

Youth in the child welfare system and juvenile justice systems face acute barriers to education success. Due in part to factors also associated with why they entered the system (such as trauma, poverty), and often compounded by a lack of appropriate services once they are in the system, these youth are more likely than their peers to be truant, face school discipline, need remedial services, perform behind their grade level, and—ultimately—drop out of high school.[153] The problem is grave—a 2005 study in Philadelphia found that 70 percent of youth with a foster care placement and 90 percent returning from a juvenile justice placement dropped out.[154] A follow-up study showed that six years later, with a focused effort and intense supports:

---

152. Udi Ofer et al., *Safety with Dignity: Alternatives to the Over-Policing of Schools*, N.Y. CIVIL LIBERTIES UNION, ANNENBERG INST. FOR SCHOOL REFORM AT BROWN UNIVERSITY, & MAKE THE ROAD NEW YORK (July 2009).

153. *See, e.g.*, Peter Leone & Lois Weinberg, *Addressing the Unmet Educational Needs of Children and Youth in the Juvenile Justice and Child Welfare Systems*, CJJR (2012), https://www.researchgate.net/publication/242728146_Addressing_the_Unmet_Educational_Needs_of_Children_and_Youth_in_the_Juvenile_Justice_and_Child_Welfare_Systems; Katherine Burdick et al., *Creating Positive Consequences: Improving Education Outcomes for Youth Adjudicated Delinquent*, 3 DUKE F. L. & SOC. CHANGE 6–13 (2011).

154. Ruth Curran Neild & Robert Balfanz, *Unfulfilled Promise: The Dimensions and Characteristics of Philadelphia's Dropout Crisis 2000–2005*, PROJECT U-TURN (2006), https://files.eric.ed.gov/fulltext/ED538341.pdf.

The graduation rate for youth with foster care involvement increased from 28 percent in the 2002–2003 cohort to 44 percent in the 2008–2009 cohort, and the graduation rate for children receiving other DHS [Department of Human Services] services increased from 32 percent in the 2002–2003 cohort to 48 percent in the 2008–2009 cohort. The graduation rate for juvenile justice–involved youth exhibited the greatest gain among high-risk students, increasing from 16 percent in the 2002–2003 cohort to 36 percent in the 2008–2009 cohort. Despite the gains for students with DHS involvement, their graduation rates remain lower than their non DHS-involved counterparts.[155]

These Standards address some of the many reasons for these educational deficits: education in out-of-home placement is deficient; students often don't have credits transferred when they return home or transfer between schools or school districts; many schools erect barriers that make it hard for foster or delinquent youth to gain entry if they have been moved from one placement to another; students returning home are often placed in schools that are difficult to reach.[156]

Youth have many education rights that, when enforced, can support them in succeeding academically and prepare them to graduate and go on to postsecondary programs or living wage employment. For example, the Fostering Connections to Success and Increasing Adoptions Act of 2008 requires the child welfare agency to work with the local education agency to ensure a dependent child continues to attend the same school even when the child's living placement changes, if it is in the child's best interests to do so.[157] The 2011 Child and Family Services Improvement Act further amended Title IV-B of the Social Security Act[158] to clarify that the agency must make efforts to achieve school stability at every change in living placement.[159]

Youth in foster care also have the right to immediate and appropriate enrollment in a new school, with all education records, if it is in their best interests to change schools when their living placement

---

155. Julia Ransom et al., *A Promise Worth Keeping: Advancing the High School Graduation Rate in Philadelphia*, PROJECT U-TURN (2015), http://www.projectuturn.net/docs/PromiseWorthKeeping.pdf.

156. These problems have been well-documented by two projects of the ABA Center on Children and the Law: one—the Legal Center for Foster Care & Education—implemented with Education Law Center-PA and Juvenile Law Center, http://www.fostercareandeducation.org/Home.aspx; the other—the Legal Center for Youth Justice and Education—with Education Law Center-PA, Juvenile Law Center and Southern Poverty Law Center, https://jjeducationblueprint.org/about.

157. 42 U.S.C. § 675(1)(G).

158. *See* Commentary to Section 2.2.

159. 42 U.S.C. § 675(1)(G).

changes.[160] The McKinney-Vento Homeless Assistance Act also offers school stability, immediate enrollment, and other protections to youth experiencing homelessness, which includes youth "awaiting foster care placement."[161]

Furthermore, the Individuals with Disabilities with Education Act (IDEA) provides a host of rights to students with disabilities—including the right to a free, appropriate public education (FAPE), to an Individualized Education Program (IEP) that is updated at least annually, to an initial evaluation upon request and re-evaluations at least every three years, to be educated in the least restrictive environment, to have a surrogate parent appointed to make education decisions if no authorized adult is filling that roll, and to transition services once the child turns 16.[162]

Title I, Part D of the Elementary and Secondary Education Act provides funding to support other initiatives to improve education outcomes for youth in both systems. Specifically, Title I, Part D has three purposes: (1) to improve educational services in institutions for neglected and delinquent youth, (2) to provide such youth with services to assist their transition to further schooling or employment, and (3) to address the dropout problem by preventing at-risk youth from dropping out and providing support services for youth returning to school after dropping out or returning to school from correctional facilities or institutions.[163] States can draw down Title I, Part D funding to support effective practices. For example, Washington state has funded education advocates to facilitate students' re-entry to school upon leaving placement.[164]

Even without additional funding, there have been local collaborative efforts, focused on youth in foster care, for example, that have produced dramatic outcomes. Led by the Legal Aid Society of Greater Cincinnati/Southwest Ohio, a multi-agency collaboration has dramatically improved outcomes for youth in foster care in Hamilton County, Ohio. The Kids in School Rule! program is a collaboration of

---

160. *Id.*

161. *Id.* §§ 11301 *et seq.*

162. 20 U.S.C. §§ 1400 *et seq.*

163. ESEA was reauthorized in 2015 as the Every Student Succeeds Act, P.L. 114-95, which maintained these core provisions of Title I, Part D. 20 U.S.C. § 1401(a).

164. Michelle M. Maike & Kristin Schutte, *Washington's Education Advocate Program Manual*, WASH. STATE OFFICE OF SUPERINTENDENT OF PUBLIC INSTRUCTION (2009), https://www.k12.wa.us/sites/default/files/public/institutionaled/pubdocs/ea_manual.pdf.

Cincinnati Public Schools, Hamilton County Job and Family Services, Hamilton County Juvenile Court, the Children's Home of Cincinnati, and the Legal Aid Society of Greater Cincinnati/Southwest Ohio. Youth in foster care have achieved greater school stability, better educational performance, and improved attendance and graduation rates. Started in 2008, the program surrounds students who are often marginalized with an empathetic network of support.[165]

---

165. Lucy May, *Here's How Hamilton County Kids in Foster Care Are Beating the Odds with Their Academic Success*, WCPO CINN (Sept. 2019), https://www.wcpo.com/news/our-community/heres -how-hamilton-county-kids-in-foster-care-are-beating-the-odds-with-their-academic-success.

PART IV: JUVENILE INTAKE AND DETENTION

Standard 4.1 Responsibilities of Probation Offices at Intake

(a) Probation staff should develop written protocols to guide intake decisions and guard against the inappropriate processing of dual-status youth in the juvenile justice system. Protocols should:

    i. encourage the diversion of dual-status youth who engage in minor delinquent behavior from the juvenile justice system; and

    ii. encourage the delivery of services through youth-serving systems other than the juvenile justice system.

(b) Consistent with Standard 2.11 of these standards concerning Information Sharing, probation staff should examine relevant databases to determine whether a youth or a youth's family is or has been involved in other youth-serving systems.

(c) In deciding whether to recommend action or inaction by the juvenile court for a youth referred from the child welfare system, probation staff should consider:

    i. the seriousness of the offense;

    ii. any information about the youth's mental health status, treatment history, prescribed medications, educational status, and care and supervision by other youth-serving agencies and systems;

    iii. whether and to what extent the alleged behavior was related to the youth's disabilities, mental health issues, exposure to violence, prior placement deficiencies, substance abuse, or other identifiable factors;

    iv. whether the child welfare system made reasonable efforts to improve the youth's placement or services and prevent the referral to juvenile court;

    v.   whether services for the youth or family, such as crisis intervention or respite, could alleviate the need for a delinquency court referral; and

    vi.   whether the juvenile justice system has non-confinement placements that are appropriate for the youth.

(d) Probation staff should not recommend a delinquency petition if the youth's conduct is more appropriately addressed by another youth-serving agency or system. Probation staff should avoid:

    i.   duplication of services when the youth is already receiving or may receive similar services from a less restrictive, less coercive agency outside of the juvenile justice system; and

    ii.   processing the youth in the juvenile justice system when the juvenile justice system cannot effectively serve the youth because of the youth's developmental limitations, disabilities, or other cognitive or mental health impairments.

(e) Probation staff should refer dual-status youth for community-based services that are suitable for the youth's age, ethnicity, gender or sexual identity, cognitive disability, and developmental stage.

Standard 4.2   Responsibilities of Judges and Probation Offices in Recommending Detention or Release

(a) Probation offices should adopt written protocols and develop risk assessment instruments to guide detention and release decisions involving dual-status youth.

(b) In deciding whether to recommend detention or release for youth referred from the child welfare system, probation staff should use the same criteria applied to other youth. Those criteria should be objective and determine whether the youth poses a risk of danger to the community or failing to appear. Other criteria should include:

      i.   the existence of services available from other youth-serving agencies to address the youth's needs and reduce the youth's risk of flight or risk to public safety; and

      ii.   whether detention will jeopardize placement or services provided by other youth-serving agencies.

(c)   Probation staff should not recommend detention:

      i.   because the youth is awaiting suitable placement in the child welfare system;

      ii.   as a respite for caregivers in the child welfare system; or

      iii. when other youth-serving systems are providing or can provide placement and services that protect the court's and the public's interests.

(d)   The intake officer should not recommend detention in a facility that cannot adequately meet a youth's special, physical, or behavioral health needs.

(e)   If a youth is detained, probation staff should, consistent with Standard 2.11 of these standards concerning Information Sharing:

      i.   advise other agencies currently serving the youth that detention is temporary, and seek to preserve the placement and services the youth is receiving from those agencies;

      ii.   provide detention staff with information about the youth's strengths, interests, preference, educational needs, and physical or behavioral health needs; and

      iii. facilitate communication between the detention staff and other agencies serving the youth.

Standard 4.3   Diverting Delinquency to Dependency and Maintaining Dual Jurisdiction

(a)   Juvenile court judges have authority to divert a delinquency petition to a child welfare or status offense petition.

(b)   The decision to dismiss or divert should be made as early as possible.

(c) A judge presiding over child welfare proceedings should be authorized, when the youth is facing delinquency proceedings or has been adjudicated delinquent, to keep the child welfare matter open so the youth may receive necessary child welfare services.

Standard 4.4   Judicial Responsibilities Regarding Detention

(a) In deciding whether to order detention or release for youth referred from the child welfare system, the juvenile court judge should use the same criteria applied to other youth. Those criteria should be objective and determine whether the youth poses a risk of danger to the community or failing to appear. Other criteria should include:

    i.   the existence of services available from other youth-serving agencies to address the youth's needs and reduce the youth's risk of flight or risk to public safety; and

    ii. whether detention will jeopardize placement or services provided by other youth-serving agencies.

(b) The juvenile court judge should not order detention:

    i.   because the youth is awaiting suitable placement in the child welfare system;

    ii. as a respite for caregivers in the child welfare system; or

    iii. when other youth-serving systems are providing or can provide placement and services protect the court's and the public's interests.

(c) The juvenile court judge should not order detention in a facility that cannot adequately meet a youth's physical or behavioral health needs.

(d) A judge who has concurrent jurisdiction over delinquency and child welfare matters may order the appropriate child welfare agencies to:

    i.   arrange a suitable nonsecure placement for a youth as an alternative to detention in the juvenile justice system; or

    ii.   continue providing services for a youth in detention.

Standard 4.5   Intake and Detention of Pregnant or Parenting Youth

(a) Juvenile justice professionals should develop protocols to ensure that pregnant or parenting youth in the juvenile justice system have:

    i.   basic support and critical services to reduce the risk that they will engage in abusive or neglectful behavior toward their own children;

    ii.   physical and behavioral health services commonly provided for high risk pregnancy and child-rearing;

    iii. alternatives to detention and pretrial release and disposition plans that address the youth's needs in caring for their own children;

    iv. opportunities for detained youth to visit with and engage their children; and

    v.   opportunities for parenting, financial management, and independent living skills training.

(b) When addressing alleged behavior by pregnant or parenting youth, juvenile justice professionals should seek to minimize harm to the health of the youth's child and minimize disruption in the child's living arrangements.

(c) Juvenile justice professionals should give special consideration to alternatives to detention during a youth's pregnancy and at least the first year of the newborn's life.

(d) When a judge detains a pregnant youth, juvenile justice professionals should address special prenatal needs of the youth by ensuring:

i.   adequate prenatal care, including regular doctor visits, child-birth classes, and dietary supplements;

ii. sanitary living conditions to reduce the risk of trauma and infection;

iii. access to reproductive health counseling; and

iv. no use of physical restraints during the term of pregnancy unless there are serious and immediate risks to the safety of the youth or others, in which case the least restrictive means of restraint should be used.

(e) During labor and delivery for detained youth, juvenile justice authorities should ensure that:

i.   the detained youth is transported to an appropriate medical facility without delay, and

ii. shackles or other restraints are not used.

(f) After delivery, juvenile justice professionals should allow the mother and child to be together at least the first year, in the least restrictive placement possible. Professionals should:

i.   develop re-entry plans that focus specifically on pregnant and parenting youth;

ii. ensure that parenting youth are provided appropriate postnatal care and services, including parenting classes, continued doctor visits, and behavioral health services as appropriate;

iii. facilitating placements that permit the child to reside with a parent or, if not possible or in the best interests of the child, facilitate visits between the youthful parent and their child, including overnight and contact visits; and

iv. facilitate visits with family or other caregivers providing care for the youth's child.

(g) Any diversion, disposition, and re-entry plan developed for pregnant or parenting youth should seek to reduce the chance that the youth's child will be placed in the child welfare system.

Part IV Commentary

4.1 Responsibilities of Probation Offices at Intake[166]

These Standards supplement the IJA-ABA Juvenile Justice Standards Relating to the Juvenile Probation Function: Intake and Predisposition Investigative Services,[167] but give special attention to the needs of crossover and multisystem youth. Standard 4.1 advances one of the core principles of these Standards by stressing the importance of diversion from the system. As stated in the Introduction, many youth who are referred to the juvenile justice system "have needs that can and should be addressed by one or more of these other systems without courts exercising delinquency jurisdiction."[168]

This recommendation calling for diversion from the juvenile system is consistent with the policy adopted by the ABA in 2008, calling for jurisdictions to "use diversion and intervention services for minor or low level acts of misbehavior committed while a youth is in foster care. . . ."[169]

Most states allow juvenile probation to divert cases, as shown by Appendix II of these Standards.[170] These Standards also recognize that there are jurisdictions in which the probation officer does not have the authority to recommend petitioning or no petitioning of cases. When they do, this Standard should be followed. Current IJA-ABA Standards provide ample guidelines to assist the probation department in determining whether to recommend the filing of a petition.[171] Probation should consider whether petitioning would cause undue harm to youth or exacerbate the problems that led to their delinquent acts,

---

166. For a thoughtful discussion of all aspects of Intake, see Tamar R. Birckhead, *Closing the Widening Net: The Rights of Juveniles at Intake*, 46 Tex. Tech L. Rev. 157 (2013).

167. Referred to hereafter as "Juvenile Probation Function."

168. *See* Introduction, p. 1 of these Standards.

169. ABA policy on Dual Jurisdiction/Crossover Youth, paragraph (a), adopted at the 2008 Annual Meeting, found in Appendix I of these Standards.

170. *See also Intake and Diversion*, JJGPS (2016), http://www.jjgps.org/juvenile-court, a product of the National Center for Juvenile Justice, the research arm of the National Council of Juvenile and Family Court Judges.

171. Juvenile Probation Function, Standard 2.8.

whether youth present a substantial danger to others, and whether referral to the court has already served as a desired deterrent.[172]

4.2   Responsibilities of Judges and Probation Offices in Recommending Detention or Release

This Standard also supplements the Juvenile Probation Function[173] by focusing on the needs of crossover and dual-jurisdiction youth.

This Standard reflects positive U.S. experience since 1992 when the Annie E. Casey Foundation launched its Juvenile Detention Alternatives Initiative (JDAI). Since JDAI began, hundreds of jurisdictions across the country have shown that they do not need to detain youth in secure pretrial settings in order to ensure their appearance at trial or to prevent their offending before the case is resolved. Skeptics predicted that youth crime would increase if jurisdictions detained fewer youth, but this has not been the case. Instead, over almost three decades, JDAI sites reduced detention by 50 percent, during an extended period of *declining* juvenile crime rates. JDAI sites use race-neutral risk assessment instruments that address the short-term risk of flight and offending.[174]

JDAI was launched because detention—although necessary in rare occasions—was overused and harmful. Detention deprives children of liberty; locking up a child should not be taken lightly. It declares to the youth they are being criminalized, and it disrupts school and employment. The mere fact of detention increases the probability a youth will be committed to an institution after trial.

Detention also has a disproportionate impact on minority youth. That impact is continued after trial. Studies of minority overrepresentation in the juvenile justice system point to detention as the place

---

172. Training of probation officers in adolescent development and neuroscience is important for the understanding of deterrence. Early 21st-century research has exposed the limits of "deterrent effects" on teenagers. *See generally* ELIZABETH S. SCOTT & LAURENCE STEINBERG, RETHINKING JUVENILE JUSTICE (Harvard University Press, 2008); David L. Myers, *Deterrence, as Delinquency Policy, in* ENCYCLOPEDIA OF JUVENILE DELINQUENCY AND JUSTICE (Wiley 2017). *See also* Roper v. Simmons, 543 U.S. 551 (2005) (rejecting deterrence as a justification for the juvenile death penalty). Deterrence is even more unlikely for youth with behavioral health (mental health or drug or alcohol) problems or intellectual disabilities.

173. *See* in particular Standards 2.8 to 2.16.

174. *See Latest JDAI Results: Significant Reductions in Juvenile Incarceration and Crime*, ANNIE E. CASEY FOUND. (Dec. 9, 2019), https://www.aecf.org/blog/latest-jdai-results-significant-reductions-in-juvenile-incarceration/. *See generally* https://www.aecf.org/work/juvenile-justice/jdai/.

with the most disparate impact in decision-making. And because it is more likely that detained youth will move deeper into the pipeline after disposition, the disproportionate effect of detention decisions affects minority youth disproportionally at each stage.

Further, detention centers are not nice places, no matter how modern. Children are often hurt in detention, by other children, and by staff. They experience violence, sexual assault, and trauma associated with post-traumatic stress.[175] Overcrowded detention centers are even more problematic.[176]

Thus, courts should never hold youth in greater confinement than is needed to protect the public and assure court attendance. Detention is not an appropriate alternative respite for caregivers who are struggling with youths' behavioral challenges. The child welfare system should make reasonable efforts to prevent out-of-home placements and to avoid using detention simply because no options have been identified in the child welfare system.

Probation staff should be aware that risk assessment instruments may overstate the risk of reoffending by dual-status or crossover youth because many of these youth do not have parents who are available to be engaged in the youth's treatment plan. Such instruments need to assess whether other systems, such as child welfare—even if it is making the referral—can manage the youth's behavior.[177]

---

175. 9.5 percent of youth detained in state juvenile facilities report at least one incident of sexual victimization by another youth or staff in the past 12 months or since admission. Of those who reported being victims of staff sexual misconduct, 85.9 percent reported more than one incident, while 20.4 percent reported being victimized more than ten times. Allen J. Beck et al., *Sexual Victimization in Juvenile Facilities Reported by Youth*, U.S. Dep't of Just. Office of Justice Programs (2013), https://www.bjs.gov/content/pub/pdf/svjfry12.pdf. Incarcerated youth are also subjected to physical abuse. Thirteen thousand claims of abuse had been reported from 2004 through 2007 in state-run juvenile facilities nationwide. An estimated 45 percent of youth confined in secure correctional facilities and camp programs report staff use unnecessary force, while 30 percent of those youth report that staff use solitary confinement as a discipline tool. Holbrook Moore, AP: *13K Claims of Abuse in Juvenile Detention Since '04* (2008), https://www.wtsp.com/article/news/ap-finds-13000-abuse-claims-in-juvenile-detention-centers-over-4-years/67-392760011.

176. Bart Lubow & Dennis Barron, *Resources for Juvenile Detention Reform Fact Sheet*, U.S. Dep't of Just., Office of Justice Programs, Office of Juvenile Justice & Delinquency Prevention (2000); Ira M. Schwartz & William H. Barton (eds), Reforming Juvenile Detention: No More Hidden Closets (Ohio State University Press 1994).

177. Both the Crossover Youth Practice Model promoted by Georgetown's CJJR, and the policies and practices promoted by the RFK National Resource Center for Juvenile Justice, cited in notes 4 and 5, *supra*, have shown that a sound collaborative process can reduce referrals to detention.

4.3   Diverting Delinquency to Dependency and Maintaining Dual Jurisdiction

This Standard promotes two themes. The first is that *delinquency* courts should make a quick decision about whether to convert a delinquency petition to a dependency petition.[178] This decision will involve a preliminary look at the youth's background before the adjudication. For the reasons stated in Standard 2.8 and Commentary, this should either happen upon motion by the youth or, if appropriate, lead to a delinquency hearing before a new judge (to avoid the fact finder considering information that may be prejudicial).[179]

The second theme is that *dependency* courts should be slow to close cases. Indeed, they should keep dependency cases open when a dependent child is arrested or has been adjudicated delinquent. There are many reasons for this policy. One is because the youth, after an arrest, may not be adjudicated delinquent. Charges may be dropped for many reasons, from witnesses failing to appear to the youth prevailing at trial. This process can take time—youth will need a place to stay while awaiting trial—or a place to return later if they are detained.[180] Second, most jurisdictions do not give delinquency courts the authority to order services that are available to dependent children. Continuity of care and services is essential. A dependency court—which may become a dual-status court as described in Standard 2.8—must retain jurisdiction to ensure that appropriate services are available.[181] Also,

---

178. This is permitted, for example, in California. CAL. CODE ANN., Welfare & Institutions § 241.1. *See* Commentary to Standard 2.1. A more common practice, even in California, is for the court reviewing the case at first appearance to request the charging authority to consider dismissal or diversion.

179. While judges often hear information about a case during pretrial proceedings, and then preside over the adjudicatory hearing, the information judges see in pretrial motions is different than that required for diversion. The latter information will often include a youth's history, including prior arrests or adjudications, as well as information related to education or behavioral health matters. There is thus greater danger of bias when a court considers a motion to divert a case than there would be, for example, in considering a motion to suppress. Questions of recusal, of course, must be made on a case-by-case basis.

180. Most foster care maintenance payments are made on a per diem basis. Thus, child welfare agencies often want to make quick use of a newly empty foster care bed; foster parents, who lose per diems when a child is not with them, may want a quick replacement. This is a policy or administrative question—how should the child welfare system be financed?—that does not diminish the importance of this Standard.

181. Obviously, closing the dependency case also undermines collaborative case planning and management that are the hallmark of the Georgetown and RFK programs cited in notes 69–72.

keeping the dependency case open—and thereby addressing a youth's needs and behavior—might obviate the need entirely for pursuing the delinquency case. Third, for older youth, being in foster care on their 18th birthday triggers numerous rights, including the right to stay in or return to foster care—in most states until age 21; and the right to Medicaid until age 26.[182]

This Standard is important for teens involved in sex trafficking.[183] Most states have statutory prohibitions to charging minors with prostitution, or they allow diversion to the dependency system.[184] Some states, however, still keep these youth in the delinquency system.[185] Thus, delinquency courts in those states must consider, pursuant to this Standard, referring the youth to child welfare; and it is crucial for dependency courts to keep jurisdiction. A high percentage of youth taken into custody for prostitution have been in foster care.[186] They are particularly vulnerable.[187]

This Standard thus advances ABA policy, which since 2011 has called for jurisdictions to aid trafficked minors by:

> Permitting their immediate protective custody as dependent children in suitable residential environments and, except in extreme and compelling circumstances, not charging children under the 18 with the crimes of engaging in prostitution or soliciting themselves, loitering with the intent to engage in prostitution, or status offenses that are incident to their trafficking situation; . . .[188]

Jurisdictions should develop protocols among defense attorneys, prosecutors, probation officers, children and youth workers, and school officials. These protocols should address when it is appropriate

182. *See supra* note 69.

183. Megan Annitto, *Consent, Coercion, and Compassion: Emerging Legal Responses to the Commercial Sexual Exploitation of Minors*, 30 Yale L.P. Rev. 1, 2011.

184. Sonia Lunn, *Safe Harbor: Does Your State Arrest Minors for Prostitution?*, Human Trafficking Search, (Oct. 18, 2018), https://humantraffickingsearch.org/safe-harbor-does-your-state-arrest-minors-for-prostitution/.

185. *Id.*

186. Rhonda McMillion, *ABA Addresses the Impact of Sex Trafficking on Foster Youths*, ABA J. (Aug. 1, 2014),https://www.abajournal.com/magazine/article/aba_addresses_the_impact_of_sex_trafficking_on_foster_youths.

187. See American Psychological Association, *Resolution on Human Trafficking in the United States, Especially of Women and Girls* (adopted Feb. 2017).

188. ABA Policy 103A: *Exploited Children Victims' Rights* (adopted Aug. 2011), on human trafficking of minor victims.

to divert a delinquency case to the dependency system or to convert a filed delinquency petition into a dependency petition.

4.4 Judicial Responsibilities Regarding Detention

This Standard supplements the Basic Principles and General Procedural Standards (Parts III and IV) of the IJA-ABA Standards Relating to Interim Status: The Release, Control and Detention of Accused Juvenile Offenders between Arrest and Disposition.[189]

The Commentary to Standard 4.2 applies here. Courts should order the least restrictive setting necessary to ensure a youth's presence in court and to reduce the risk of reoffending before the adjudicatory hearing. Courts have additional authority that is not available to probation officers. As discussed in the Commentary to Standard 4.3, judges can order child welfare agencies to keep cases open and to retain custody of a youth who has been arrested. Judges can order those agencies to supervise the youth and bring the youth to court, thereby eliminating the need for detention by replicating, through child welfare, detention's risk management justifications. Judges should consider family or family-like placements, including kin and therapeutic foster homes, as alternatives to detention.

In addition to making decisions in individual cases, judges are leaders who are critical to successful state and local efforts to reduce unnecessary detention. Judges have a leadership role in establishing policies and changing practices for all youth, including dual-status youth.[190]

4.5 Intake and Detention of Pregnant or Parenting Youth

This Standard provides detailed guidance to practitioners and policy makers in an area long fraught with difficulties.

> Pregnant and Parenting teens often are balancing their lives and being a parent. Ensuring that adolescent parents receive adequate social and

---

189. *See* §§ 1.1–4.7.

190. *Strategies for the Successful Expansion of JDAI*, Annie E. Casey Found. (Mar. 18, 2019), https://www.aecf.org/blog/strategies-for-the-successful-expansion-of-jdai/.

emotional, medical, and academic support is essential to the parent and the baby's future.[191]

While the starting point for this Standard is the comprehensive Criminal Justice Standard, Standards on Treatment of Prisoners,[192] this Standard goes further. It addresses the policies and practices that must be in place to deliver the range of services that a pregnant or parenting teenager needs. Alternatives to detention become even more important for this population, since detention staff who care for adolescents are rarely trained to (1) provide services to infants; (2) promote mother-baby bonding; while (3) ensuring that the young mother receives the critical services that are increasingly available to new parents; and (4) making sure that the new mother has all of the other services, such as education and behavioral health services, that are available to youth in the general population.

Juvenile justice services were late in coming to the care of large numbers of females. Designed for boys, the juvenile system was not equipped for the girls who emerged at the turn of the 21st century as a fast-growing juvenile justice population.[193] In addition, pregnant girls have often been victims of physical and sexual abuse and neglect, conditions for which the child welfare system is better suited.[194]

The importance of infant-parent bonding is well-established. The public system must avoid unnecessarily separating that bond since a broken bond is difficult to repair.[195] The Family First Prevention Services Act of 2018 places a renewed federal emphasis on promoting the well-being of infants and their parents, on preventing their unnecessary separation, and on ensuring that they receive appropriate services. The act requires that states, to be eligible for federal financial support of its child welfare system,[196] include the following:

---

191. Child Welfare Information Gateway, *Supporting Pregnant and Parenting Teens*, U.S. Dep't of Health & Human Services, Administration for Children & Families, Children's Bureau, https://www.childwelfare.gov/topics/preventing/promoting/parenting/pregnant-teens/.

192. Standard 23-6.9 Pregnant prisoners and new mothers.

193. Leslie Acoca, *Introduction to the National Girls Health Screen Project; the Findings from the Medical Case File Review of Girls Being Held in Detention and the Preliminary Analysis of Health/ Mental Health Studies of Girls in the Juvenile Justice System*, Nat'l Juvenile Just. Network (Sept., 2005), https://www.njjn.org/uploads/digital-library/resource_247.pdf.

194. American Academy of Pediatrics, *Health Care for Youth in the Juvenile Justice System*, 128 Pediatrics (March 2012).

195. *See* Joseph Goldstein et al., Beyond the Best Interest of the Child (The Free Press 1973).

196. 42 U.S.C. § 671 State plan for foster care and adoption assistance.

(e) Prevention and family services and programs . . .

(4) Requirements related to providing services and programs
Services and programs specified in paragraph (1) may be provided
under this subsection only if specified in advance in the <u>child</u>'s prevention plan described in subparagraph (A) and the requirements in
subparagraphs (B) through (E) are met:

> **(A) Prevention plan** The State maintains a written prevention plan
> for the <u>child</u> that meets the following requirements (as applicable):
> …
>
> > **(ii) Pregnant or parenting foster youth** In the case of a <u>child</u>
> > who is a pregnant or parenting foster youth described in para-
> > graph (2)(B), the prevention plan shall—
> >
> > > **(I)** be included in the <u>child</u>'s <u>case plan</u> required under <u>sec-
> > > tion 675(1) of this title</u>;
> > >
> > > **(II)** list the services or programs to be provided to or on
> > > behalf of the youth to ensure that the youth is prepared (in
> > > the case of a pregnant foster youth) or able (in the case of a
> > > parenting foster youth) to be a parent;
> > >
> > > **(III)** describe the foster care prevention strategy for any
> > > <u>child</u> born to the youth; and
> > >
> > > **(IV)** comply with such other requirements as the <u>Secretary</u>
> > > shall establish.[197]

Any diversion, disposition, or re-entry plan involving pregnant and
parenting youth should use evidence-based programs that implement
public health models of intervention. There is a large literature on
how to serve this population.[198]

---

197. *Id.*

198. *See, e.g.,* Stefanie Mollborn, *Teenage Mothers Today: What We Know and How It Matters*, Soc'y for Rsch. in Child Dev., (Nov, 7, 2016), https://srcd.onlinelibrary.wiley.com/doi/abs/10.1111/c dep.12205.

PART V: REFERRING YOUTH FOR SERVICES

Standard 5.1 Accessing Behavioral Health Services

(a) To reduce the high rates of mental health and substance abuse conditions among dual-status youth, every jurisdiction should have a system that:

    i.   provides for early identification of youth in the child welfare and juvenile justice systems who have mental health or substance abuse conditions;

    ii.   seeks to prevent the unnecessary involvement in the juvenile justice system of children who need mental health or substance abuse services; and

    iii. provides for timely access by youth in the child welfare system to appropriate mental health treatment by qualified professionals within the least restrictive setting that is consistent with public needs and reduces the risk of delinquent behavior by these youth.

(b) A comprehensive system to address youth with mental health or substance abuse disorders should provide:

    i.   screening and assessment at entry and key points in the child welfare and juvenile justice processes;

    ii.   a continuum of evidence-based services at all stages of the youth's involvement in the child welfare and juvenile justice systems, including short-term interventions and crisis services, on-going supportive services, and continuity of care;

    iii. family involvement in the least restrictive setting;

    iv. protections against self-incrimination when youth participate in court-ordered mental health or substance abuse screening, assessment, and treatment; and

    v.   sustainable funding mechanisms to support the above.

(c) **Juvenile justice authorities should have authority to obtain services from other youth-serving systems, including state and local child welfare, physical and behavioral health, physical health, educational, and alcohol and drug abuse treatment systems.**

(d) **Juvenile and child welfare courts should have authority to obtain services for youth with mental health and substance abuse conditions without having to alter the legal custody of the youth or transfer jurisdiction to another court or system.**

PART V COMMENTARY

5.1   Accessing Behavioral Health Services

The 1980 IJA-ABA Juvenile Justice Standards failed to address behavioral health[199] issues. There is only an allusion to mental health services along with "mental retardation" in the standards governing Court Organization and Administration:

> Mental illness and retardation commitment proceedings concerning juveniles and adults should be governed by the law of the jurisdiction applicable to such proceedings for non-adjudicated persons.[200]

This Standard marks a significant improvement on the 1980 volumes by building on 40 years of research into the links between behavioral health and juvenile justice. It recognizes the significant investment in behavioral health services at the federal and state levels.[201] The core principles in this Standard are taken from the Mental

---

199. "[B]behavioral health" is defined by SAMHSA as the promotion of mental health, resilience, and well-being; the treatment of mental and substance use disorders; and the support of those who experience and/or are in recovery from these conditions, along with their families and communities. *Behavioral Health Integration*, SAMHSA, https://www.samhsa.gov/sites/default/files/samhsa-behavioral-health-integration.pdf. Congress created the Substance Abuse and Mental Health Services Administration (SAMHSA) in 1992 to make substance use and mental disorder information, services, and research more accessible. *See generally* SAMHSA, https://www.samhsa.gov/about-us.

200. *See* Standard 1.1(a).

201. SAMHSA, https://www.samhsa.gov/.

Health/Juvenile Justice Joint Policy Statement adopted by the Pennsylvania executive branch and judicial leaders in 2006.[202]

Reports and studies document that the failure of multiple systems to effectively serve youth in their communities has driven youth with behavioral health disorders into the child welfare and juvenile justice systems in large numbers.[203] Recent large-scale empirical studies suggest that as many as 65 percent to 75 percent of youth involved in the juvenile justice system have one or more diagnosable psychiatric disorders.[204] Most of these youth do not have mental health issues that are acute enough to justify involuntary mental health commitment. Even if they do, appropriate therapeutic placements are difficult to find. Thus, these Standards address the vast majority of youth who are referred to juvenile court because their problems have been undiagnosed, or they have not received mental health services elsewhere. Left untreated, court-involved youth with behavioral disorders sink deeper into the juvenile justice system as they struggle to comply with terms of probation, skip school, or do not adjust to the requirements of placement facilities. Unidentified, untreated youth in such facilities pose a safety risk to both themselves and other youth. The longer youths' needs are unmet, the more acute the issues may become, increasing the difficulty of addressing the underlying behavioral health issue.

Behavioral health issues are even more pronounced for dual-jurisdiction youth than they are for the child welfare or juvenile justice population alone. Behavioral health specialists should be actively involved in case assessment, case planning, and case management

---

202. The statement was developed under the umbrella of Models for Change, a juvenile justice initiative supported by the John D. and Catherine T. MacArthur Foundation. The complete policy statement is at http://www.modelsforchange.net/publications/142. The policy statement drew on principles set forth in greater detail in Kathleen R. Skowyra and Joseph J.

203. *See, e.g.*, United States House of Representatives, Committee on Government Reform Minority Staff, Special Investigations Division (July 2004). Incarceration of Youth Who Are Waiting for Community Mental Health Services in the United States. Washington, D.C.: House of Representatives; United States General Accounting Office (2003). Child Welfare and Juvenile Justice: Federal Agencies Could Play a Stronger Role in Helping States Reduce the Number of Children Placed Solely to Obtain Mental Health Services. Washington, D.C. U.S. Government Accounting Office (2003).

204. Jennie L. Shufelt & Joseph J. Cocozza, Youth with Mental Health Disorders in the Juvenile Justice System: Results from a Multi-State Prevalence Study, National Center for Mental Health and Juvenile Justice (2006).

processes for these youth.[205] This problem is especially true for Black and Latinx youth. "[L]ow SES and minority children and adolescents have an even greater difficulty in receiving quality mental and behavioral health care" than the population at large.[206] "In addition to the mental and behavioral health burden experienced by racial/ethnic minority children and adolescents, significant barriers exist in their access to and utilization of mental and behavioral health services. . . ."[207]

This Standard also takes into consideration the concern of parents, advocates, and system professionals: that parents turn too often to the child welfare system and juvenile justice system because they have nowhere else to turn. Youth should not be referred to either system merely to obtain mental health services.

> [W]henever safe and appropriate, youth with mental health needs should be prevented from entering the juvenile justice system in the first place. For youth who do enter the system, a first option should be to refer them to effective treatment within the community. For those few who require placement, it is important to ensure that they have access to effective services while in care to help them re-enter society successfully.[208]

Screening and assessment are essential to divert youth from the child welfare and juvenile justice systems, or, if they are in either of those systems, to link them with appropriate services in the community or placement. Screening and assessment come with perils, however. First, they must be normed for the population that is entering these systems.[209] Second, many states fail to offer self-incrimination protections when youth are screened or assessed. These failures to

---

205. Denise Herz and her colleagues have written extensively about the many behavioral health problems faced by dual jurisdiction youth. *See, e.g.*, Denise Herz et al., *Addressing the Needs of Multi-System Youth: Strengthening the Connection between Child Welfare and Juvenile Justice*, CENTER FOR JUVENILE JUSTICE REFORM & ROBERT F. KENNEDY CHILDREN'S ACTION CORPS (2012).

206. American Psychological Association, *Child and Adolescent Mental and Behavioral Health Resolution*, (June 2019), https://www.apa.org/about/policy/child-adolescent-mental-behavioral-health.

207. *Id.* Youth involved with the child welfare and juvenile justice system are at enhanced risk of behavioral health challenges. As the APA notes, ". . . it is important to appreciate the magnified effects of intersectionality (i.e., intersecting identities and multiple minority status, such as being a person of color as well as female, a gender identity and sexual orientation minority, an immigrant or a person with a disability) on mental and behavioral health and disparities."

208. Mental Health and Juvenile Justice Collaborative for Change, *Better Solutions for Youth with Mental Health Needs in the Juvenile Justice System*, NATIONAL CENTER FOR MENTAL HEALTH AND JUVENILE JUSTICE & RESOURCE CENTER PARTNERS (2014), http://www.modelsforchange.net/publications/519.

209. *Supra* note 18, at 33.

protect from self-incrimination are even more acute when youth receive treatment in these systems. There is a paradox, of course, as treatment that is supposed to prepare youth for success in the community can lead to deeper system involvement.[210] This Standard squarely addresses these issues.

For discussion of juvenile court authority to obtain services from other youth-serving systems, see Commentary to Standard 2.1.[211]

---

210. Lourdes M. Rosado & Riya S. Shah, Protecting Youth from Self-Incrimination When Undergoing Screening, Assessment and Treatment within the Juvenile Justice System (Juvenile Law Center, 2007). This is a comprehensive examination of the problems, with solutions.

211. *See supra* note 69, in particular, references to California and South Carolina law.

PART VI: DELINQUENCY ADJUDICATION OF DUAL-STATUS YOUTH

Standard 6.1   Due Process at Adjudicatory Hearing

Charges of delinquency should be adjudicated at a full due process hearing by a judge who is a neutral fact-finder. The juvenile court judge should:

(a) not be influenced by knowledge of or prior interactions with the youth or the youth's family in a dependency case or other legal matters;

(b) make a determination of delinquency based on admissible evidence in the delinquency record; and

(c) not review information relating to the youth's involvement in a dependency case unless:

   i. review is requested by a party to the delinquency case, and

   ii. the information is relevant and appropriate for judicial review under applicable rules of evidence.

Standard 6.2   Legal Representation in a Delinquency Case

(a) Youth charged with delinquency are entitled to competent, loyal, and zealous representation by defense counsel. A "best interests" advocate for a child in a dependency proceeding should not also serve as the youth's defense counsel in a delinquency case.

(b) Incriminating statements made by a youth to a best interest advocate who is not bound by the rules of the attorney-client confidentiality should be inadmissible in a delinquency hearing absent a knowing, voluntary, and intelligent waiver.

146

PART VI COMMENTARY

6.1   Due Process at Adjudicatory Hearing

The IJA-ABA Standards Relating to Adjudication of youth charged with delinquency apply with equal force to all youth charged with delinquency, including crossover and dual-jurisdiction youth. Due process rights at an adjudicatory hearing should never be compromised in order to secure services for multi-jurisdiction youth.[212]

The 1980 IJA-ABA Standards incorporated the major due process rights to which youth became entitled in the aftermath of *In re Gault*.[213] This Standard is limited to addressing due process through the lens of delinquency hearings in which the youth is already under court jurisdiction through involvement in the child welfare system. Information about the youth's child welfare history—which in many states includes status offenses, such as running away, truancy, or ungovernability—should be barred at adjudication unless the dependent youth, through counsel, gives consent. Absent consent, other information in the child welfare file—such as a youth's school discipline record or mental health history—should be similarly barred. There may be situations in which the prosecution believes that information about the youth's dependent child status or history is relevant to the delinquency adjudication. Under such circumstances the juvenile court, upon motion by the prosecution, should develop a system for in camera inspection of social files by a judge or court official not assigned to adjudicate the delinquency case.

6.2   Legal Representation in a Delinquency Case

ABA policies are opposed to "best interest" representation of dependent children, in particular those who are teenagers and most likely to cross over to the juvenile justice system.[214] Thus, the Definitions section of these Standards distinguishes between a "Best Interest Advocate," who is not a lawyer, and Delinquency Counsel and Dependency

---

212. On the importance of a neutral fact-finder, *see supra* notes 65 and 66, Commentary to Standard 2.7. As noted in that section, there are special challenges in rural counties, or in small venues in which a single judge hears both dependency and delinquency cases.

213. 387 U.S. 1 (1967); *In re* Winship, 397 U.S. 358 (1970); Breed v. Jones, 421 U.S. 519 (1975).

214. *See* Commentary to Standard 2.6.

Counsel, who are lawyers who must advocate for a client's "expressed interest."

Youth will often trust and confide in their guardians ad litem,[215] without realizing that a GAL is a best interest advocate who is not normally bound by the rules of attorney-client confidentiality. As a result, a youth may not realize that his or her incriminating statements may be repeated to the court or law enforcement officials.

Because a GAL or Best Interest Advocate typically has no duty to preserve client confidentiality, such an advocate should be prohibited from representing a youth in a delinquency case. Clients who have seen their lawyers share confidential information may have no reason to believe that those lawyers will suddenly start protecting such information. These Standards thus follow the IJA-ABA Juvenile Justice Standards and the ABA Model Act on Representation of Dependent Children.[216]

If, for some compelling reason, a person who has acted as a GAL or Best Interest Advocate for a youth is subsequently appointed as the youth's lawyer in a delinquency case, the lawyer should explain to the youth—and state on the record in court—that the lawyer's role has changed and he or she is no longer acting in the best interest of the youth but will instead be bound by rules of professional conduct that require zealous representation of the youth's stated interests.

---

215. Many jurisdictions refer to the Best Interest Advocate as a guardian ad litem (GAL). The GAL's role in dependency proceedings is often inconsistent with the role of attorney for the youth in delinquency proceedings. *See, e.g.*, Pennsylvania Juvenile Act, 42 Pa. Cons. Stat. § 6311 Guardian ad litem for child in court proceedings.

In these jurisdictions, the guardian ad litem acts in the best interest of the youth and is not bound by attorney-client confidentiality, while counsel for the youth in a delinquency proceeding must strictly adhere to the rules of confidentiality—including those governing the attorney-client privilege and client "secrets"—and must zealously advocate for the youth's stated interest.

216. *See, generally* William Vaughn Stapleton & Lee E. Teitelbaum, In Defense of Youth: A Study of the Role of Counsel in American Juvenile Courts (Russell Sage Foundation, 1972). Lee Teitelbaum was the Reporter for the 1980 IJA-ABA Standards Relating to Counsel for Private Parties.

PART VII: DISPOSITION OF DELINQUENCY CASES

Standard 7.1   Information Gathering and Information Sharing For Disposition

After adjudication, records relating to a youth's child welfare case may be reviewed by the juvenile court to:

(a)   avoid conflicting court orders;

(b)   ensure effective case management; and

(c)   assist in the development of an effective disposition plan.

Standard 7.2   Disposition Process

(a)   If a youth is adjudicated delinquent, the court should hold a full due process hearing to determine the youth's appropriate disposition. The youth's disposition hearing should be consolidated with child welfare proceedings involving the youth if the court determines that such proceedings will advance the best interests of the youth and promote efficient and effective coordination of services. Youth and family members with disabilities should receive accommodations necessary for meaningful participation in the proceedings.

(b)   Risk or needs assessment tools used in disposition planning for dual-status youth should be validated and targeted to achieve the youth's best long-term interests in either the child welfare or delinquency system.

(c)   Results of any risk or needs assessment tools should be in writing and provided to the parties, and any persons who administered the tool should be available for examination by the parties.

(d)   Jurisdictions should develop protocols and teams to aid disposition planning for dual-status youth. Such teams should include representatives from youth-serving agencies necessary to address the youth's needs, as well as the youth, the youth's parents, guardian or caretaker, defense counsel, best interest advocate, service provider, and representatives from the state, such as a probation officer or prosecutor.

(e) When a youth participates in a disposition team meeting, the youth should be advised that the team will consider any information the youth provides in making placement decisions.

(f) The juvenile court judge should:

    i.   designate a lead agency responsible for coordinating services for the youth;

    ii.   direct that disposition team meetings be completed before disposition, and expedited when a youth is detained pending disposition; and

    iii. order that the team prepare a written disposition report with a statement of reasons explaining how the recommendations will advance the best interests of the youth and the goals of the state's juvenile justice code. That report should be distributed to all parties including the youth and defense counsel in advance of the disposition hearing. The author of the report should be available for examination at or before the hearing.

(g) All parties should be permitted to review and respond to any information or testimony that will be or is presented to the court at the disposition hearing.

Standard 7.3   Postponement of Disposition

(a) The court may temporarily postpone disposition in a delinquency case and recommend referral to the appropriate child welfare agency that can serve the youth with minimal risk to public safety, when a delinquent youth is in immediate need of services from or awaiting placement by the child welfare system. Any such referral should be expedited if possible.

(b) The child welfare system should develop processes for expediting cases for delinquent youth who are pending disposition in a delinquency proceeding.

Standard 7.4   Disposition Options

(a) Courts ordering disposition for dual-status youth should be aware of and utilize all disposition options that are legislatively available for youth in the child welfare and delinquency systems.

(b) The juvenile court should order the least restrictive disposition that furthers the best interests of the youth and the goals of the juvenile justice system.

(c) Disposition options should include:

    i.   termination of the delinquency jurisdiction;

    ii.   referral to other youth-serving systems;

    iii. maintaining dual jurisdiction; or

    iv. disposition within the delinquency system while providing access to other youth-serving services, systems or agencies.

(d) Juvenile courts should have authority to

    i.   review service, rehabilitative, and disposition plans developed in the child welfare system;

    ii.   modify child welfare plans that are in conflict with the goals of the juvenile justice system; and

    iii. require child welfare and juvenile justice agencies to coordinate planning to satisfy their obligations to the youth.

(e) All youth who are adjudicated delinquent should have access to the same publicly-funded services that are available to non-delinquent youth.

(f) Juvenile court judges and probation officers should assist youth in obtaining services from other youth-serving systems and develop protocols for expeditious service delivery from such systems and agencies.

Standard 7.5   Disposition Orders

(a) Disposition orders that place the youth out of the home should include:

    i. a plan to maintain the youth's connection to parents, caregivers, or others who are important to the youth;

    ii. a reunification or permanency plan that seeks to reunite the youth with family, caregivers or other significant supportive adult, to identify some other permanent stable living arrangement; and

    iii. a re-entry and discharge plan that specifies where and how, after release from detention or residential placement, the youth will be educated, work, and receive appropriate services.

(b) Disposition orders should set forth the services expected from each agency and set regular status review hearings to assess compliance with the order.

Standard 7.6   Modification of Disposition Orders

(a) Juvenile courts should have authority to review and modify if necessary, any component of a disposition order for dual-status youth.

(b) Courts should not modify any disposition ordered until after notice to, and opportunity to be heard by, all parties.

(c) After disposition, any party in a delinquency case should have authority to petition the court, and the court should have authority to:

    i. reduce the restrictiveness or duration of disposition when more appropriate and less restrictive options have become available; or

    ii. increase the restrictiveness or duration of disposition only when the youth has violated the terms or conditions of disposition and the services being provided are not adequately addressing the youth's needs or ensuring public safety and no equally or less restrictive options are available.

(d)   The court should not have authority to increase the restrictiveness or duration of disposition for a dual-status youth until after a full due process hearing, with counsel and an opportunity for the youth to be heard. Youth and family members with disabilities should receive accommodations necessary for meaningful participation in the proceedings.

(e)   Absent informed consent by the youth, neither the restrictiveness nor the duration of disposition should be increased just to ensure the youth's access to funding.

PART VII COMMENTARY

7.1   Information Gathering and Information Sharing for Disposition

These Standards have two broad goals. One is to keep children *out* of the juvenile justice system when their needs, and public safety risks, can be managed by other systems. The second is to ensure that youth who *are* in the delinquency system (1) have access to services from other systems; (2) have coordinated and integrated development of disposition plans; (3) receive effective case management; and (4) aren't hurt by competing court calendars, mixed messages, and conflicting orders.

Part VII addresses the second goal. Standard 7.1 is a corollary to Standards 2.10 to 2.12;[217] it sets forth three core objectives of a dual-status court, for which shared information will be necessary.

---

217. The dual-status court, at disposition, is a cousin of the Unified Children and Family Court, which the ABA officially endorsed in 1980 and to which it reaffirmed its commitment in 1994. *Text of American Bar Association Policies Related to Children 1979–2014*, ABA, https://www.american bar.org/content/dam/aba/administrative/child_law/ABAPolicies1979-2014.pdf. These dual-status standards caution against having a single fact-finder *at adjudication*. They are thus consistent with STANDARDS RELATING TO DISPOSITIONAL PROCEDURES, 2.1.A. (I.J.A. A.B.A. 1980). They recognize, however, that procedural rights are different at disposition, and there is value, as in the unified family court, in having a single judge as "case manager" who has access to information that is necessary to further the goals of these Standards.

7.2   Disposition Process

Dispositions should promote access to opportunities for personal and social growth. Dispositions should help youth improve their decision-making about their futures. Dispositions should hold youth accountable in developmentally appropriate ways. They should reduce re-offending and promote public safety through means that are individualized, culturally competent, trauma informed, fair, just, and recognize youths' needs and strengths.

This Standard gives the court flexibility in furthering those ends. It gives the court the option of consolidating the delinquency disposition with that of the dependency court. This is particularly important because child welfare dispositions engage older teens in decision-making, build on youths' strengths, and give them a pathway to adulthood. In most states, dependency courts have access to a wider range of services than are available to delinquency courts.

The 1980 Standards caution:

> It should not be assumed that more information is also better information, or that the accumulation of dispositional information, particularly of the subjective and evaluative type, is necessarily an aid to decision making.[218]

"Subjective and evaluative" information can be biased, as can the interpretation of objective information. Racial bias—explicit or implicit—is an obvious factor in distorted decision-making.

Implicit in this Standard is one of the goals of this volume: the elimination of racial and ethnic disparities in the juvenile justice system. Bias can lead to harmful dispositions, such as unnecessary placement outside of the home, where racial and ethnic disparities in placement have been well-documented. Decision-makers have been shown to be influenced by explicit or implicit bias,[219] which can affect their judgment about Black and brown youth (as well as youth with disabilities and LGBTQ youth). As one commentator has noted in a discussion of racial disparities in the juvenile justice system, implicit bias is the predisposition of the public and juvenile justice decision-makers "to

---

218. Standards Relating to Dispositional Procedures, 2.1.D (I.J.A A.B.A. 1996).
219. Kristin Henning, *Criminalizing Normal Adolescent Behavior in Communities of Color: The Role of Prosecutors in Juvenile Justice Reform*, 98 Cornell L. Rev. 383, 419 et seq. (Jan. 2013).

consciously or subconsciously associate black youth with crime and dangerousness."[220]

This Standard's recommendations for the careful use of validated risk assessments, and for written reports with their authors subject to cross-examination, are measures that are meant to increase the reliability of information used by the court at disposition.

Standard 7.2 addresses how risk or needs assessment tools should be used at disposition. Such tools are not uncontroversial. Some critics note that many risk and needs assessment tools have not been validated in ways that consider race, ethnicity, or gender.[221] Others argue that a validated risk assessment tool "can minimize bias in judgments about youths' risk to public safety and their case management needs."[222]

These Standards recognize that risk assessment tools can be useful. To have value, however, the Standards require tools that have been validated, which means validated for all populations. In addition, *"Risk assessment tools are NOT prescriptive. They will not tell the user exactly what course of action should be taken with a youth."*[223] Risk assessment tools should *guide* decision-making, but they should not mandate a particular decision. Even so, because within these tools there is the potential for bias, this Standard requires that the person who administered the tool be available for examination, that is, as a witness in court.[224]

Notwithstanding the preference for multi-agency teams to assist in disposition planning, a youth remains entitled to due process at the delinquency disposition hearing. Thus, a lawyer representing a youth in a delinquency disposition should advocate for the youth's stated

---

220. *Id.* at 419. Henning, at 419 n.207, lists some of the many studies on the association of Black youth with dangerousness.

221. *See, e.g.,* Fredrick Butcher & Jeff M. Kretschmar, *How Juvenile Justice Systems Must Balance Risk Assessment with Racial Equity*, JUVENILE JUST. INFO. EXCH. (Feb. 4, 2020), https://jjie.org/2020/02/04/how-juvenile-justice-systems-must-balance-risk-assessment-with-racial-equity/.

222. Gina M. Vincent et al., *Risk Assessment in Juvenile Justice: A Guidebook for Implementation*, MODELS FOR CHANGE 6 (2012), http://njjn.org/uploads/digital-library/Risk_Assessment_in_Juvenile_Justice_A_Guidebook_for_Implementation.pdf.

223. *Id.* Emphasis in original.

224. As of 2017, 38 states had adopted a single risk assessment tool for state level use. The four most common tools were Youth Level of Service/Case Management Inventory (YLS/CMI); Structured Assessment of Violence Risk in Youth (SAVRY); Youth Assessment and Screening Instrument (YASI); and Positive Achievement Change Tool (PACT). *See Juvenile Justice Services*, JJGPS, http://www.jjgps.org/juvenile-justice-services#evidence-based-practices?tabId=2&view=risk-instruments.

legal interests and defer to the youth in decisions about whether to make or agree to a specific dispositional recommendation.[225]

The parties should minimize delays in disposition. However, a short delay may be necessary to ensure that appropriate referrals are made, and appropriate services are available. To avoid unnecessary delay, the parties should engage the child welfare system as soon as appropriate under the rules of confidentiality delineated in these Standards. The child welfare system should develop an expedited response system for youth who are facing disposition in a delinquency proceeding.

As recognized in the Standards relating to Cross-System Training,[226] effective disposition planning requires that all juvenile court judges, probation officers, and lawyers be trained about the availability of resources in the community, including services available from community-based, school-based, faith-based, nonprofit, and other public and private agencies. To assist youth in obtaining these services, the juvenile court should work with youth-serving agencies to develop protocols and procedures, memoranda of understanding, purchase of service agreements, and contracts for interagency referrals and expedited service delivery from public and private entities.

7.4   Disposition Options

It is essential that crossover and dual jurisdiction youth have access to all of the services and placements that are appropriate to meet their needs.[227]

7.6   Modification of Disposition Orders

In the juvenile justice system, courts can compel a youth's involuntary stay in care, usually to the 21st birthday.[228] However, for obvious reasons, youth rarely want to remain in the juvenile justice system, when missteps can lead to incarceration or re-incarceration. Sometimes, however, youth wish to continue with services, treatment,

---

225. *See* STANDARDS RELATING TO COUNSEL FOR PRIVATE PARTIES (I.J.A. A.B.A 1980), CRIMINAL JUSTICE STANDARDS FOR THE DEFENSE FUNCTION, 5.2 CONTROL AND DIRECTION OF THE CASE (I.J.A. A.B.A. 2017), and STANDARDS RELATING TO COUNSEL FOR PRIVATE PARTIES, 9.3(A) COUNSELING PRIOR TO DISPOSITION (I.J.A. A.B.A 1980).

226. *See* Standard 2.15.

227. *See supra* note 66.

228. A few states, like California, allow the court to keep a youth in the delinquency system past the 21st birthday.

and even placement after a delinquency disposition is scheduled to conclude. The virtue of a concurrent dependency jurisdiction is that it transfers control of the case *to the youth* when the youth turns 18. In dependency cases, youth may ask to extend duration of a disposition to ensure continued funding and continuity of services. State law should ensure that youth who have completed the requirements of disposition have a right to stay put in a program or placement, if they so desire, *as a dependent child*. When the coercive authority of the delinquency court is no longer needed, the delinquency court should close its case. The Commentary to Standard 2.2 describes the opportunities for youth in the dependency system past age 18, and particular benefits that accrue to foster youth if they are in the foster care system on their 18th birthday.

In many states, delinquency courts lose jurisdiction after disposition if they place youth in out-of-home care. States should amend their laws to ensure that this does not happen in the cases of dual-status youth. Regular court reviews are required by federal law when states claim Title IV-E dollars for a delinquent youth's care.[229] These Standards assume that the delinquency court will retain jurisdiction after disposition.

---

229. 42 U.S.C. § 670(a)16) requires a case review system to be a part of every state's IV-E plan.

PART VIII: POST-DISPOSITION AND RE-ENTRY

Standard 8.1 Key Principles Governing Re-entry and Discharge Planning

(a) Re-entry into the community and discharge from the juvenile justice system should be planned to include coordination with the child welfare system and ensure that dual-status youth receive all services they may need and all benefits to which they may be entitled.

(b) Re-entry and discharge planning should provide youth with a stable residential placement with appropriate services, support, and supervision from the child welfare and juvenile justice systems to promote their success in the community after discharge.

(c) Re-entry and discharge planning should:

  i. require the juvenile justice system to begin re-entry and discharge planning at or before disposition and complete it well in advance of the re-entry or discharge;

  ii. identify and implement services that, at a minimum, address continuity of education (including special education), housing, employment, and the need for physical and behavioral health services; and that are timely and coordinated across systems and agencies;

  iii. allow the filing of a petition for dependency, voluntary placement, or re-entry into foster care before a youth's 18th birthday, or whatever older age state law permits, if it appears the youth will need housing or other services when juvenile court jurisdiction terminates;

  iv. specify that delay in identifying, securing, or arranging appropriate post-discharge services may not be relied on to extend the duration of a residential placement; and

  v. allow the youth and the youth's family and counsel to participate fully in the development and periodic reviews of the re-entry plan.

Standard 8.2   Implementation of Re-Entry and Discharge Plan

(a) Youth discharged from residential placement but remaining under supervision of either the child welfare or delinquency system should have case managers assigned and trained to ensure timely and coordinated implementation of the youth's re-entry and discharge plan.

(b) Each agency with responsibility to the youth should:

   i. participate in a discharge planning meeting with other service providers at least thirty (30) days in advance of the anticipated discharge date;

   ii. ascertain, before discharge, the youth's strengths, interests, preferences and needs regarding services;

   iii. identify and secure, before discharge, a residence for the youth, to avoid delay in discharge; and

   iv. assist youth in obtaining important documents (such as identification or driver's license and birth certificates) as well as coverage for essential services such as healthcare.

PART VIII COMMENTARY

If the youth is in both the delinquency and dependency systems, implementation of Part VIII Standards will be best done when a single judge is responsible for the delinquency and dependency dockets.[230]

If the youth is only in the delinquency system, Standard 8.1(c)iii emphasizes the importance of filing a dependency petition before a child's 18th birthday ("or whatever older age state law permits") to promote stability, permanence, and youth well-being. The dependency petition may be necessary to ensure that a youth has a place to live—to avoid homelessness—or to ensure access to medical care or, in some instances, Special Immigrant Juvenile Status.

Part VIII Standards build on principles developed in Standards 2.2, 2.6, and 7.6. It draws heavily on Pennsylvania's 2005 Joint Policy

---

230. *See* Standard 2.7 and STANDARDS RELATING TO COURT ORGANIZATION AND ADMINISTRATION, 1.1.B. (I.J.A. A.B.A. 1982).

Statement on Aftercare[231] along with material from the National Reentry Resource Center.[232]

> Estimates suggest that up to two-thirds of youth and young adults who are involved in the juvenile justice system are also involved in the child welfare system. In most states, young adults age out of foster care between the ages of 18 and 21, meaning that they potentially exit the child welfare and juvenile justice systems at the same time. This concurrence often leaves youth and young adults to face the transition to independence on their own, making it that much more difficult to find stable housing. Further, youth and young adults experiencing homelessness may be at greater risk of continued contact with the justice system.[233]

Pennsylvania's Joint Policy Statement was a multi-agency effort that was part of the MacArthur Foundation's Models for Change juvenile justice reform initiative. Signatories to the Statement included the state secretaries in charge of child welfare, juvenile justice, education, and children's mental health, as well as leaders of the state's juvenile court judges and juvenile probation officers. The signers called aftercare "a key element in promoting public safety," defining it as:

> . . . the combination of services, planning, support and supervision that begins at disposition, continues while a youth is in placement, anticipates the youth's release from placement, continues until the youth is discharged from juvenile court supervision, and extends thereafter through connections to other opportunities, supports or services, such as those provided to dependent children.[234]

Part VIII Standards are designed to implement that definition. For example, they recognize the importance of joint planning of juvenile justice with child welfare. Although there are fewer delinquent youth in placement today than there have been in many years,[235] there are still thousands of youth in delinquency placements on any day. Careful assessment and planning while those youth are in care will enable

---

231. Commonwealth of Pennsylvania, *Joint Policy Statement on Aftercare* (Jan. 13, 2009), http://www.modelsforchange.net/publications/153.

232. *See generally* THE NATIONAL REENTRY RESOURCE CENTER, https://nationalreentryresourcecenter.org/.

233. Webinar: Addressing the Housing Needs of Youth and Young Adults in Contact with the Justice System (National Reentry Resource Center and the Coalition for Juvenile Justice 2016), https://nationalreentryresourcecenter.org/events/addressing-housing-needs-youth-and-young-adults-contact-justice-system.

234. Joint Policy Statement on Aftercare, *supra* note 232.

235. The annual one-day census in 1997 found 105,055 youth in residential care; in 2017 the count was down to 43,580. https://www.ojjdp.gov/ojstatbb/ezacjrp/.

eligible youth to receive continued services from the child welfare system. Such planning will also require the filing of a dependency petition for some youth, which must occur before their 18th birthdays, in order for this subset of delinquent youth to have a place to live and receive the benefits described earlier.[236]

Post-disposition planning should promote stability and plan for permanency. Whether convened in the child welfare case or in the delinquency case (for states receiving Title IV-E funding for delinquents), permanency hearings are required under federal AFSA and are critically important vehicles for re-entry planning and for engaging youth in their cases.[237]

In addition to promoting stability in a youth's life, aftercare planning should boost the youth's well-being. This includes a particular emphasis on education. The Standards emphasize continuity of education, which is particularly difficult for delinquent youth in placement.

> Youth in juvenile facilities face countless barriers to educational success. Placement in a facility usually requires a youth to change schools, and the educational programs provided in facilities typically lack the academic rigor of community-based schools. Youth may be assigned to the wrong grade, given coursework below grade level, or simply placed in front of a computer and expected to teach themselves. Although a large percentage of youth in the juvenile justice system are eligible for special education, many facilities fail to provide mandated services.
>
> When they are discharged from facilities, youth often struggle to transition back to community schools. Many find that they are unable to transfer the credits they earned or that all their courses are counted as elective hours. Unsurprisingly, these barriers lead to abysmal educational outcomes: a majority of youth do not return to school after release from custody, and only 1% of justice-involved youth graduate from college.
>
> These outcomes are particularly tragic given that many youth enter the justice system due to school-related issues, such as truancy or school-based offenses. Rather than help youth meet their educational goals, system involvement sets them further behind.[238]

---

236. Again, see commentary to Standards 2.2, 2.6. and 7.6.
237. *See* Family First Prevention Services Act, Pub. L. No. 115-123 (2018), Sections 50731 *et seq.*, at 42 U.S.C. §§ 670 *et seq.*
238. These observations come from justice-involved youth who are part of Juvenile Law Center's Juveniles for Justice youth engagement program. See their eloquent publication: Juveniles for Justice, *Broken Bridges: How Juvenile Placements Cut Off Youth from Communities and Successful Futures*, JUVENILE LAW CENTER (2018), https://jlc.org/sites/default/files/attachments/2018-12/2018Broken Bridges-FINAL-WEB_0.pdf.

The American Bar Association Center on Children and the Law, Juvenile Law Center, Education Law Center-PA, and Southern Poverty Law Center have proposed comprehensive solutions to these problems,[239] which jurisdictions should incorporate in their discharge planning. In particular, re-entry planning should ensure that educational credits earned in placement will be appropriately allocated or transferred to the youth's school upon discharge, consistent with Standard 3.4 of these Standards.

Implementation of Standard 8.2(b) may present difficulty for some agencies or systems that have responsibility for youths' success. Thus, the probation officer as case manager must find ways to involve those entities in active re-entry planning. The case manager should consider involving those entities in multidisciplinary teams, or in family team decision-making, to increase youths' opportunities for successful return to their communities. Modern technology makes this increasingly possible, as inexpensive video conferencing will make it easy for every relevant entity—including community-based providers—to participate meaningfully in planning.

Some youth will need assistance with immigration related issues, such as an application for Special Juvenile Immigration Status (SJIS), which requires an adjudication of dependency. American Bar Association policy since 2017 has called on Congress to:

> Preserve the availability of and the current statutory framework for Special Immigrant Juvenile Status ("SIJ") that protects noncitizen children when reunification is not viable with one or both parents due to abuse, abandonment, neglect, or a similar basis under state law . . .[240]

The Special Immigrant Juvenile (SIJ) classification provides that specified children who have been subject to state juvenile court child welfare proceedings may seek lawful permanent residence in the United States.[241]

---

239. *See* THE LEGAL CENTER FOR YOUTH JUSTICE AND EDUCATION, https://jjeducationblueprint.org/about.

240. *Protections for Immigrant and Asylum Seeking Children*, ABA Pol'y Resolution 301 (adopted Feb. 2017), https://www.americanbar.org/groups/public_interest/child_law/resources/attorneys/protections-for-immigrant-and-asylum-seeking-children/.

241. *Green Card Based on Special Immigrant Juvenile Classifications*, U.S. CITIZENSHIP & IMMIGRATION SERVICES (2018), https://www.uscis.gov/green-card/special-immigrant-juveniles/green-card-based-special-immigrant-juvenile-classification.

Part IX: Appeals

Standard 9.1   Right to Appeal

(a)   Dual-status youth should have the same right to appeal any order of the Family Court as any other youth. The right to appeal should include a review of the facts, law, and disposition order. Procedural safeguards should exist to ensure that youth are not penalized due to delays and other consequences arising out the youth's involvement in multiple legal matters.

(b)   A youth involved in multiple legal matters should be entitled to appellate review of, at a minimum:

   i.   all orders of a juvenile or dependency court that dispose of any portion of any case or matter;

   ii.   inconsistent orders in the youth's delinquency, dependency or other matters; and

   iii.   orders that do not embody the least restrictive alternative to achieve the best interests of the youth and the goals of multiple systems.

Standard 9.2   Written Court Orders and Advice of Rights

(a)   At the conclusion of any judicial proceeding involving dual-status youth and their families, the judge should:

   i.   prepare a final written order delineating the court's rulings, the facts found, the law applied, the disposition ordered, and the reasons therefore;

   ii.   advise the youth (and family) of the right to appeal;

   iii.   advise the parent or guardian of the right to appeal in dependency proceedings; and

   iv.   inquire of the youth's financial status, appoint appellate counsel if youth is indigent, or instruct defense counsel to secure the appointment of appellate counsel.

(b) **At or before the conclusion of the matter, the youth and the youth's counsel should be entitled to a copy of any document in the court file, as well as a verbatim transcript or recording of any relevant hearing.**

PART IX COMMENTARY

The principles set forth in this Part apply to all cases, but they warrant emphasis in the context of youth and families with multiple needs. Appellate rights are easily overlooked when dependency and delinquency cases are consolidated. Indeed, appeals are almost nonexistent in child welfare or juvenile justice when cases are heard separately. There is little reason to think that the right to appeal will be exercised more frequently when cases are heard together. Thus, while this Part affirms a *right* to appeal, there are obstacles to that right being exercised. In appropriate cases, counsel must find ways to assert the right by overcoming those obstacles.

These Standards supplement the IJA-ABA Standards Relating to Appeal and Collateral Review. That volume, at five pages, was the slenderest of the 20 volumes approved by the ABA in 1980. Yet, it offers broad grounds for appeal,[242] with a right to appellate counsel.[243] It also provides for stays of placement—and release from placement—pending appeal unless a court orders otherwise.[244] In practice, this volume has been largely ignored; it has had little impact "on the core appellate court functions: error correction, law-making, and uniformity."[245] The lack of appeals from juvenile court dispositions undermines "the legitimacy of the judicial process for litigants and the public."[246]

---

242. STANDARDS RELATING TO APPEAL AND COLLATERAL REVIEW 2.1 (I.J.A. A.B.A. 1979).

243. *Id.* at Standard 3.1.

244. *Id.* at Standard 5.1 *et seq.*

245. Megan Annitto, *Juvenile Justice Appeals*, 66 U. MIAMI L. REV. 671, 677 (2012).

246. Donald J. Harris, *Due Process v. Helping Kids in Trouble: Implementing the Right to Appeal from Adjudications of Delinquency in Pennsylvania*, 98 DICKINSON L. REV. 209, 212 (1994). This is particularly important because youth who believe a process is fair are more likely to embrace the law and comply with it. Jeffrey Fagan & Tom R. Tyler, *Legal Socialization of Children and Adolescents*, 18 SOC. JUST. RSCH., 217–41 (Sept. 2005).

Although youth have a right to appeal, appeals from juvenile court are rare:

> An alarming aspect of juvenile defense is the infrequency with which appeals are taken. Public defenders rarely take appeals in juvenile cases. . . . Appointed lawyers also take appeals rarely.[247]

Appeals are rare in part because counsel is, in most states, effectively unavailable after disposition.[248] Thus, one solution is for jurisdictions to ensure access to counsel following disposition.

The problem goes deeper than that, even when youth have counsel, because the juvenile court culture is inimical to appellate review. This culture relies on plea bargaining; renders court orders of disposition virtually unreviewable; and considers appeals as counter-therapeutic. State appellate procedures reinforce that culture by making it difficult to have timely reviews—that is, by failing to have a system that recognizes that speed matters when making decisions about children's lives.

Despite a call from some quarters to end plea bargaining in juvenile court,[249] too many juvenile court cases end in pleas, often impulsively.[250] Plea colloquies often fail to mention a right to appeal.[251] In addition, most plea bargains in juvenile court end in orders of probation. It is rare that youth know, when they agree to being placed on probation, what the conditions of probation will be. A high percentage of youth who are eventually incarcerated are those who have been found to have violated one or more of those conditions. In Philadelphia, for example, in 2019, almost three-quarters of youth who

---

247. Patricia Puritz et al., A Call for Justice: An Assessment of Access to Counsel and Quality of Representation in Delinquency Proceedings (A.B.A. Juvenile Justice Center, et al., 1995). The ABA Juvenile Justice Center later became the National Juvenile Defender Center, whose state-level assessments of counsel for delinquent youth show similar inattention to appellate practice.

248. *See generally* Nat'l Juvenile Defender Ctr.., Access Denied: A National Snapshot of States' Failure to Protect Children's Right to Counsel 32–35 (2017).

249. Steven C. Teske, *The Contrariness of Plea Bargaining in Juvenile Courts*, Juvenile Just. Info. Exch. (Dec. 3, 2019), https://jjie.org/2019/12/03/part-1-the-contrariness-of-plea-bargaining-in-juve nile-courts/.

250. Erika N. Fountain & Jennifer L. Woolard, *How Defense Attorneys Consult with Juvenile Clients about Plea Bargains*, 24 Psych., Pub. Pol'y, & Law 2 (2018).

251. Elizabeth Gladden Kehoe & Kim Brooks Tandy, *Indiana: An Assessment of Access to Counsel & Quality of Representation in Delinquency Proceedings*, Nat'l Juvenile Defender Ctr., Central Juvenile Defender Ctr., Children's Law Ctr., Inc. (2006) (more than half of respondents "indicated the right to appeal was never discussed in the colloquy . . .") at 32.

were sent to out-of-home placement were confined because of probation violations.[252]

Although appellate courts routinely render decisions in cases of child abuse and neglect, or termination of parental rights, those appeals are generally brought by parents. Older foster youth rarely take appeals.[253]

To the extent that appeals are taken, they rarely challenge a court's order of disposition.[254] Even though many state appellate courts expedite appeals in cases involving children, appeals still take too long to make a difference in children's lives.[255]

There is also a judicial culture that sees appeals as interfering with rehabilitation. Appellate courts give juvenile courts wide latitude. The "abuse of discretion" standard of appellate review gives little promise of success on appeal.[256] Such a standard effectively insulates dispositions from appellate review, contributing to the lack of consistency across courts within a jurisdiction, and across jurisdictions within a state. The lack of appeals exacerbates justice by geography.

For many of the preceding reasons, the ABA in 2014 adopted policy that called for youth to have access to effective appellate representation.[257] The policy made four recommendations for governmental bodies regarding juvenile appellate representation. They are:

---

252. *See* Robert G. Schwartz, *A 21st Century Developmentally Appropriate Juvenile Probation Approach*, 69 Juvenile & Fam. Ct. J. 1, 41–54 (Mar. 2018); Penn. JCJC, *2019 Juvenile Court Annual Report*, https://www.jcjc.pa.gov/Research-Statistics/Disposition%20Reports/2019%20Juvenile%20Court%20Annual%20Report.pdf, at 39. In Allegheny County, in 2019, over two-thirds of placements were for those of youth who had earlier been placed on probation. *Id.*

253. California tends to be an outlier, in that there have been several appeals on the issue of extending foster care past the 18th birthday. *See, e.g., In re* H.C., 226 Cal. Rptr. 3D 424, Fourth Appellate District, Division One (2017); *In re* AARON S., 235 Cal. App. 4 507, Sixth Appellate District (2015). Even in California, though, appeals are few and far between.

254. Juvenile Law Ctr., Lessons from Luzerne County: Promoting Fairness, Transparency and Accountability Recommendations to the Interbranch Commission on Juvenile Justice 16 (2010).

255. In the wake of the Luzerne County "Kids for Cash" scandal, the Pennsylvania Supreme Court adopted Rule of Appellate Procedure 1770, which gives expedited review of challenges to out-of-home placements. In practice, almost no appeals are taken pursuant to this rule.

256. For a discussion of the many obstacles to juvenile appeals, see Megan Annitto, *Juvenile Justice on Appeal*, 66 U. Miami L. Rev. 671 (2012), at https://papers.ssrn.com/sol3/papers.cfm?abstract_id=2106059..

257. ABA Policies, Juvenile Justice, Appellate Representation, https://www.americanbar.org/groups/public_interest/child_law/resources/attorneys/.

1) Training should be provided to judges and attorneys to recognize that, in juvenile representation, control and direction of the case is the same as for a criminal defendant.
2) Adequate resources should be provided so that juveniles, including those qualifying for public defender services, have access to effective appellate representation.
3) Appellate review should occur within the time frame that the juvenile is completing the court-ordered disposition.
4) Data on juvenile appeals should be collected to identify possible geographic disparities and institutional barriers to appellate representation.[258]

These Standards reemphasize the importance of appeals. Appeals are necessary to address inconsistent orders between and among different courts. Those orders may be for placement in different locations or involve conflicting levels of restrictiveness in placement. There may be conflicting orders around education, or counseling. Appellate relief may be necessary if lower courts do not resolve these issues on their own. (Of course, courts that adopt a dual status docket pursuant to Standard 2.7 are less likely to confront these problems.)

Because of the possibility of competing or inconsistent orders, these Standards encourage judges to give statements of reasons on the record for their orders of adjudication, disposition, or other significant orders.

To implement these Standards, procedural safeguards are necessary to ensure that youth are not penalized because of delays or missed appellate deadlines caused by the youth's involvement in multiple legal matters.

---

258. Debra Cassens Weiss, *ABA Resolution Backs Access to Effective Appellate Representation for Juveniles*, ABA J. (Feb. 10, 2014), https://www.abajournal.com/news/article/aba_resolution_backs _access_to_effective_appellate_representation_for_juven

PART X: RECORDS EXPUNGEMENT

Standard 10.1 Expungement of Juvenile and Family Court Records

(a) Expungement of delinquency records should require the complete deletion of records from all files and databases in all courts as well as any agency that obtained the records from the juvenile justice system.

(b) Youth entitled to expungement of delinquency records should retain that right even when the youth is under the jurisdiction of other youth-serving agencies or systems.

(c) The juvenile court should establish procedures to ensure effective notification to other youth-serving agencies and systems that a youth's delinquency records should be expunged.

(d) In jurisdictions where the juvenile court or law enforcement agency is required to notify a youth's school of an arrest, adjudication, or disposition, the juvenile court should also be required to notify the school when any juvenile court record has been expunged, and the school should be required to destroy its records relating to any expunged matter.

PART X COMMENTARY

This Part responds to three overlapping themes that emerged over the past few decades. First, in the mid-1990s, states that made their juvenile justice systems more punitive increased public access to law enforcement records for many categories of youth for whom such records had previously been closed.[259] Second—which is why these

---

259. *See, e.g.*, Linda A. Szymanski, *Juvenile Court Confidentiality Issues*, NCJJ SNAPSHOT (Sept. 1996), http://ncjj.org/PDF/Snapshots/1996/vol1_no5_confidentialityissues.pdf; Linda A. Szymanski, *Can Sealed Juvenile Court Records Ever Be Unsealed or Inspected?*, NCJJ SNAPSHOT (May 2010), http://ncjj.org /PDF/Snapshots/2010/vol15_no5_Sealedrecordsthatcanbeunsealed.pdf.

Dual Jurisdiction Standards were adopted—more and more youth were being referred to juvenile court by other youth-serving systems, were being served by those systems while under juvenile court supervision, or were returning to them after being discharged by the court. Third, states increased collateral consequences that accrued following arrest or adjudication.[260]

In addition, state law redefined the relationship between law enforcement and schools. Schools today are often required to notify police when certain offenses occur on school property,[261] and police are often required to notify schools when students are arrested anywhere for certain offenses.[262]

Thus, youth's school records, or social service records, may include information about arrests, even if there is no adjudication of delinquency. Records of arrest or adjudication may linger for years, as states vary in their mix of opportunities and barriers to expungement or sealing.[263]

Because youth's arrest records float so easily among service providers and between them and the cloud, expungement of juvenile court records is more important than ever: private, for-profit corporations are gathering records, including those of juveniles, and selling them to employers.[264] It is important that records be expunged promptly, as delays can lead to unjust circulation of information that can go viral.

To respond to this evolving world, this Standard builds on the American Bar Association's long history of protecting juvenile confidentiality through appropriate expungement of records. It supplements the comprehensive 1980 IJA-ABA Standards Relating to Juvenile Records and Information Services.

---

260. NJDC, *A Juvenile Defender's Guide to Conquering Collateral Consequences* (2018), https://njdc .info/wp-content/uploads/2018/10/Collateral-Consequences-Checklist-for-Juvenile-Defenders.pdf.

261. *See, e.g.,* Pennsylvania's rule requiring a memorandum of understanding between schools and police. State Board of Education, *Rules and Regulations,* 42 Penn. Bulletin (2012), https://www .education.pa.gov/Documents/K-12/Safe%20Schools/Chapter%2010%2042%20PaB%204574.pdf.

262. *See, e.g.,* Texas Code of Criminal Procedure Act 15.27. Notification to schools required.

263. Riya Saha Shah & Lauren A. Fine, Failed Policies, Forfeited Futures: A Nationwide Scorecard on Juvenile Records (Juvenile Law Ctr., 2014).

264. Natane Eaddy & Riya Saha Shah, *Future Interrupted: Infographics on the Impact of Juvenile Records,* Juvenile Law Ctr. (Apr. 3, 2018), https://jlc.org/resources/future-interrupted-infographics -impact-juvenile-records.

The Standard also embraces a 2014 Juvenile Law Center national report on the impact of inappropriate access to juvenile records;[265] and it builds on the ABA's Model Act Governing the Confidentiality and Expungement of Juvenile Delinquency Records ("Model Act"), adopted as policy in 2015.[266]

Juvenile Law Center's 2014 report set forth concerns:

> Public access to records of juvenile arrests, court proceedings and dispositions can impede successful transitions to adulthood for many youth, especially when these records remain available long after the youth's involvement with the juvenile justice system has ended. These records can create obstacles for youth seeking employment, education, housing and other opportunities.
>
> The common belief that juvenile records are confidential because of the juvenile justice system's historic goal of protecting children from the traditional consequences of criminal behavior is false. Many states disclose information about youth involvement with the juvenile justice system and fail to provide opportunities for sealing or expungement. Sealing refers to closing records to the public but keeping them accessible to a limited number of court or law enforcement personnel connected to a child's case, while expungement involves the physical destruction and erasure of a juvenile record.
>
> A growing number of states no longer limit access to records or prohibit the use of juvenile adjudications in subsequent proceedings. While many states have laws that limit the exposure of a juvenile record through sealing or expungement, they are ineffective if they provide access to juvenile records beyond the time of juvenile court involvement, carve out exceptions or include onerous requirements that hamper the ability of young people to take advantage of their protections.[267]

The ABA Model Act:

> . . . is intended to protect juvenile and adult citizens against the damage stemming from their juvenile delinquency records, and the unauthorized use or disclosure of confidential records and any potential stigma that would result from their disclosure.[268]

---

265. Riya Saha Shah et al., *Juvenile Records: A National Review of State Laws on Confidentiality, Sealing and Expungement*, Juvenile Law Ctr. (2014), https://jlc.org/resources/juvenile-records-national-review-state-laws-confidentiality-sealing-and-expungement.

266. A.B.A., *Report to the House of Delegates*, Aug. 2015, https://www.americanbar.org/content/dam/aba/directories/policy/annual-2015/2015-annual-103a.pdf. Note that the Model Act applies to records. It does not address other matters, such as access to courtrooms that hear cases involving youth. Model Act, Section II. Scope.

267. *Id.* at 6.

268. Model Act, *supra* note 267. Section I. Purpose.

The best protection against inappropriate use of juvenile and family court records and the potential for unfair collateral consequences is expungement of the record. Youth-serving agencies should be notified when records should be expunged. When a youth is a dual-jurisdiction or multisystem youth, several agencies may need to be notified.

Expungement becomes more difficult when records involving youth are shared, consolidated, or otherwise commingled with those of other youth-serving agencies. The juvenile court should take steps to notify other agencies and systems and facilitate the expungement of all juvenile justice records that have been shared or disseminated.

Part XI: Responsibilities of Prosecuting Attorneys

Standard 11.1 Policies and Protocols

(a) Prosecutors should develop policies to guide intake decisions involving dual-status youth. Such policies should encourage diversion or non-intervention for youth who engage in minor delinquent behavior and who can obtain appropriate services from other youth-serving agencies and systems.

(b) Prosecutors should, in conjunction with state and local law enforcement officers and youth-serving agencies, develop policies governing referrals to the juvenile justice system from other youth-serving agencies and systems. Such policies should seek to reduce referrals to the juvenile justice system for minor delinquent behavior.

Standard 11.2 Training

Prosecutors should participate in cross-system training as set forth in Standard 2.15 of these standards concerning the Need for Cross-System Training.

Standard 11.3 Charging Decisions

(a) Consistent with Standard 2.11 of these standards concerning Information Sharing, when youth are referred to the juvenile justice system, prosecutors should review available Family Court records to determine whether the youth or the youth's family is or has been served by other youth-serving systems.

(b) The prosecutor should not file a delinquency petition:

   i.   when the alleged delinquent behavior is minor and the youth can obtain appropriate services from other agencies;

   ii. when it is clear that the youth did not have the mental capacity, cognitive ability, or intent necessary to be held responsible for his behavior; or

      iii.   to secure services or placement for a youth when a delin-quency charge would not otherwise be warranted.

(c)   The prosecutor should not prosecute delinquent behavior in juvenile or criminal court when the prosecutor determines that the purposes of the delinquency process can be accomplished outside of the juvenile or criminal justice system.

(d)   The prosecutor should make every effort to ensure that a delinquency petition will not result in the termination or disruption of appropriate services for the youth from other youth-serving systems. The prosecutor should discourage other government attorneys handling dependency cases from closing dependency proceedings just because a delinquency petition is filed.

Standard 11.4   Communicating with Victims

The prosecutor should advise victims, to the extent required by law or permitted under confidentiality laws or rules, of circumstances involving dual-status youth that lead to specific charging decisions and proposed resolutions. The prosecutor should advise victims of statutory, rule or other limitations on disclosure of information about the accused youth.

Standard 11.5   Diversion

(a)   The prosecutor should consider information regarding the youth's access to services from the child welfare system when deciding whether to divert a youth from the juvenile justice system.

(b)   If the prosecutor decides to divert a dual-status youth from the juvenile justice system, the prosecutor should:

      i.   refer the youth to a program suitable for the youth's age, ethnicity, culture, gender or sexual identification, disability, and developmental or cognitive ability; and

      ii.   consider diversion programs that allow the youth to participate in community service in lieu of a delinquency petition.

Standard 11.6   Detention

(a) In deciding whether to request detention of an accused youth, the prosecutor should:

    i.   not seek detention for alleged minor delinquent behavior; and

    ii. consider whether other youth-serving agencies outside the juvenile justice system can protect the youth and serve public safety.

(b) The prosecutor should not seek detention just because no suitable child welfare placement has been identified.

(c) The prosecutor should not seek detention when detention will likely cause the youth to lose placement or services from other youth-serving systems and public safety can be served without detention.

Standard 11.7   Communicating and Coordinating with Youth-Serving Agencies

(a) If the prosecutor declines to file a delinquency petition, the prosecutor should communicate that decision to any referring agency.

(b) The prosecutor should develop policies to govern the effective referral of youth to the child welfare system and other youth-serving agencies.

Standard 11.8   Disposition and Post-Disposition Planning

(a) The prosecutor should participate in placement, re-entry, and disposition planning team meetings consistent with Standard 7.2 of these standards concerning the Disposition Process.

(b) The prosecutor should not seek an out-of-home placement when the youth's supervision and service needs can be met in the community.

(c) After disposition, the prosecutors should periodically review the case.

    i. If it appears that additional or alternate services are needed to meet the needs of the youth or to ensure public safety, the prosecutor may seek to modify the dispositional plan as described above.

    ii. If it appears that the youth no longer needs care and rehabilitation from the juvenile court and does not pose a risk to public safety, the prosecutor should file a request to terminate the delinquency disposition early.

Part XI Commentary

11.1 Policies and Protocols, 11.3 Charging Decisions, and 11.5 Diversion

Prosecutors have enormous discretion. They have a unique opportunity to divert minor delinquent behavior from the juvenile justice system.

Georgetown Law Professor Kristin Henning describes a case from her experience in Washington, D.C.'s juvenile court:

> Sixteen-year-old Shannon is riding a public bus with five classmates from her special education school when she notices one of the teacher's aides from her school at the back of the bus. Shannon snatches the aide's hat and tosses it to one of her classmates. After playing a game of catch with the hat through peals of laughter, the children drop the hat and get off the bus. Police arrest Shannon at school the next day. Prosecutors charge her with robbery.[269]

While this may to some seem like an extreme example, it highlights a commonplace challenge for the juvenile justice system: normal adolescent behavior can, if someone makes the effort, be classified as criminal. Henning discusses Shannon's arrest, saying that it, like

---

269. Kristin Henning, *Criminalizing Normal Adolescent Behavior in Communities of Color: The Role of Prosecutors in Juvenile Justice Reform*, 98 Cornell L. Rev. 383, 427 (Jan. 2013).

others she cites, involves "allegations that, if true, meet the statutory elements for the crimes listed. Yet, as with any decision in the juvenile justice system, police and prosecutors have discretion *not* to act. . . ."[270]

Henning acknowledges the role that school officials and police have in referring youth—or not—to juvenile court. Prosecutors, however, have a unique role as gatekeepers of juvenile court jurisdiction:

> Prosecutors who recognize that youth of color are routinely referred from one or more schools for drug use, disorderly conduct, or other low- to midlevel offenses may decline to prosecute and encourage schools and community leaders to identify responses to adolescent offending that do not impose the stigma and collateral consequences of a juvenile court adjudication. By declining to prosecute categories of adolescent behavior, prosecutors set the standard for juvenile court intake and over time may significantly influence patterns of arrest and referral.[271]

In early 2020, the Annie E. Casey Foundation produced a webinar on prosecutors as leaders.

> During the webinar, John Jordan, the juvenile division chief of the Harris County, Texas District Attorney's Office noted that his office has changed the criteria prosecutors must apply in determining whether to accept charges from police. Beyond probable cause, prosecutors must now consider the nature of the misconduct—whether it represents normal youth behavior, for example. They must also consider individual factors such as age, disability, mental health and child welfare status and whether an appropriate diversion program is available.[272]

These Dual Jurisdiction Standards give new meaning to what it means to "seek justice" in cases of minor, normative misbehavior that can—and should—be addressed by schools or other youth serving systems rather than by juvenile court. They are consistent with the ethical obligations set forth in the ABA Model Rules for Professional Conduct[273] and the 1980 IJA-ABA Juvenile Justice Standards: "[t]he primary duty of the juvenile prosecutor is to seek justice: to fully and

---

270. *Id.* (emphasis in original).

271. *Id.* at 430 (citation omitted).

272. *Webinar Highlights Prosecutor-Led Juvenile Justice Reforms*, Annie E. Casey Foundation (Feb. 25, 2020), https://www.aecf.org/blog/webinar-highlights-prosecutor-led-juvenile-justice-reforms/. Harris County includes Houston.

273. Rule 3.8 (Special Responsibilities of a Prosecutor).

faithfully represent the interests of the state, without losing sight of the philosophy and purpose of the family court."[274]

These Standards suggest steps that prosecutors should consider when confronted with the case of a dual-jurisdiction—or potentially dual-jurisdiction—youth. They are consistent with "policy positions and guidelines" adopted in 2016 by the National District Attorneys Association (NDAA).[275] These guidelines remind prosecutors that diversion is appropriate even when probable cause exists—cases that Professor Henning described above as meeting the "statutory elements" of a crime.

> The decision to divert a case is a charging decision because it is a determination that sufficient evidence exists to file a charge in court but that the goals of prosecution can be reasonably reached through diversion.[276]

Similarly, referring to principles of adolescent development, Fair and Just Prosecution recommends:

> Do not prosecute kids for typical adolescent behavior such as fist fights, smoking marijuana, disorderly conduct, or other infractions at school that don't result in serious physical harm.[277]
>
> Advocate for diversion programs . . .

---

274. STANDARDS RELATING TO PROSECUTION 1.1(B). They are also consistent with the ABA's 2008 Policy on Crossover and Dual Jurisdiction Youth, set forth in Appendix I.

275. National Juvenile Justice Prosecution Center, Juvenile Prosecution Policy Positions and Guidelines, July 5, 2016, approved by NDAA's Board on November 12, 2016. This document was prepared by Caren Harp, Susan Broderick and Jennifer White. James C. Backstrom, Dakota County Attorney, Hastings, Minnesota, and former Co-Chair of the National District Attorneys Association's Juvenile Justice Committee also assisted in preparing this document, National Juvenile Justice Prosecution Center, *Juvenile Prosecution Policy Positions and Guidelines*, (July 5, 2016), http://ndaa.org /wp-content/uploads/Juvenile-Prosecution-Policy-Positions-and-Guidelines-11-12-2016.pdf.

276. *Id.* n.20, quoting, at 7, from page 7 of the National District Attorneys Association, NDAA Resource Manual and Policy Positions on Juvenile Crime Issues. Diverting a case before a charge is filed is a way to mitigate collateral consequences, reduce systems delay, and connect youth with appropriate and timely community-based services.

277. Nationally, offenses like these result in large numbers of arrests. In 2018, over 125,000 youth were arrested for simple assault; over 90,000 for drug abuse violations; over 57,000 for disorderly conduct; over 26,000 for liquor law violations. Charles Puzzanchera, *Juvenile Justice Statistics National Report: Juvenile Arrests, 2018*, OFFICE OF JUSTICE PROGRAMS (June, 2020), https://ojjdp.ojp.gov /sites/g/files/xyckuh176/files/media/document/254499.pdfm, at 3. While some of these offenses might have resulted in serious harm, or warranted prosecution, many surely fall into the category of "minor delinquent behavior" as defined by these Standards.

Recognize that young people accused of crimes often have experienced trauma . . .[278]

Youth in the child welfare system are often overlooked or considered inappropriate for diversion programs or deferred adjudications. This is a variation of "foster care bias" that sends dependent youth to—and more deeply into—the juvenile justice system. The needs of a youth should not tilt the scales toward formal filing. Prosecutors considering diversion should consider youths' dually involved status and the supports they may need to complete diversion successfully. This may involve—when imposing conditions of diversion—that prosecutors recognize these youths' situations, for example, lack of transportation, inability to pay fees, or lack of an adult to sign for their participation. Prosecutors will sometimes view these barriers as reasons to reject diversion, rather than find ways to overcome them. This happens, too, when prosecutors see low risk youth with high needs—some prosecutors refer these youth to court, rather than diverting their cases, overlooking the possibility of collaborating with child welfare in fashioning a diversion plan.

When youth have been referred to the juvenile justice system by other youth-serving agencies, the prosecutor should carefully review and consider information known at the time of screening about the youth's mental health status, treatment history, prescribed medications, educational status, cognitive capacity, and care and supervision from other youth-serving systems. The prosecutor should also attempt to determine whether and to what extent the youth's behavior is attributable or related to the youth's disabilities. For example, youth who engage in aggressive behavior in a mental health facility may need an alternative treatment plan in lieu of intervention from the juvenile justice system. Likewise, a youth who has been identified as a special education student and engages in aggressive or disorderly behavior may need a new educational placement or plan rather than intervention from the juvenile justice system.

---

278. *21 Principles for the 21st Century Prosecutor*, Fair and Just Prosecution (FJP), the Justice Collaborative, and the Brennan Center for Justice (2018), https://www.brennancenter.org /sites/default/files/2019-08/Report_21st_century_prosecutor.pdf, at 9.

11.2   Training

Specialized training for juvenile prosecutors can often be an after-thought, if it is done at all. In small and rural jurisdictions, prosecutors are generalists who may not have time for in-depth training. In other jurisdictions, many prosecutors begin their careers in juvenile court, with no expectation that they will remain there. Those novices both lack rigorous training, or they fail to invest in it, knowing that they will soon be "promoted" to criminal court. Despite such obstacles, prosecutors, like other decision-makers, should have training on matters described in Standard 2.15. NDAA notes the importance of prosecutors knowing that teens are different:

> Not only do they need to know how to prosecute various criminal offenses, they must have an understanding of factors specific to juvenile offenders such as adolescent brain development, adjudicative competency, the effects of exposure to violence on children, and effective, evidence-based interventions with youth. Training in prevention and early intervention should also be included. The family dynamic is an inescapable component of juvenile court, which makes specialized training in family violence and adolescent sex offending, which is often interfamilial, an essential aspect of juvenile prosecutor training.[279]

11.4   Communicating with Victims

To the extent necessary and permissible by law, the prosecutor may explain why diversion for youth with multisystem needs is appropriate. In some cases, restorative justice programs such as victim-offender mediation may be useful, if the victim agrees and the youth is able to participate, in resolving delinquency matters that involve crossover or multisystem youth. Prosecutors should be attentive, however, to the challenges that youth with disabilities face in complying with restorative justice models.

---

279. National Juvenile Justice Prosecution Center, Juvenile Prosecution Policy Positions and Guidelines, July 5, 2016, approved by NDAA's Board on November 12, 2016, at 7.

11.6 Detention

In addition to being involved in individual detention decisions, prosecutors have a role in shaping the way jurisdictions use detention.[280]
Prosecutors can help develop their jurisdiction's detention risk-
assessment instruments, which affect whether youth are detained for
minor misbehavior;[281] and they can help ensure that detention centers are safe for youth who are detained.[282]

11.7 Communicating and Coordinating
with Youth-Serving Agencies

In order to develop policies regarding referrals to child welfare, prosecutors should build relationships with the child welfare system.[283]
Prosecutors should encourage child welfare officials to expedite a
dependency investigation when delinquency proceedings are pending. Prosecutors should also participate in court-facilitated interagency
planning meetings that address dual-jurisdiction issues.[284]

11.8 Disposition and Post-Disposition Planning

When youth are adjudicated delinquent, prosecutors should be
actively engaged at disposition, increasing the likelihood that dual-
jurisdiction youth have access to appropriate services. Placement will
be rare for youth who are found delinquent for minor misbehavior. If
in those rare cases a dual jurisdiction youth is placed in a delinquency

---

280. Kathleen Feely, Collaboration and Leadership in Juvenile Detention Reform
(Annie E. Casey Foundation, 1999).

281. *See generall,* Jennifer Fratello et al., *Juvenile Detention Reform in New York City Measuring Risk
through Research,* Vera Institute of Justice (2011), https://www.vera.org/downloads/publica
tions/RAI-report-v7.pdf, at 11.

282. *See generally* Juvenile Detention Alternatives Initiative, *Juvenile Detention Facility Assessment:
Standards Instrument 2014 Update,* Annie E. Casey Found. (2014), https://www.aecf.org/resources
/juvenile-detention-facility-assessment. CCLP and YLC recommend that prosecutors be part of
teams that conduct routine assessments of conditions in detention centers. *Id.* at 17.

283. This will obviously be easy in those jurisdictions in which prosecutors are also the state's
attorneys in child welfare cases.

284. Gene Siegel & Rachael Lord, *When Systems Collide: Improving Court Practices and Programs in
Dual Jurisdiction Cases,* Juvenile & Fam. Ct. J. (2005); Gregory Halemba & Rachael Lord, *Effectively
Intervening with Dual Jurisdiction Youth in Ohio,* Nat'l Ctr. for Juvenile Just. (2005).

facility, prosecutors at disposition should promote services—including "age appropriate rehabilitative efforts" that will facilitate re-entry.[285]

In particular, prosecutors should be attentive to the re-entry principles advanced earlier in Part VIII.[286]

---

285. Juvenile Prosecution Policy Positions and Guidelines, *supra* note 276, at 13.

286. Pennsylvania's Joint Policy Statement on Aftercare, *supra* note 232, envisions prosecutors attending all disposition review hearings in order to promote effective reentry.

PART XII: RESPONSIBILITIES OF DEFENSE COUNSEL

Standard 12.1 Ethical Obligations of Defense Counsel

Defense counsel representing dual-status youth should abide by all applicable professional and ethical obligations for defense counsel generally.

Standard 12.2 Training

Defense counsel should participate in cross-system training consistent with Standard 2.13 of these standards concerning Access to Court Records.

Standard 12.3 Investigation and Confidentiality Waivers

(a) Consistent with Standard 2.14 of these standards concerning Waivers of Confidentiality, defense counsel and dependency counsel should advise the youth in age-appropriate language, and when permitted and appropriate, inform the youth's parent or guardian, about the need for a signed waiver to allow counsel access to child welfare records and the implications of such waiver. Youth, parents, or guardians with disabilities should receive accommodations necessary to provide informed consent to the waiver.

    i. The juvenile justice system should provide, and defense counsel should obtain, necessary interpretive services. Defense counsel should ensure that any written waiver form and other documents are appropriately translated.

    ii. When the youth is developmentally or cognitively limited or limited in his or her literacy skills, counsel should explain and obtain the waiver in a manner the youth can best understand.

(b) Defense counsel should gather and review all information that would likely affect the youth's custody, legal status, or services in the juvenile justice system.

Standard 12.4   Pre-Petition Advocacy by Delinquency Counsel

(a) Defense counsel should advise the youth regarding the possibility of initiating a referral from the juvenile justice system to the child welfare system and the possible implications of such a referral.

(b) Defense counsel should provide decision-makers all relevant information militating against, and advocate against, the filing of a delinquency petition and the inclusion of particular charges in a petition with the youth's voluntary and informed consent. Defense counsel should consider and recommend alternatives to provide needed services for the youth and, if necessary, to protect the public.

(c) Defense counsel should communicate with the youth's dependency counsel and the youth's best interest advocate when the youth consents and such communication would not undermine the youth's rights in the delinquency case.

Standard 12.5   Advocacy at Detention Hearing

(a) In and before a detention hearing, defense counsel should present facts and arguments to support placement in the community or in the custody of youth-serving agencies, if consistent with the youth's objectives. Facts and arguments should include evidence from youth-serving agencies regarding the availability of specific placements or services.

(b) If the youth is detained or sent to another out-of-home placement, defense counsel should advocate for comparable or better education, physical or behavioral health, and other services than the youth had been receiving prior to the placement.

(c) If the youth is ordered detained, defense counsel should, as soon as possible provide detention or shelter care staff with information about the youth's needs and advocate for the proper care and safety of the youth.

Standard 12.6   Disposition Advocacy

(a) Defense counsel representing dual-status youth should zeal-ously advocate for the youth's stated objectives at all stages, including any multi-agency planning team meeting or dispo-sition hearing.

(b) Counsel should protect the youth's due process interests, including in cases when the disposition hearing is consoli-dated with other Family Court proceedings.

(c) If necessary to advance the youth's objectives, counsel should challenge any evidence or reports submitted to the juvenile court at the disposition hearing, including items submitted by the multi-agency team.

Standard 12.7   Post-Disposition Advocacy

(a) Defense counsel's advocacy on behalf of dual-status youth should not end at the entry of a disposition order. Counsel should maintain contact with both the youth and the agency or agencies responsible for implementing the court's order, and:

   i.   counsel the youth and inform the youth's family con-cerning the order and its implementation;

   ii. ensure the timely and appropriate implementation of the order; and

   iii. ensure the youth's rights are protected as the youth's disposition is implemented.

(b) Defense counsel should monitor the implementation of the youth's disposition order.

   i.   If it appears that additional or different services are needed to meet the needs of the youth, counsel should seek to modify the dispositional plan or order, as consis-tent with the youth's stated interests.

   ii. If it appears the youth no longer needs rehabilitative services from the juvenile court and does not pose a risk to public safety, defense counsel should seek to modify or terminate disposition early.

(c) Relevant government jurisdictions should ensure that defense counsel have the authority and funding to continue representation after disposition consistent with these standards.

Standard 12.8   Appellate Advocacy

(a) After adjudication and disposition, defense counsel should

    i.   explain to the youth the meaning and consequences of the court's judgment and the youth's right to appeal any delinquency disposition or other court orders;

    ii.   give the youth a professional judgment as to whether there are meritorious grounds for appeal and the probable results of an appeal; and

    iii. explain to the youth the advantages and disadvantages of an appeal.

(b) Defense counsel should take whatever steps are necessary to protect the youth's right to appeal any illegal disposition or other court order, as consistent with the youth's stated objectives.

Part XII Commentary

12.1   Ethical Obligations of Defense Counsel

In all matters pertaining to representation of a dual-jurisdiction or crossover youth, defense counsel should abide by:

- the IJA-ABA Standards Relating to Counsel for Private Parties;
- the ABA Rules of Professional Conduct;
- the stated interests of the youth; and
- state and federal laws and regulations regarding confidentiality.

Counsel defending a youth with multisystem needs in a delinquency proceeding must be vigilant not to assume the role of guardian ad litem for the youth. The role of defense counsel differs

significantly from that of a guardian ad litem.[287] Because of the constitutional underpinnings of delinquency representation, lawyers for
multisystem youth must avoid substituting their judgment for that
of their clients, and must avoid a "best interest" standard of representation that applies in some jurisdictions to guardians ad litem or
attorneys for dependent youth. ABA policy applies the same ethical
responsibility to lawyers who represent dependent teens, but this
view is not universally shared among children's lawyers.[288] These
Standards are designed to avoid the ethical and professional responsibility quandaries that arise when counsel have different standards of
representation.[289]

12.3 Investigation and Confidentiality Waivers

Defense counsel should help youth understand the differences
between *involuntary* systems, in which courts have power to order
the youth to behave in certain ways, or to receive specified services,
and *voluntary* systems in which the youth or parent has more control.
The latter include special education, most behavioral health services,
and any social service that a youth can enter or leave at will. Involuntary systems—such as juvenile justice or child welfare—can dictate
through court order the type of service, its intensity and its duration, and the degree and nature of the youth's participation. Counsel
should help the youth understand the consequences of noncompliance
with child welfare or juvenile justice services that have been ordered
by courts. Although delinquency courts have available a range of

---

287. An early, exhaustive ABA description of the role of juvenile defense counsel appears in
Patricia Puritz & Robin Walker Sterling, The Role of. Defense Counsel in Delinquency Court, 25
CRIM. JUST. 16 (Spring 2010). The ABA Juvenile Justice Center was succeeded by the independent
National Juvenile Defender Center, now renamed The Gault Center.

288. *See* text associated with *supra* notes 59–61.

289. *See* ROBIN WALKER STERLING ET AL., ROLE OF JUVENILE DEFENSE COUNSEL IN DELINQUENCY
COURT (National Juvenile Defender Center 2009); Lisa Thurau et al., *National Juvenile Defense Standards*, National Juvenile Defender Center (2012); Kristin Henning, *Loyalty, Paternalism and Rights: Client Counseling Theory and the Role of Child's Counsel in Delinquency Cases*, 81 NOTRE DAME L. REV. 245
(Nov. 2005).

"graduated responses" when court-ordered services are unavailing,[290] courts always have the authority to order out-of-home placement. Defense counsel's obligations during the initial stages are set forth in the IJA-ABA Standards Relating to Counsel for Private Parties.[291]

The youth's defense counsel will often need to communicate or coordinate with other counsel involved in dual-jurisdiction cases, including dependency counsel, guardians ad litem (GAL), or Court Appointed Special Advocates (CASA). The scope and nature of that communication will be limited by the lawyer's obligation to maintain attorney-client confidentiality and loyalty to the client. The defense lawyer may be able to obtain information from other lawyers and advocates without violating client confidences. When information sharing is more advantageous than harmful to the youth and the youth's delinquency case—in particular when counsel seeks to transfer the case to child welfare or keep a child welfare case open—the lawyer may share information after obtaining the youth's knowing and voluntary consent.

12.4   Pre-Petition Advocacy by Delinquency Counsel

Although it is challenging, given caseloads and limited time, counsel must develop a lawyer-client relationship as soon as possible:

> In order to be effective, both in meeting charges against clients and in dealing with social and family issues, juvenile defenders must establish good relationships with their clients. This takes considerable time and effort. Young people charged with crimes are often distrustful of adults, including their own attorneys. Counsel must patiently explain and emphasize that what clients tell them is confidential. Attorneys must build relationships with clients that will enable them to share deeply personal information.[292]

---

290. Jason Szanyi & Dana Shoenberg, *Graduated Responses Tool Kit: New Resources and Insights to Help Youth Succeed on Probation*, CTR. FOR CHILDREN'S LAW & POL'Y (2016), https://www.cclp.org/wp-content/uploads/2016/06/Graduated-Responses-Toolkit.pdf.

291. Sections 4.1–6.4.

292. Patricia Puritz et al., *supra* note 289, at 30 (citation omitted). *See also Ten Core Principles for Providing Quality Delinquency Representation through Public Defense Delivery Systems*, NAT'L JUVENILE DEFENDER CTR. AND NAT'L LEGAL AID & DEFENDER ASS'N (2d ed. 2008), https://www.njjn.org/uploads/digital-library/resource_760.pdf.

This may be difficult, too, because youth may have had GALs, CASAs, or best-interest lawyers in the dependency system who did *not* keep confidences, or who were not client directed.

Defense counsel may advocate that a youth be diverted from the juvenile justice system to other more appropriate youth-serving agencies and systems, such as the child welfare, mental health, substance abuse treatment, education, or special education systems. To accomplish diversion appropriately, these standards strongly endorse holistic advocacy by the defense bar.[293] Holistic representation is comprehensive advocacy that requires defenders to become aware of services, placements, and treatment opportunities outside of the juvenile justice system and encourages defenders to assist families in navigating the bureaucracies of other youth-serving systems or refer youth to organizations that may assist them in this way. Defender training should include information on how clients can obtain services from other systems. Many large defender offices employ social workers who help link youth to services from those systems. If defenders cannot provide holistic advocacy themselves—perhaps because of contractual limits—they may be able to link with lawyers who can assist.[294]

In determining whether to disclose information to any person regarding a client's involvement in one or more youth-serving systems, defense counsel must abide by the rules of professional conduct in maintaining the attorney-client privilege and protecting client "secrets." Counsel owes a duty of loyalty and confidentiality to the client and may not disclose information without the youth's consent, except as permitted by the disciplinary rules of the ABA Code of Professional Conduct or as otherwise required by law. Unless required by applicable statute or court rule, defense counsel should not disclose information that would be contrary to the youth's stated interests in the delinquency proceedings.[295]

Whenever counsel discloses information about the youth's medical, mental health, educational, or other needs, and such information becomes part of the juvenile delinquency record, counsel should request that information be kept separate and confidential from other

---

293. *See* Robin Walker Sterling et al., *supra* note 289, at 20–21.

294. *See, e.g.*, the exemplary work of TeamChild in Washington State, TEAM CHILD, https://teamchild.org/.

295. *See* STANDARDS RELATING TO COUNSEL FOR PRIVATE PARTIES (I.J.A. A.B.A. 1980).

delinquency records unless state or federal law allows public access to that information.

12.6   Disposition Advocacy

Although defense counsel is expected to actively participate in the multi-agency planning team, counsel remains bound to advance the stated interests of the youth. Thus, defense counsel cannot support or advocate in favor of the team recommendation if the youth remains opposed. At the team meeting, counsel should make sure that the youth understands the potential implications of each option and should help the youth express his or her views to the rest of the team. Counsel should provide the team with facts and arguments that will advance the youth's desired outcome.

If the youth ultimately disagrees with the team's final recommendation, counsel's advocacy must continue at the disposition hearing. While other team members will be present at the hearing to advance the team's recommendation, counsel owes a duty of loyalty to the client to correct misinformation and to present alternatives that are consistent with the youth's stated interest.

12.7   Post-Disposition Advocacy

These standards supplement IJA-ABA Standards Relating to Counsel for Private Parties.[296]

When youth have both a guardian ad litem and a defense counsel, defense counsel should not delegate their responsibilities to the guardian ad litem, unless the youth consents after full explanation of their differing ethical obligations. The youth should also be allowed to withdraw that consent at any time.

Despite strong support for post-dispositional representation by organizations like the ABA and the National Juvenile Defender Center,[297] many states either do not allow or do not fund defense advocacy after the entry of the disposition orders.[298] Jurisdictions should ensure that youth are represented by counsel advocating for

---

296. *See* in particular Part IX of those Standards.

297. *See supra* note 289; *Ten Core Principles, supra* 294; NJD standards supra; Nat'l Juvenile Defense Center, *National Juvenile Defense Standards* (2013) at https://njdc.info/wp-content/uploads/2013/09/NationalJuvenileDefenseStandards2013.pdf.

298. *See, e.g., State ex rel. O.S.*, 2011 N.J. Super., Unpub. LEXIS 955.

the stated interests of the youth at all stages of the juvenile court process. Defense counsel should have legal authority and payment to represent the youth until termination of juvenile court jurisdiction.

12.8   Appellate Advocacy

This Standard is a corollary to Part IX, Appeals. The IJA-ABA Juvenile Justice Standards say that trial counsel should normally be the lawyer who conducts the appeal.[299]

---

299. Standard 10.3. The Standard recognizes that there may be circumstances when it is appropriate to have the appeal done by other "competent counsel," so long as that "will not work substantial disadvantage to the client's interests. . . ." *Id.*

APPENDIX I

ABA 2008 POLICY ON CROSSOVER AND DUAL JURISDICTION YOUTH

BE IT RESOLVED, that the American Bar Association urges the federal, state, territorial, and tribal governments to revise laws, court rules, policies, and practices related to "dual jurisdiction" youth (abused and neglected youth with juvenile "dependency" cases who are charged with acts of delinquency) to:

a) Use diversion and intervention services for minor or low level acts of misbehavior committed while a youth is in foster care;

b) Eliminate statutory and legal restrictions inhibiting dual jurisdiction;

c) Create a legal preference enabling youth to have their dependency proceedings remain open with continued child and family support;

d) Provide, when feasible, that a single judge hear post-adjudication dispositional matters involving dual jurisdiction cases and that continuity of legal representation for the child in both court proceedings be secured;

e) Promote training for all juvenile defense counsel on foster care issues;

f) Ensure that an adult responsible for the youth attend hearings in both proceedings to address issues related to the child and family;

g) Encourage information-sharing among dependency and delinquency courts and agencies, establish confidentiality protections for all child welfare information shared, and restrict the use of information gathered from foster youth as part of screening, assessment, or treatment in the pending or future delinquency or criminal proceedings;

h) Promote the prompt post-arrest involvement of providers, case-workers, or advocates acting on the youth's behalf; ensure fair treatment of foster youth in juvenile detention, incarceration, or probation decisions; and eliminate practices that result in detention or prolonged incarceration of youth due to foster care status or an absence of suitable placement options;

i) Provide clear authority for continued social services/child welfare support for children and families when youth cross from dependency to delinquency court/juvenile justice, and eliminate funding barriers that inhibit multiple agency support of these youth and their families;

j) Apply protections afforded foster youth under Titles IV-E of the Social Security Act to youth placed through delinquency or status offense proceedings, in foster care or other non-penal settings, under court authority or under the auspices of juvenile justice agencies; and

k) Fully implement 2002 and 2003 amendments to the Juvenile Justice and Delinquency Prevention Act and the Child Abuse Prevention and Treatment Act to: 1) make youths' child welfare records known to the juvenile court for effective treatment planning; 2) provide effective treatment and service continuity when youth transition between child welfare and juvenile justice systems; 3) assure that when youth are placed in settings funded through Title IV-E of the Social Security Act they receive full protections afforded under that law; and 4) collect state data on all youth transferred from one system to another.

APPENDIX II

STATE STATUTES PROMOTING DIVERSION

Standard 1.1   Definitions

(m) "Diversion" is the referral of an accused youth, without adjudication of criminal or delinquency charges, to a youth service agency or other program, accompanied by a formal termination of all legal proceedings against the youth in the juvenile justice system upon successful completion of the program requirements.

Every state's youth justice code provides for pre-petition diversion of youth. While state statutes vary in their specificity, all provide that juvenile probation officers or prosecutors have the authority to divert youth from the juvenile justice system. Sometimes the diversion is unconditional; sometimes the youth must complete program requirements. Some state laws prescribe diversion in great detail. Others are more elliptical or mention diversion in passing.

Following are relevant "diversion" sections of state statutes, as of March 2020.

ALASKA
1. Alaska Statutes
2. Title 47. Chapter 12. Article 1. Juvenile Delinquency (§§ 47.12.010–47.12.270)

Sec. 47.12.060. Informal action to adjust matter.
(a) The provisions of this section apply to a minor who is alleged to be a delinquent minor under AS 47.12.020 and for whom the department or an entity selected by it has made a preliminary inquiry as required by AS 47.12.040(a)(1). Following the preliminary inquiry,

(1) the department or the entity selected by it may dismiss the matter with or without prejudice; or

(2) the department or the entity selected by it may take informal action to adjust the matter.

(b) When the department or the entity selected by it decides to make an informal adjustment of a matter under (a)(2) of this section, that informal adjustment

(1) must be made with the agreement or consent of the minor and the minor's parents or guardian to the terms and conditions of the adjustment;

(2) must give the minor's foster parent an opportunity to be heard before the informal adjustment is made;

(3) must include notice that informal action to adjust a matter is not successfully completed unless, among other factors that the department or the entity selected by it considers, as to the victim of the act of the minor that is the basis of the delinquency allegation, the minor pays restitution in the amount set by the department or the entity selected by it or agrees as a term or condition set by the department or the entity selected by it to pay the restitution; . . .

ALABAMA
Michie's Alabama Code, Title 12 Courts:
§ 12-15-101. Purpose of the Alabama Juvenile Justice Act; short title; goals for the juvenile court.

(b) In furtherance of this purpose, the following goals have been established for the juvenile court:

...

(5) To promote a continuum of services for children and their families from prevention to aftercare, considering wherever possible, prevention, diversion, and early intervention.

ARKANSAS
AR—Arkansas Code Annotated > Title 9 Family Law > A.C.A. § 9-27-323

(a) If the prosecuting attorney, after consultation with the intake officer, determines that a diversion of a delinquency case is in the best interests of the juvenile and the community, the officer with the consent of the juvenile and his or her parent, guardian, or custodian may attempt to make a satisfactory diversion of a case.

(b) If the intake officer determines that a diversion of a family in need of services case is in the best interest of the juvenile and the community, the officer with the consent of the petitioner, juvenile, and his or her parent, guardian, or custodian may attempt to make a satisfactory diversion of a case.

ARIZONA
AZ—Arizona Annotated Revised Statutes A.R.S. § 8-321, 8-328
Title 8 Child Safety > Chapter 3 Juvenile Offenders > Article 2. Delinquency and Alcohol Offense Complaints and Hearings

8-321. Referrals; diversions; conditions; community based alternative programs
A. Except as provided in subsection B of this section, before a petition is filed or an admission or adjudication hearing is held, the county attorney may divert the prosecution of a juvenile who is accused of committing a delinquent act or a child who is accused of committing an incorrigible act to a community based alternative program or to a diversion program administered by the juvenile court.

8-328. Juvenile diversion programs; reporting
A. A city or town attorney or prosecutor or a law enforcement agency shall not establish or conduct a diversion program or community based alternative program for juvenile offenders unless the program is authorized by the county attorney and notice is provided to the presiding judge of the juvenile court.

B. Beginning January 1, 2011, a city or town attorney or prosecutor or a law enforcement agency that establishes or conducts a diversion program or community based alternative program shall report the citation number, name and date of birth of each juvenile who participates in a diversion program or community based alternative program to the juvenile court in a format approved by the presiding judge of the juvenile court.

CALIFORNIA
Deering's California Codes Annotated
WELFARE AND INSTITUTIONS CODE (§§ 1–25200)

§ 626. Alternative procedures as to disposition of minor; Governing consideration in selecting alternative

An officer who takes a minor into temporary custody under the provisions of Section 625 may do any of the following:

(a) Release the minor.

(b) Deliver or refer the minor to a public or private agency with which the city or county has an agreement or plan to provide shelter care, counseling, or diversion services to minors so delivered. A placement of a child in a community care facility as specified in Section 1530.8 of the Health and Safety Code shall be made in accordance with Section 319.2 or 319.3, as applicable, and with paragraph (8) or (9) of subdivision (e) of Section 361.2, as applicable.

COLORADO
CO—Colorado Revised Statutes Annotated C.R.S. 19-2-303
TITLE 19. CHILDREN'S CODE > ARTICLE 2. THE COLORADO JUVENILE JUSTICE SYSTEM

19-2-303. Juvenile diversion program - authorized - report - legislative declaration - definitions

(1) (a) In order to more fully implement the stated objectives of this title 19, the general assembly declares its intent to establish a juvenile diversion program that, when possible, integrates restorative justice practices to provide community-based alternatives to the formal court system that will reduce juvenile crime and recidivism and improve positive juvenile outcomes, change juvenile offenders' behavior and attitudes, promote juvenile offenders' accountability, recognize and support the rights of victims, heal the harm to relationships and the community caused by juvenile crime, and reduce the costs within the juvenile justice system. (b) . . .

19-2-510. Preliminary investigation
(1) Whenever it appears to a law enforcement officer or any other person that a juvenile is or appears to be within the court's jurisdiction, as provided in section 19-2-104, the law enforcement officer or other person may refer the matter conferring or appearing to confer jurisdiction to the district attorney, who shall determine whether the interests of the juvenile or of the community require that further action be taken.

(2) Upon the request of the district attorney, the matter may be referred to any agency for an investigation and recommendation.

CONNECTICUT
　　Connecticut Annotated Statutes
　　Title 46b Family Law (Chs. 815–817)
　　Chapter 815t Juvenile Matters (Pts. I–II)

Sec. 46b-121s. Community based diversion system.
There shall be a community-based diversion system developed pursuant to subsection (k) of section 46b-121n.

DELAWARE
　　Delaware Code Annotated
　　Title 10 Courts and Judicial Procedure (Pts. I–VII)
　　Part A Proceedings in the Interest of a Child (§§ 1001–1020)

§ 1004A. Juvenile Offender Civil Citation Program.
(a) There is hereby established a juvenile offender civil citation option to provide a civil alternative to arrest and criminal prosecution for eligible youth who have committed minor misdemeanor acts of delinquency as set forth herein. The Juvenile Offender Civil Citation Program shall be coordinated by a statewide Civil Citation Coordinator within the Division of Youth Rehabilitative Services and shall include assessment and intervention services that a juvenile voluntarily agrees to complete in lieu of formal arrest and prosecution.

DISTRICT OF COLUMBIA
Title 16. Particular Actions, Proceedings and Matters. (Chs. 1–55)
Chapter 23. Family Division [Family Court] Proceedings.
(Subchs. I–V)
Subchapter I. Proceedings Regarding Delinquency, Neglect, or
Need of Supervision. (§§ 16-2301–16-2340)

§ 16-2305.02. Preliminary probation conferences; adjustment process.
(a) For the purposes of this section, the term:

(1) "Adjustment process" means the process by which the Social Services Division and the Office of the Corporation Counsel may proceed where a determination is made that the filing of a delinquency or persons in need of supervision petition is not in the best interests of the child or public.

(2) "Nonviolent offenses" means those offenses identified as such by the Office of the Corporation Counsel in an interagency agreement with the Social Services Division, but shall not include a "crime of violence" as defined in section 1(f) of An Act To control the possession, sale, transfer, and use of pistols and other dangerous weapons in the District of Columbia, to provide penalties to prescribe rules of evidence, and for other purposes, approved July 8, 1932 (47 Stat. 650; § 22-4501(f)), or possessory firearm offenses.

(b) Where the Director of Social Services recommends, after a preliminary inquiry is conducted pursuant to § 16-2305(a), that it is not in the best interests of the child or public to recommend the filing of a delinquency or persons in need of supervision petition, the Director of Social Services shall so recommend to the Office of the Corporation Counsel, and the Corporation Counsel shall make a determination of the suitability of the case for adjustment, which may include diversion. The Director of Social Services shall permit any participant who is represented by a lawyer to be accompanied by the lawyer at any preliminary conference.

FLORIDA
Florida Statutes Annotated, Title XLVII. Criminal Procedure and
Corrections. (Chs. 900–985)

§ 985.12. Civil citation or similar prearrest diversion programs.
(1) Legislative findings and intent. — The Legislature finds that the
creation and implementation of civil citation or similar prearrest
diversion programs at the judicial circuit level promotes public safety,
aids interagency cooperation, and provides the greatest chance of success for civil citation and similar prearrest diversion programs. The
Legislature further finds that the widespread use of civil citation and
similar prearrest diversion programs has a positive effect on the criminal justice system and contributes to an overall reduction in the crime
rate and recidivism in the state. The Legislature encourages but does
not mandate that counties, municipalities, and public or private educational institutions participate in a civil citation or similar prearrest
diversion program created by their judicial circuit under this section.

(2) Judicial circuit civil citation or similar prearrest diversion program
development, implementation and operation.

(a) A civil citation or similar prearrest diversion program for misdemeanor offenses shall be established in each judicial circuit in
the state. The state attorney and public defender of each circuit, the
clerk of the court for each county in the circuit, and representatives
of participating law enforcement agencies in the circuit shall create
a civil citation or similar prearrest diversion program and develop
its policies and procedures. In developing the program's policies
and procedures, input from other interested stakeholders may be
solicited. The department shall develop and provide guidelines
on best practice models for civil citation or similar prearrest diversion programs to the judicial circuits as a resource.

(b) Each judicial circuit's civil citation or similar prearrest diversion program must specify:

1. The misdemeanor offenses that qualify a juvenile for participation in the program;

2. The eligibility criteria for the program;

3. The program's implementation and operation;

4. The program's requirements, including, but not limited to, the completion of community service hours, payment of restitution, if applicable, and intervention services indicated by a needs assessment of the juvenile, approved by the department, such as family counseling, urinalysis monitoring, and substance abuse and mental health treatment services; and

5. A program fee, if any, to be paid by a juvenile participating in the program. If the program imposes a fee, the clerk of the court of the applicable county must receive a reasonable portion of the fee.

(c) The state attorney of each circuit shall operate a civil citation or similar prearrest diversion program in each circuit. A sheriff, police department, county, municipality, locally authorized entity, or public or private educational institution may continue to operate an independent civil citation or similar prearrest diversion program that is in operation as of October 1, 2018, if the independent program is reviewed by the state attorney of the applicable circuit and he or she determines that the independent program is substantially similar to the civil citation or similar prearrest diversion program developed by the circuit. If the state attorney determines that the independent program is not substantially similar to the civil citation or similar prearrest diversion program developed by the circuit, the operator of the independent diversion program may revise the program and the state attorney may conduct an additional review of the independent program.

(d) A judicial circuit may model an existing sheriff's, police department's, county's, municipality's, locally authorized entity's, or public or private educational institution's independent civil citation or similar prearrest diversion program in developing the civil citation or similar prearrest diversion program for the circuit.

(e) If a juvenile does not successfully complete the civil citation or similar prearrest diversion program, the arresting law enforcement officer shall determine if there is good cause to arrest the juvenile for the original misdemeanor offense and refer the case to the state attorney to determine if prosecution is appropriate or allow the juvenile to continue in the program.

(f) Each civil citation or similar prearrest diversion program shall enter the appropriate youth data into the Juvenile Justice Information System Prevention Web within 7 days after the admission of the youth into the program.

(g) At the conclusion of a juvenile's civil citation or similar prearrest diversion program, the state attorney or operator of the independent program shall report the outcome to the department. The issuance of a civil citation or similar prearrest diversion program notice is not considered a referral to the department.

(h) Upon issuing a civil citation or similar prearrest diversion program notice, the law enforcement officer shall send a copy of the civil citation or similar prearrest diversion program notice to the parent or guardian of the child and to the victim.

GEORGIA
Official Code of Georgia Annotated
TITLE 15. COURTS, CHAPTER 11. JUVENILE CODE
ARTICLE 6. DELINQUENCY, PART 5. INFORMAL
ADJUSTMENT

Section 15-11-515. Informal adjustment; circumstances; admissions; exceptions
(a) Before a petition for informal adjustment is filed, a probation officer or other officer designated by the court, subject to the court's direction, may inform the parties of informal adjustment if it appears that:

(1) The admitted facts bring the case within the jurisdiction of the court;

(2) Counsel and advice without an adjudication would be in the best interests of the public and a child, taking into account at least the following factors:

(A) The nature of the alleged offense;

(B) The age and individual circumstances of such child;

(C) Such child's prior record, if any;

(D) Recommendations for informal adjustment made by the complainant or the victim; and

(E) Services to meet such child's needs and problems may be unavailable within the formal court system or may be provided more effectively by alternative community programs; and

(3) A child and his or her parent, guardian, or legal custodian consent with knowledge that consent is not obligatory.

(b) The giving of counsel and advice shall not extend beyond three months unless extended by the court for an additional period not to exceed three months and shall not authorize the detention of a child if not otherwise permitted by this article.

(c) An incriminating statement made by a participant in an informal adjustment to the person giving counsel or advice and in the discussion or conferences incident thereto shall not be used against the declarant over objection in any hearing except in a hearing on disposition in a juvenile court proceeding or in a criminal proceeding upon conviction for the purpose of a presentence investigation.

(d) If a child is alleged to have committed a class A designated felony act or class B designated felony act, the case shall not be subject to informal adjustment, counsel, or advice without the prior consent of the district attorney or his or her authorized representative.

HAWAII
Michie's™ Hawaii Revised Statutes Annotated
Title 31 Family (Chs. 571–588)
Chapter 571 Family Courts (Pts. I–IX)

§ 571-31.2. Juvenile intake and diagnostic services.
(a) The court or other designated agency shall:

(1) Notify the child's parent, guardian or legal custodian or take reasonable action to ensure that such notice has been given;

(2) Require the child, the child's parent, the child's guardian or legal custodian, or both, to appear at the court or other designated agency as soon as practicable for a family counseling session to attempt a quick resolution of their problem;

(3) Investigate, evaluate, make necessary determination, and take appropriate actions regarding:

(A) Diversion from justice system processing, formal or informal, and closure of the case;

(B) Release of a child to the care of the child's parent or other responsible adult;

(C) Extending to or making arrangement for the securing of suitable informal adjustment under section 571-31.4, 571-31.5 or 571-31.6;

(D) Initiation of the filing of a complaint or petition;

(E) Detention of a child, utilizing the standard set out in section 571-31.1 or temporary shelter in a nonsecure shelter; and

(F) Making such other informal disposition as may be suitable.

(b) If the intake officer believes it desirable, such officer may take action to obtain the child or the written promise of a parent, guardian, or legal custodian to take the child to the court or other designated agency as in section 571-31(c). The failure of a parent, guardian, or other legal custodian to produce the child in court or at the other designated agency as required by an authorized notice may be pursued as provided in section 571-31(d).

(c) For cases diverted under subsection (a)(3)(A), intake officers shall compile reports at least monthly enumerating the aggregate number of cases diverted and the types of alleged offenses precipitating the referral of the child to the court. These reports shall be submitted to the administrator of the juvenile client services branch in each judicial circuit, who shall compile the reports into an annual report for each judicial circuit, to be submitted to the board of family court judges and the Hawaii juvenile justice state advisory council.

IDAHO
Idaho Code Annotated
TITLE 20. STATE PRISON AND COUNTY JAILS
CHAPTER 5. JUVENILE CORRECTIONS ACT

§ 20-511. Diversion or informal disposition of the petition
(1) Prior to the filing of any petition under this act, the prosecuting attorney may request a preliminary inquiry from the county probation officer to determine whether the interest of the public or the juvenile requires a formal court proceeding. If court action is not required, the prosecuting attorney may utilize the diversion process and refer the case directly to the county probation officer or a community-based diversion program for informal probation and counseling. If the diversion process is utilized pursuant to this subsection, then statements made by a juvenile in a diversion proceeding shall be inadmissible at an adjudicative proceeding on the underlying charge as substantive evidence of guilt. If community service is going to be utilized pursuant to this subsection, the prosecuting attorney shall collect a fee of sixty cents (60 cent(s)) per hour for each hour of community service work the juvenile is going to perform and remit the fee to the state insurance fund for the purpose of securing worker's compensation insurance for the juvenile offender performing community service. However, if a county is self-insured and provides worker's compensation insurance for persons performing community service pursuant to the provisions of this chapter, then remittance to the state insurance fund is not required.

ILLINOIS
Illinois Compiled Statutes Annotated
Chapter 705 COURTS (§§ 5/0.01–510/2),
Juvenile Court Act of 1987 (Arts. I–VII),
Part 1. General Provisions (§§ 405/5-101–405/5-170)

705 ILCS 405/5-105 Definitions
As used in this Article:

. . .

(6) "Diversion" means the referral of a juvenile, without court intervention, into a program that provides services designed to educate the juvenile and develop a productive and responsible approach to living in the community.

705 ILCS 405/5-301 Station adjustments

A minor arrested for any offense or a violation of a condition of previous station adjustment may receive a station adjustment for that arrest as provided herein. In deciding whether to impose a station adjustment, either informal or formal, a juvenile police officer shall consider the following factors:

(A) The seriousness of the alleged offense.

(B) The prior history of delinquency of the minor.

(C) The age of the minor.

(D) The culpability of the minor in committing the alleged offense.

(E) Whether the offense was committed in an aggressive or premeditated manner.

(F) Whether the minor used or possessed a deadly weapon when committing the alleged offenses. . . .

705 ILCS 405/5-305 Probation adjustment

(1) The court may authorize the probation officer to confer in a preliminary conference with a minor who is alleged to have committed an offense, his or her parent, guardian or legal custodian, the victim, the juvenile police officer, the State's Attorney, and other interested persons concerning the advisability of filing a petition under Section 5-520 [705 ILCS 405/5-520], with a view to adjusting suitable cases without the filing of a petition as provided for in this Article, the probation officer should schedule a conference promptly except when the State's Attorney insists on court action or when the minor has indicated that he or she will demand a judicial hearing and will not comply with a probation adjustment. . . .

INDIANA
Burns' Indiana Statutes Annotated, Title 31 Family Law and Juvenile Law (Arts. 1–41), Article 37 Juvenile Law: Delinquency (Chs. 1–25)
Chapter 8 Information About Delinquent Children, Investigation, and Preliminary Inquiry (§§ 31-37-8-1–31-37-8-6)

31-37-8-5. Duties of intake officer.
(a) The intake officer shall do the following:

(1) Send the prosecuting attorney a copy of the preliminary inquiry.

(2) Recommend whether to:

(A) file a petition;

(B) file a petition and recommend that the child be referred for an assessment by a dual status assessment team as described in IC 31-41-1-5;

(C) informally adjust the case;

(D) informally adjust the case and recommend that the child be referred for an assessment by a dual status assessment team as described in IC 31-41-1-5;

(E) refer the child to another agency; or

(F) dismiss the case.

31-37-8-6. Decision regarding filing of petition.
The prosecuting attorney shall decide whether to file a petition.

IOWA
Title VI Human Services (Subtits. 1–6), Subtitle 5 Juveniles (Chs. 232–233B)
Chapter 232 Juvenile Justice (Divs. I–XII)
Part 3 Intake (§§ 232.28–232.34)

232.28 Intake.
***

6. The intake officer, after consultation with the county attorney when necessary, shall determine whether the complaint is legally sufficient for the filing of a petition. A complaint shall be deemed legally sufficient for the filing of a petition if the facts as alleged are sufficient to establish the jurisdiction of the court and probable cause to believe that the child has committed a delinquent act. If the intake officer determines that the complaint is legally sufficient to support the filing of a petition, the officer shall determine whether the interests of the child and the public will best be served by the dismissal of the complaint, the informal adjustment of the complaint, or the filing of a petition.

7. If the intake officer determines that the complaint is not legally sufficient for the filing of a petition or that further proceedings are not in the best interests of the child or the public, the intake officer shall dismiss the complaint.

KANSAS
Kansas Annotated Statutes
Chapter 38. Minors (Arts. 1–24)
Article 23. Revised Kansas Juvenile Justice Code
(§§ 38-2301–38-23,101)

38-2346. Immediate intervention programs.
(a) Each director of juvenile intake and assessment services in collaboration with the county or district attorney shall adopt a policy and establish guidelines for an immediate intervention process by which a juvenile may avoid prosecution. The guidelines may include information on any offenders beyond those enumerated in subsection (b)(1) that shall be referred to immediate intervention. In addition to juvenile intake and assessment services adopting policies and guidelines for the immediate intervention process, the court, the county or district attorney, the director of the intake and assessment center and other relevant individuals or organizations, pursuant to a written agreement, shall collaboratively develop local programs to:

(1) Provide for the direct referral of cases to immediate intervention programs by the county or district attorney and the intake and assessment worker.

(2) Allow intake and assessment workers to issue a summons, as defined in subsection (e) and if juvenile intake and assessment services has adopted appropriate policies and guidelines, allow law enforcement officers to issue such a summons.

(3) Allow the intake and assessment centers and other immediate intervention program providers to directly purchase services for the juvenile and the juvenile's family.

(4) Allow intake and assessment workers to direct the release of a juvenile prior to a detention hearing after the completion of the intake and assessment process pursuant to K.S.A. 75-7023, and amendments thereto.

(b)

(1) A juvenile who goes through the juvenile intake and assessment process pursuant to K.S.A. 75-7023, and amendments thereto, shall be offered the opportunity to participate in an immediate intervention program and avoid prosecution if the juvenile is charged with a misdemeanor that is not an offense described in chapter 55 of article 21 of the Kansas Statutes Annotated, and amendments thereto, or a violation of K.S.A. 2016 Supp. 21-5507, and amendments thereto, the juvenile has no prior adjudications, and the offer is made pursuant to the guidelines developed pursuant to this section. Participation in an immediate intervention program is not required to be offered to a juvenile who was originally charged with an offense which, if committed by an adult, would constitute a felony and, as a result of a plea agreement reached between the juvenile and prosecuting attorney, the charge has been amended to a misdemeanor. A juvenile who has participated in an immediate intervention program for a previous misdemeanor may, but is not required to, be offered participation in an immediate intervention program.

(2) A juvenile may also participate in an immediate intervention program if the juvenile is referred for immediate intervention by the county or district attorney pursuant to subsection (d).

(3) Any juvenile referred to immediate intervention by juvenile intake and assessment services shall, upon acceptance, work together with court services, community corrections, juvenile intake

and assessment services or any other entity designated as a part of the written agreement in subsection (a) to develop an immediate intervention plan. Such plan may be supervised or unsupervised by any of the aforementioned entities. The county or district attorney's office shall not be required to supervise juveniles participating in an immediate intervention program.

(4) The immediate intervention plan shall last no longer than six months from the date of referral, unless the plan requires the juvenile to complete an evidence-based mental health or substance abuse program that extends beyond the six-month period. In such case, the plan may be extended up to two additional months.

(5) If the juvenile satisfactorily complies with the immediate intervention plan, such juvenile shall be discharged and the charges dismissed at the end of the time period specified in paragraph (4).

(6) If the juvenile fails to satisfactorily comply with the immediate intervention plan, the case shall be referred to a multidisciplinary team for review. The multidisciplinary team created pursuant to K.S.A. 2016 Supp. 38-2393, and amendments thereto, shall review the immediate intervention plan within seven days and may revise and extend such plan or terminate the case as successful. Such plan may be extended for no more than four additional months.

(7) If the juvenile fails to satisfactorily comply with the revised plan developed pursuant to paragraph (6), the intake and assessment worker, court services officer or community corrections officer overseeing the immediate intervention shall refer the case to the county or district attorney for consideration.

(c) The parent of a juvenile may be required to be a part of the immediate intervention program.

(d) For all juveniles that have fewer than two prior adjudications, the county or district attorney shall review the case upon receipt of a complaint to determine if the case should be referred for immediate intervention or whether alternative means of adjudication should be designated pursuant to K.S.A. 2016 Supp. 38-2389, and amendments thereto. The county or district attorney shall consider any recommendation of a juvenile intake and assessment worker, court services officer or community corrections officer.

(e) "Summons" means a written order issued by an intake and assessment worker or a law enforcement officer directing that a juvenile appear before a designated court at a stated time and place to answer a pending charge.

(f) A juvenile who is eligible for an immediate intervention shall not be denied participation in such a program or terminated unsuccessfully due to an inability to pay fees or other associated costs. Fees assessed from such a program shall be retained by the program and shall not be used for any purpose, except development and operation of the program.

(g) If a juvenile substantially complies with an immediate intervention program, charges in such juvenile's case shall not be filed.

(h) The policies and guidelines developed pursuant to subsection (a) shall adhere to standards and procedures for immediate intervention developed by the department of corrections pursuant to K.S.A. 2016 Supp. 38-2395, and amendments thereto, and be based on best practices.

(i) Nothing in this section shall require a juvenile to participate in an immediate intervention program when the county or district attorney has declined to continue with prosecution of an alleged offense.

KENTUCKY
   Michie's™ Kentucky Revised Statutes
   TITLE LI Unified Juvenile Code (Chs. 600–645)
   CHAPTER 635 Public Offenders (§§ 635.010–635.545)

635.010. Complaint—Duties of county attorney and court-designated worker.
(1) The county attorney shall cause a review to be made of each complaint alleging that a public offense has been committed. The purpose of this review shall be to determine from the available evidence whether there are reasonable grounds to believe that the alleged facts would constitute a public offense. The county attorney may elect not to proceed with the complaint, regardless of whether reasonable grounds exist, and dismiss the complaint.

(2) The county attorney, upon receipt of a request for special review, shall consider the facts presented by the complainant and by the court-designated worker who made the recommendation that no petition be filed, before the county attorney makes a final decision as to whether a public offense petition shall or shall not be filed.

(3) In all cases in which the child is alleged to have committed a public offense and is not detained, the court-designated worker shall submit his written recommendation to the county attorney or designee within twenty (20) days, exclusive of weekends and holidays, from the date the child was taken into custody or the complaint was filed. In cases where the child is detained, the court-designated worker's report shall be submitted within seventy-two (72) hours of the time the child is ordered detained.

(4) The county attorney may not file a petition if the complaint is a misdemeanor and the child who is the subject of the diversion agreement has no prior adjudications and no prior diversions. . . .

LOUISIANA
LexisNexis® Louisiana Annotated Statutes, Louisiana Children's Code
Title 8. Delinquency (Chs. 1–18)
Chapter 8. Informal adjustment procedure (Arts. 839–841)

Art. 839. Availability of an informal adjustment agreement
A. Prior to the filing of a petition, the district attorney or the court with the consent of the district attorney may authorize an informal adjustment agreement.

B. After the filing of a petition but before the attachment of jeopardy pursuant to Article 811, the court may authorize the district attorney or probation officer to effect an informal adjustment agreement if the child and district attorney have no objection. The court may, with concurrence of the district attorney, dismiss the petition or allow the petition to remain pending during the period of informal adjustment.

C. When entering an informal adjustment agreement, the court may, with concurrence of the district attorney, utilize or initiate a teen or youth court program and may assess a fee to a participant in the program to offset costs.

D.

(1) Where a petition involves an allegation of an act of prostitution pursuant to R.S. 14:82, prostitution by massage pursuant to R.S. 14:83.3 or 83.4, or crimes against nature by solicitation pursuant to R.S. 14:89.2 and it is the child's first offense and the child expresses a willingness to cooperate and receive specialized services for sexually exploited children, the district attorney may effect an informal adjustment agreement which includes specialized services for the child.

(2) If, however, the child has previously been adjudicated a delinquent in violation of R.S. 14:82, 83.3, 83.4, or 89.2 or is unwilling to cooperate with specialized services for sexually exploited children, continuing with the delinquency proceeding shall be within the discretion of the district attorney.

(3) The specialized services referenced in Subparagraph (1) of this Paragraph may include but are not limited to safe and stable housing, comprehensive on-site case management, integrated mental health and chemical dependency services, including specialized trauma recovery services, education and employment training, and referrals to off-site specialized services, as appropriate.

MAINE
Maine Revised Statutes Annotated by LexisNexis®
Title 15. Court Procedure—Criminal (Pts. 1–8)
Part 6. Maine Juvenile Code (Chs. 501–513)
Chapter 507. Petition, Adjudication and Disposition
(§§ 3301–3319)

§ 3301. Preliminary investigation, informal adjustment and petition initiation
1. Preliminary Investigation.

When a juvenile accused of having committed a juvenile crime is referred to a juvenile community corrections officer, the juvenile community corrections officer shall, except in cases in which an investigation is conducted pursuant to Title 5, section 200-A, conduct a preliminary investigation to determine whether the interests of the juvenile or of the community require that further action be taken.

On the basis of the preliminary investigation, the juvenile community corrections officer shall:

A. Decide that action requiring ongoing supervision is not required either in the interests of the public or of the juvenile;

B. Make whatever informal adjustment is practicable without a petition; or

C.

Request a petition to be filed.

...

5. Juvenile Community Corrections Officer Alternatives. On the basis of the preliminary investigation, the juvenile community corrections officer shall choose one of the following alternatives:

A. Decide that action requiring ongoing supervision is not required either in the interests of the public or of the juvenile. If the juvenile community corrections officer determines that the facts in the report prepared for the community corrections officer by the referring officer pursuant to section 3203-A, subsection 3 are sufficient to file a petition, but in the community corrections officer's judgment the interest of the juvenile and the public will be served best by providing the juvenile with services voluntarily accepted by the juvenile and the juvenile's parents, guardian or legal custodian if the juvenile is not emancipated, the juvenile community corrections officer may refer the juvenile for that care and treatment and not request that a petition be filed;

B. Make whatever informal adjustment is practicable without a petition. The juvenile community corrections officer may effect whatever informal adjustment is agreed to by the juvenile and the juvenile's parents, guardian or legal custodian if the juvenile is not emancipated, including a restitution contract with the victim of the crime and the performance of community service. Informal adjustments may extend no longer than 6 months and may not be commenced unless:

(1) The juvenile community corrections officer determines that the juvenile and the juvenile's parents, guardian or legal custodian, if the juvenile is not emancipated, were advised of their

constitutional rights, including the right to an adjudicatory hearing, the right to be represented by counsel and the right to have counsel appointed by the court if indigent;

(2) The facts establish prima facie jurisdiction, except that any admission made in connection with this informal adjustment may not be used in evidence against the juvenile if a petition based on the same facts is later filed; and

(3) Written consent to the informal adjustment is obtained from the juvenile and the juvenile's parents, guardian or legal custodian if the juvenile is not emancipated; ...

C. If the juvenile community corrections officer determines that the facts are sufficient for the filing of a petition, the juvenile community corrections officer shall request the prosecuting attorney to file a petition; or

D. If the juvenile community corrections officer makes a determination pursuant to paragraph A or B, the community corrections officer shall notify the juvenile and the juvenile's parents, guardian or legal custodian at least 2 weeks prior to the date for which they are summonsed. . . .

6. Review by Attorney for the State.

If the juvenile community corrections officer decides not to request the attorney for the State to file a petition, the juvenile community corrections officer shall inform the attorney for the State, the complainant, the law enforcement officer and the victim of the decision and of the reasons for the decision as soon as practicable. The juvenile community corrections officer shall advise the complainant, the law enforcement officer and the victim that they may submit their complaint to the attorney for the State for review.

If the juvenile community corrections officer makes a determination pursuant to subsection 5, paragraph A or B and decides not to request the attorney for the State to file a petition for a violation of Title 22, section 2389, subsection 2 or Title 28-A, section 2052, the juvenile community corrections officer shall inform the Secretary of State of the violation. The Secretary of State shall suspend for a period of 30 days that juvenile's license or permit to operate a motor vehicle, right to operate a motor vehicle and right to apply for and obtain a license. After the suspension is terminated, any record of the suspension is confidential and may be released only to a law enforcement officer or the courts for prosecution of violations of Title 29-A, section 2412-A.

The attorney for the State on that attorney's own motion or upon receiving a request for review by the law enforcement officer, the complainant or the victim, shall consider the facts of the case, consult with the juvenile community corrections officer who made the initial decision and then make a final decision as to whether to file the petition. The attorney for the State shall notify the juvenile community corrections officer of the final decision within 30 days of being informed by the juvenile community corrections officer of the initial decision. If a juvenile community corrections officer has not yet made an initial decision, the attorney for the State may file a petition at any time more than 30 days after the juvenile community corrections officer has been given notice pursuant to section 3203-A.

MARYLAND
Annotated Code of Maryland
TITLE 3. COURTS OF GENERAL JURISDICTION— JURISDICTION/SPECIAL CAUSES OF ACTION
SUBTITLE 8A. JUVENILE CAUSES—CHILDREN OTHER THAN CINAS AND ADULTS

Section 3-8A-10. Complaint; preliminary procedures
. . .

(c) Jurisdictional inquiry. —

(1) Except as otherwise provided in this subsection, in considering the complaint, the intake officer shall make an inquiry within 25 days as to whether the court has jurisdiction and whether judicial action is in the best interests of the public or the child.

(2) An inquiry need not include an interview of the child who is the subject of the complaint if the complaint alleges the commission of an act that would be a felony if committed by an adult or alleges a violation of Section 4-203 or Section 4-204 of the Criminal Law Article.

(3) In accordance with this section, the intake officer may, after such inquiry and within 25 days of receiving the complaint:

(i) Authorize the filing of a petition or a peace order request or both;

(ii) Propose an informal adjustment of the matter; or

(iii) Refuse authorization to file a petition or a peace order request or both.

(4)

(i) If a complaint is filed that alleges the commission of an act which would be a felony if committed by an adult or alleges a violation of Section 4-203 or Section 4-204 of the Criminal Law Article, and if the intake officer denies authorization to file a petition or proposes an informal adjustment, the intake officer shall immediately:

1. Forward the complaint to the State's Attorney; and

2. Forward a copy of the entire intake case file to the State's Attorney with information as to any and all prior intake involvement with the child.

(ii) The State's Attorney shall make a preliminary review as to whether the court has jurisdiction and whether judicial action is in the best interests of the public or the child. The need for restitution may be considered as one factor in the public interest. After the preliminary review the State's Attorney shall, within 30 days of the receipt of the complaint by the State's Attorney, unless the court extends the time:

1. File a petition or a peace order request or both;

2. Refer the complaint to the Department of Juvenile Services for informal disposition; or

3. Dismiss the complaint.

(iii) This subsection may not be construed or interpreted to limit the authority of the State's Attorney to seek a waiver under Section 3-8A-06 of this subtitle.

MASSACHUSETTS
Annotated Laws of Massachusetts
TITLE XVII PUBLIC WELFARE (Chs. 115–123B)
Chapter 119 Protection and Care of Children, and Proceedings
Against Them (§§ 1–89)

§ 54A. Delinquency — Determination — Diversion.
(a) A juvenile court shall have jurisdiction to divert from further court processing a child who is subject to the jurisdiction of the juvenile court as the result of an application for complaint brought pursuant to section 54. The court may divert a child to a program as defined in section 1 of chapter 276A.

(b) A child complained of as a delinquent child may, upon the request of the child, undergo an assessment prior to arraignment to enable the judge to consider the suitability of the child for diversion. If a child chooses to request a continuance for the purpose of such an assessment, the child shall notify the judge prior to arraignment. Upon receipt of such notification, the judge may grant a 14-day continuance. The department of probation may conduct such assessment prior to arraignment to assist the judge in making that decision. If the judge determines it is appropriate, a determination of eligibility by the personnel of a program may substitute for an assessment. If a case is continued pursuant to this subsection, the child shall not be arraigned and an entry shall not be made into the criminal offender record information system until a judge issues an order to resume the ordinary processing of a delinquency proceeding. A judge may order diversion without first ordering an assessment in any case in which the court finds that sufficient information is available without an assessment.

(c)

 (1) After the completion of the assessment, the probation officer or, where applicable, the director of a program to which the child has been referred shall submit to the court and to the counsel for the child a recommendation as to whether the child would benefit from diversion.

 Upon receipt of the recommendation, the judge shall provide an opportunity for both the commonwealth and counsel for the child to be heard regarding diversion of the child. The judge shall then make a final determination as to the eligibility of the child for diversion. The proceedings of a child who is found eligible for diversion shall be stayed for 90 days unless the judge determines that the interest of justice would best be served by a lesser period of time or unless extended under subsection (f).

(2) A stay of proceedings shall not be granted under this section unless the child consents in writing to the terms and conditions of the stay of proceedings and knowingly executes a waiver of the child's right to a speedy trial on a form approved by the chief justice of the juvenile court department. Consent shall be given only upon the advice of counsel.

(3) The following shall not be admissible against the child in any proceedings: (i) a request for assessment; (ii) a decision by the child not to enter a program; (iii) a determination by probation or by a program that the child would not benefit from diversion; and (iv) any statement made by the child or the child's family during the course of assessment. Any consent by a child to a stay of proceedings or any act done or statement made in fulfillment of the terms and conditions of a stay of proceedings shall not be admissible as an admission, implied or otherwise, against the child if the stay of proceedings was terminated and proceedings were resumed on the original complaint. A statement or other disclosure or a record thereof made by a child during the course of assessment or during the stay of proceedings shall not be disclosed at any time to a commonwealth or other law enforcement officer in connection with the investigation or prosecution of any charges against the child or a codefendant.

(4) If a child is found eligible for diversion pursuant to this section, the child shall not be arraigned and an entry shall not be made into the criminal offender record information system unless a judge issues an order to resume the ordinary processing of a delinquency proceeding. If a child is found eligible pursuant to this section, the eligibility shall not be considered an issuance of a criminal complaint for the purposes of section 37H½ of chapter 71.

(d) A district attorney may divert any child for whom there is probable cause to issue a complaint, either before or after the assessment procedure set forth in subsection (b), with or without the permission of the court and without regard to the limitations in subsection (g). A district attorney who diverts a case pursuant to this subsection may request a report from a program regarding the child's status in and completion of the program.

(e) If during the stay of proceedings a child is charged with a subsequent offense, a judge in the court that entered the stay of proceedings may issue such process as is necessary to bring the child before the court. When the child is brought before the court, the judge shall afford the child an opportunity to be heard. If the judge finds probable cause to believe that the child has committed a subsequent offense, the judge may order that the stay of proceedings be terminated and that the commonwealth be permitted to proceed on the original complaint as provided by law.

(f)

(1) Upon the expiration of the initial 90-day stay of proceedings, the probation officer or the program director shall submit to the court a report indicating the successful completion of diversion by the child or recommending an extension of the stay of proceedings for not more than an additional 90 days so that the child may complete the diversion program successfully.

(2) If the probation officer or the program director indicates the successful completion of diversion by a child, the judge may dismiss the original complaint pending against the child. If the report recommends an extension of the stay of proceedings, the judge may, on the basis of the report and any other relevant evidence, take such action as the judge deems appropriate, including the dismissal of the complaint, the granting of an extension of the stay of proceedings or the resumption of proceedings.

(3) If the conditions of diversion have not been met, the child's attorney shall be notified prior to the termination of the child from diversion and the judge may grant an extension to the stay of proceedings if the child provides good cause for failing to comply with the conditions of diversion.

(4) If the judge dismisses a complaint under this subsection, the court shall, unless the child objects, enter an order directing

expungement of any records of the complaint and related proceedings maintained by the clerk, the court, the department of criminal justice information services and the court activity record index.

(g) A child otherwise eligible for diversion pursuant to this section shall not be eligible for diversion if the child is indicted as a youthful offender or if the child is charged with a violation of 1 or more of the offenses enumerated in the second sentence of section 70C of chapter 277, other than the offenses in subsection (a) of section 13A of chapter 265 and sections 13A and 13C of chapter 268, or if the defendant is charged with an offense for which a penalty of incarceration greater than 5 years may be imposed or for which there is a minimum term penalty of incarceration or which may not be continued without a finding or placed on file. Diversion of juvenile court charges under this chapter shall not preclude a subsequent indictment on the same charges in superior court.

MICHIGAN
Michigan Compiled Laws Service
Chapter 722 Children (§§ 722.1–722.1567)
Act 13 of 1988 (§§ 722.821–722.831)

Act 13 of 1988 Juvenile Diversion Act
AN ACT to permit certain minors to be diverted from the court system having jurisdiction over minors; to establish diversion criteria and procedures; to require certain records to be made and kept; to prescribe certain powers and duties of courts having jurisdiction over minors and of law enforcement agencies; and to prescribe certain penalties.

MINNESOTA
Minnesota Annotated Statutes
Counties, County Officers, Regional Authorities (Chs. 370–403)
Chapter 388. County Attorney (§§ 388.01–388.25)

388.24 PRETRIAL DIVERSION PROGRAMS FOR JUVENILES
Subdivision 1. *Definition.* — As used in this section:

(1) a child under the jurisdiction of the juvenile court is an "offender" if:

(i) the child is petitioned for, or probable cause exists to petition or take the child into custody for, a felony, gross misdemeanor, or misdemeanor offense, other than an offense against the person, but has not yet entered a plea in the proceedings;

(ii) the child has not previously been adjudicated in Minnesota or any other state for any offense against the person; and

(iii) the child has not previously been petitioned for an offense in Minnesota and then had the petition dismissed as part of a diversion program, including a program that existed before July 1, 1995; and

(2) "pretrial diversion" means the decision of a prosecutor to refer an offender to a diversion program on condition that the delinquency petition against the offender will be dismissed or the petition will not be filed after a specified period of time if the offender successfully completes the program.

Subd. 2. *Establishment of program*. — By July 1, 1995, every county attorney shall establish a pretrial diversion program for offenders. If the county attorney's county participates in the Community Corrections Act as part of a group of counties under section 401.02, the county attorney may establish a pretrial diversion program in conjunction with other county attorneys in that group of counties. The program must be designed and operated to further the following goals:

(1) to provide eligible offenders with an alternative to adjudication that emphasizes restorative justice;

(2) to reduce the costs and caseload burdens on juvenile courts and the juvenile justice system;

(3) to minimize recidivism among diverted offenders;

(4) to promote the collection of restitution to the victim of the offender's crime;

(5) to develop responsible alternatives to the juvenile justice system for eligible offenders; and

(6) to develop collaborative use of demonstrated successful culturally specific programming, where appropriate.

Subd. 3. ***Program components.*** — A diversion program established under this section may:

(1) provide screening services to the court and the prosecuting authorities to help identify likely candidates for pretrial diversion;

(2) establish goals for diverted offenders and monitor performance of these goals;

(3) perform chemical dependency assessments of diverted offenders where indicated, make appropriate referrals for treatment, and monitor treatment and aftercare;

(4) provide individual, group, and family counseling services;

(5) oversee the payment of victim restitution by diverted offenders;

(6) assist diverted offenders in identifying and contacting appropriate community resources;

(7) provide educational services to diverted offenders to enable them to earn a high school diploma or GED; and

(8) provide accurate information on how diverted offenders perform in the program to the court, prosecutors, defense attorneys, and probation officers.

Subd. 4. ***Reporting of data to Bureau of Criminal Apprehension.*** — Effective August 1, 1997, every county attorney who establishes a diversion program under this section shall report the following information to the Bureau of Criminal Apprehension:

(1) the name and date of birth of each diversion program participant and any other identifying information the superintendent considers necessary;

(2) the date on which the individual began to participate in the diversion program;

(3) the date on which the individual is expected to complete the diversion program;

(4) the date on which the individual successfully completed the diversion program, where applicable; and

(5) the date on which the individual was removed from the diversion program for failure to successfully complete the individual's goals, where applicable.

The superintendent shall cause the information described in this subdivision to be entered into and maintained in the criminal history file as defined in section 13.87.

MISSISSIPPI
Mississippi Code 1972 Annotated, Title 43. Public Welfare (Chs. 1–61)
Chapter 21. Youth Court (§§ 43-21-143-21-915)
Intake (§§ 43-21-351 — 43-21-357)

§ 43-21-357. Intake procedure.
(1) After receiving a report, the youth court intake unit shall promptly make a preliminary inquiry to determine whether the interest of the child, other children in the same environment or the public requires the youth court to take further action. As part of the preliminary inquiry, the youth court intake unit may request or the youth court may order the Department of Human Services, the Department of Youth Services, any successor agency or any other qualified public employee to make an investigation or report concerning the child and any other children in the same environment, and present the findings thereof to the youth court intake unit. If the youth court intake unit receives a neglect or abuse report, the youth court intake unit shall immediately forward the complaint to the Department of Human Services to promptly make an investigation or report concerning the child and any other children in the same environment and promptly present the findings thereof to the youth court intake unit. If it appears from the preliminary inquiry that the child or other children in the same environment are within the jurisdiction of the court, the youth court intake unit shall recommend to the youth court:

(a) That the youth court take no action;

(b) That an informal adjustment be made;

(c) The Department of Human Services, Division of Family and Children Services, monitor the child, family and other children in the same environment;

(d) That the child is warned or counseled informally;

(e) That the child be referred to the youth court intervention court; or

(f) That a petition be filed.

(2) The youth court shall then, without a hearing:

(a) Order that no action be taken;

(b) Order that an informal adjustment be made;

(c) Order that the Department of Human Services, Division of Family and Children Services, monitor the child, family and other children in the same environment;

(d) Order that the child is warned or counseled informally;

(e) That the child be referred to the youth intervention court; or

(f) Order that a petition be filed.

(3) If the preliminary inquiry discloses that a child needs emergency medical treatment, the judge may order the necessary treatment.

MISSOURI
Missouri Annotated Statutes
Title 12. Public Health and Welfare (Chs. 188–215)
Chapter 211. Juvenile Courts (§§ 211.011–211.500)

§ 211.081. Preliminary inquiry as to institution of proceedings— approval of division necessary for placement outside state— institutional placements, findings required, duties of division, limitations on judge, financial limitations [Effective until January 1, 2021]
1. Whenever any person informs the juvenile officer in writing that a child appears to be within the purview of applicable provisions

of section 211.031 or that a person seventeen years of age appears to be within the purview of the provisions of subdivision (1) of subsection 1 of section 211.031, the juvenile officer shall make or cause to be made a preliminary inquiry to determine the facts and to determine whether or not the interests of the public or of the child or person seventeen years of age require that further action be taken. On the basis of this inquiry, the juvenile officer may make such informal adjustment as is practicable without a petition or file a petition. Any other provision of this chapter to the contrary notwithstanding, the juvenile court shall not make any order for disposition of a child or person seventeen years of age which would place or commit the child or person seventeen years of age to any location outside the state of Missouri without first receiving the approval of the children's division.

MONTANA
Montana Code Annotated, Title 41 Minors (Chs. 1–7)
Chapter 5 Youth Court Act (Pts. 1–25)
Part 13 Informal Proceeding (§§ 41-5-1301–41-5-1304)

41-5-1301 Informal disposition.
After a preliminary inquiry under 41-5-1201, the juvenile probation officer or assessment officer upon determining that further action is required and that referral to the county attorney is not required may:

(1) provide counseling, refer the youth and the youth's family to another agency providing appropriate services, or take any other action or make any informal adjustment that does not involve probation or detention; or

(2) provide for treatment or adjustment involving probation or other disposition authorized under 41-5-1302 through 41-5-1304 if the treatment or adjustment is voluntarily accepted by the youth's parents or guardian and the youth, if the matter is referred immediately to the county attorney for review, and if the juvenile probation officer or assessment officer proceeds no further unless authorized by the county attorney.

NEBRASKA
Revised Statutes of Nebraska Annotated, Chapter 43 Infants and Juveniles (Arts. 1–48), Article 2 Juvenile Code (§§ 43-201–43-2,130)
(c) Law Enforcement Procedures (§§ 43-248–43-252)
(d) Preadjudication Procedures (§§ 43-253–43-273)

§ 43-248.02. Juvenile offender civil citation pilot program; peace officer issue civil citation; contents; advisement; peace officer; duties; juvenile report to juvenile assessment center; failure to comply; effect.
A juvenile offender civil citation pilot program as provided in this section and section 43-248.03 may be undertaken by the peace officers and county and city attorneys of a county containing a city of the metropolitan class. The pilot program shall be according to the following procedures:

> (1) A peace officer, upon making contact with a juvenile whom the peace officer has reasonable grounds to believe has committed a misdemeanor offense, other than an offense involving a firearm, sexual assault, or domestic violence, may issue the juvenile a civil citation;

***

§ 43-260.02. Juvenile pretrial diversion program; authorized.
A county attorney may establish a juvenile pretrial diversion program with the concurrence of the county board. If the county is part of a multicounty juvenile services plan under the Nebraska County Juvenile Services Plan Act, the county attorney may establish a juvenile pretrial diversion program in conjunction with other county attorneys from counties that are a part of such multicounty plan. A city attorney may establish a juvenile pretrial diversion program with the concurrence of the governing body of the city. Such programs shall meet the requirements of sections 43-260.02 to 43-260.07.

§ 43-260.07. Juvenile pretrial diversion program; data; duties.
(1) On January 30 of each year, every county attorney or city attorney of a county or city which has a juvenile pretrial diversion program shall report to the Director of Juvenile Diversion Programs the information pertaining to the program required by rules and regulations

adopted and promulgated by the Nebraska Commission on Law Enforcement and Criminal Justice.

(2) Juvenile pretrial diversion program data shall be maintained and compiled by the Director of Juvenile Diversion Programs.

NEVADA
Nevada Revised Statutes Annotated, Title 5. Procedure in Juvenile Cases. (Chs. 62–63)
Chapter 62C. Procedure Before Adjudication.
(§§ 62C.010–62C.400)

62C.200. Informal supervision by probation officer: Conditions for placement; written agreement; duration; effect on filing petition.

1. When a complaint is made alleging that a child is delinquent or in need of supervision, the child may be placed under the informal supervision of a probation officer if:

(a) The child voluntarily admits participation in the acts alleged in the complaint; and

(b) The district attorney gives written approval for placement of the child under informal supervision, if any of the acts alleged in the complaint are unlawful acts that would have constituted a gross misdemeanor or felony if committed by an adult.

2. If the probation officer recommends placing the child under informal supervision, the probation officer must advise the child and the parent or guardian of the child that they may refuse informal supervision.

3. The child must enter into an agreement for informal supervision voluntarily and intelligently:

(a) With the advice of the attorney for the child; or

(b) If the child is not represented by an attorney, with the consent of the parent or guardian of the child.

4. If the child is placed under informal supervision:

(a) The terms and conditions of the agreement for informal supervision must be stated clearly in writing. The terms and conditions of the agreement may include, but are not limited to, the requirements set forth in NRS 62C.210.

(b) The agreement must be signed by all parties.

(c) A copy of the agreement must be given to:

(1) The child;

(2) The parent or guardian of the child;

(3) The attorney for the child, if any; and

(4) The probation officer, who shall retain a copy in the probation officer's file for the case.

5. The period of informal supervision must not exceed 180 days. The child and the parent or guardian of the child may terminate the agreement at any time by requesting the filing of a petition for formal adjudication.

6. The district attorney may not file a petition against the child based on any acts for which the child was placed under informal supervision unless the district attorney files the petition not later than 180 days after the date the child entered into the agreement for informal supervision. If the district attorney files a petition against the child within that period, the child may withdraw the admission that the child made pursuant to subsection 1.

7. If the child successfully completes the terms and conditions of the agreement for informal supervision, the juvenile court may dismiss any petition filed against the child that is based on any acts for which the child was placed under informal supervision.

NEW HAMPSHIRE
New Hampshire Revised Statutes Annotated
Title XII Public Safety and Welfare (Chs. 153–174)
Chapter 169-B Delinquent Children (§§ 169-B:1–169-B:47)

169-B:10. Juvenile Diversion.
I. An officer authorized under RSA 169-B:9 to take a minor into custody may dispose of the case without court referral by releasing the minor to a parent, guardian, or custodian. The officer shall make a

written report to the officer's department identifying the minor, specifying the grounds for taking the minor into custody and indicating the basis for the disposition.

I-a. Prior to filing a delinquency petition with the court, the arresting agency or prosecutor shall screen the petition for participation in diversion. The petitioner shall identify why diversion was not an appropriate disposition prior to seeking court involvement.

II. At any time before or at arraignment pursuant to this chapter, a minor and the minor's family may be referred to a court-approved diversion program or other intervention program or community resource. Referral may be made by the arresting or prosecuting agency or juvenile probation and parole officer, prior to filing a petition with the court or after the filing of a petition by such agency with the court's approval, or by the court on its own, or any party's motion. When the arresting or prosecuting agency, or juvenile probation and parole officer suspects that a minor has a disability, an administrator at the responsible school district shall be notified. If appropriate, the school district shall refer the minor for evaluation to determine if the child is in need of special education and related services.

II-a. The administrative judge of the judicial branch family division shall have the authority to approve diversion referral procedures for use in all juvenile matters throughout the state.

III. Referral to diversion or other community resource after filing is appropriate if:

(a) The facts bring the case within the jurisdiction of the court;

(b) Referral of the case is in the best interest of the public and the minor; and

(c) The minor and the parents, guardian, or other custodian give knowing, informed, and voluntary consent.

IV. Referral after filing shall stay the proceedings for a period not to exceed 6 months from the date of referral, unless extended by the court for an additional period not to exceed 6 months and does not authorize the detention of the minor.

V. During the period of referral, the court may require further conditions of conduct on the part of the minor and the minor's parents.

VI. No person who performs public service as part of his or her participation in a court approved diversion program under this chapter shall receive any benefits that such employer gives to its employees, including, but not limited to, workers' compensation and unemployment benefits and no such employer shall be liable for any damages sustained by a person while performing such public service or any damages caused by that person unless the employer is found to be negligent.

NEW JERSEY
New Jersey Annotated Statutes, Title 2A. Administration of Civil and Criminal Justice (Subtits. 1–12), Chapter 4A. Juvenile Justice (Arts. 1–4)
Article 4. Court Approved Juvenile Services (§§ 2A:4A-70–2A:4A-92)

§ 2A:4A-72. Recommendation of diversion
a. Where court intake services recommends diverting the juvenile, the reasons for the recommendation shall be submitted by intake services and approved by the court before the case is deemed diverted.

b. Where, in determining whether to recommend diversion, court intake services has reason to believe that a parent or guardian is a drug dependent person, as defined in section 2 of the "New Jersey Controlled Dangerous Substances Act," P.L.1970, c. 226 (C. 24:21-2) or an alcoholic as defined by P.L.1975, c. 305 (C. 26:2B-8), the basis for this determination shall be stated in its recommendation to the court.

c. The county prosecutor shall receive a copy of each complaint filed pursuant to section 11 of P.L. 1982, c. 77 promptly after the filing of the complaint.

d. Within 5 days after receiving a complaint, the intake services officer shall advise the presiding judge and the prosecuting attorney of intake services' recommendation as well as recommendation or objections received as to the complaint. In determining whether to divert, the court may hold a hearing to consider the recommendations and any objections submitted by court intake services in light of the factors provided in this section. The court shall give notice of the hearing to the juvenile, his parents or guardian, the prosecutor, arresting police officer and complainant or victim. Each party shall have the right to be heard on the matter. If the court finds that not enough information has been received to make a determination, a further hearing may be ordered. The court may dismiss the complaint upon a finding that the facts as alleged are not sufficient to establish jurisdiction, or that probable cause has not been shown that the juvenile committed a delinquent act.

§ 2A:4A-73. Diverting complaints

a. The court may divert a complaint filed pursuant to section 11 of P.L. 1982, c. 77 (C. 2A:4A-30), to intake conferences or juvenile conference committees. Where the complaint alleges a disorderly persons or petty disorderly persons offense the court may dispose of the case as a juvenile-family crisis pursuant to P.L. 1982, c. 80 (C. 2A:4A-76 et seq.) The county prosecutor shall be promptly notified of the diversion of a complaint.

b. The complainant or victim of any offense committed by a juvenile diverted by the court, which offense would be a crime if committed by an adult, shall receive a statement as to the reasons for the proposed diversion.

NEW MEXICO
Michie's ™ Annotated Statutes of New Mexico
Chapter 32A Children's Code (Arts. 1–26)
Article 2 Delinquency (§§ 32A-2-1–32A-2-33)

32A-2-5. Juvenile probation and parole services; establishment; juvenile probation and parole officers; powers and duties.
A. Juvenile probation and parole services shall be provided by the department.

B. To carry out the objectives and provisions of the Delinquency Act, but subject to its limitations, the department has the power and duty to:

(1) receive and examine complaints and allegations that a child is a delinquent child for the purpose of considering beginning a proceeding pursuant to the provisions of the Delinquency Act;

(2) make case referrals for services as appear appropriate or desirable;

(3) make predisposition studies and assessments and submit reports and recommendations to the court;

(4) supervise and assist a child placed on probation or supervised release or under supervision by court order or by the department;

(5) give notice to any individual who has been the subject of a petition filed pursuant to the provisions of the Delinquency Act of the sealing of that individual's records in accordance with that act;

(6) informally dispose of up to three misdemeanor charges brought against a child within two years;

(7) give notice to the children's court attorney of the receipt of any felony complaint and of any recommended adjustment of such felony complaint;

(8) identify an Indian child for the purpose of contacting the Indian child's tribe in delinquency cases; and

(9) upon receipt of a referral, contact an Indian child's tribe to consult and exchange information for the purpose of collaborating on appropriate referrals for services along with case planning throughout the period of involvement with juvenile justice services. . . .

NEW YORK
New York Consolidated Laws Service, Family Court Act (§ 111)
Article 3 Juvenile Delinquency (Pts. 1–8)
Part 1 Jurisdiction and Preliminary Procedures (§§ 301.1–315.3)

§ 308.1. Rules of court for preliminary procedure

1. Rules of court shall authorize and determine the circumstances under which the probation service may confer with any person seeking to have a juvenile delinquency petition filed, the potential respondent and other interested persons concerning the advisability of requesting that a petition be filed.

2. Except as provided in subdivisions three and four of this section, the probation service may, in accordance with rules of court, adjust suitable cases before a petition is filed. The inability of the respondent or his or her family to make restitution shall not be a factor in a

decision to adjust a case or in a recommendation to the presentment agency pursuant to subdivision six of this section. Nothing in this section shall prohibit the probation service or the court from directing a respondent to obtain employment and to make restitution from the earnings from such employment. Nothing in this section shall prohibit the probation service or the court from directing an eligible person to complete an education reform program in accordance with section four hundred fifty-eight-l of the social services law.

3. The probation service shall not adjust a case in which the child has allegedly committed a designated felony act unless it has received the written approval of the court.

4. The probation service shall not adjust a case in which the child has allegedly committed a delinquent act which would be a crime defined in section 120.25, (reckless endangerment in the first degree), subdivision one of section 125.15, (manslaughter in the second degree), subdivision one of section 130.25, (rape in the third degree), subdivision one of section 130.40, (criminal sexual act in the third degree), subdivision one or two of section 130.65, (sexual abuse in the first degree), section 135.65, (coercion in the first degree), section 140.20, (burglary in the third degree), section 150.10, (arson in the third degree), section 160.05, (robbery in the third degree), subdivision two, three or four of section 265.02, (criminal possession of a weapon in the third degree), section 265.03, (criminal possession of a weapon in the second degree), or section 265.04, (criminal possession of a dangerous weapon in the first degree) of the penal law where the child has previously had one or more adjustments of a case in which such child allegedly committed an act which would be a crime specified in this subdivision unless it has received written approval from the court and the appropriate presentment agency.

5. The fact that a child is detained prior to the filing of a petition shall not preclude the probation service from adjusting a case; upon adjusting such a case the probation service shall notify the detention facility to release the child.

6. The probation service shall not transmit or otherwise communicate to the presentment agency any statement made by the child to a probation officer. However, the probation service may make a

recommendation regarding adjustment of the case to the presentment agency and provide such information, including any report made by the arresting officer and record of previous adjustments and arrests, as it shall deem relevant.

7. No statement made to the probation service prior to the filing of a petition may be admitted into evidence at a fact-finding hearing or, if the proceeding is transferred to a criminal court, at any time prior to a conviction.

8. The probation service shall consider the views of the complainant and the impact of the alleged act or acts of juvenile delinquency upon the complainant and upon the community in determining whether adjustment under this section would be suitable.

9. Efforts at adjustment pursuant to rules of court under this section may not extend for a period of more than three months without leave of the court, which may extend the period for an additional two months.

10. If a case is not adjusted by the probation service, such service shall notify the appropriate presentment agency of that fact within forty-eight hours or the next court day, whichever occurs later.

11. The probation service may not be authorized under this section to compel any person to appear at any conference, produce any papers, or visit any place.

12. The probation service shall certify to the division of criminal justice services and to the appropriate police department or law enforcement agency whenever it adjusts a case in which the potential respondent's fingerprints were taken pursuant to section 306.1 in any manner other than the filing of a petition for juvenile delinquency for an act which, if committed by an adult, would constitute a felony, provided, however, in the case of a child eleven or twelve years of age, such certification shall be made only if the act would constitute a class A or B felony.

13. The provisions of this section shall not apply where the petition is an order of removal to the family court pursuant to article seven hundred twenty-five of the criminal procedure law.

NORTH CAROLINA
NC—General Statutes of North Carolina Annotated
CHAPTER 7B. JUVENILE CODE
DIVISION 02. UNDISCIPLINED AND DELINQUENT
JUVENILES
ARTICLE 17. SCREENING OF DELINQUENCY AND
UNDISCIPLINED COMPLAINTS

Section 7B-1701. Preliminary inquiry
When a complaint is received, the juvenile court counselor shall make a preliminary determination as to whether the juvenile is within the jurisdiction of the court as a delinquent or undisciplined juvenile. If the juvenile court counselor finds that the facts contained in the complaint do not state a case within the jurisdiction of the court, that legal sufficiency has not been established, or that the matters alleged are frivolous, the juvenile court counselor, without further inquiry, shall refuse authorization to file the complaint as a petition.

If a complaint against the juvenile has not been previously received, as determined by the juvenile court counselor, the juvenile court counselor shall make reasonable efforts to meet with the juvenile and the juvenile's parent, guardian, or custodian if the offense is divertible.

When requested by the juvenile court counselor, the prosecutor shall assist in determining the sufficiency of evidence as it affects the quantum of proof and the elements of offenses.

The juvenile court counselor, without further inquiry, shall authorize the complaint to be filed as a petition if the juvenile court counselor finds reasonable grounds to believe that the juvenile has committed one of the following nondivertible offenses:

(1) Murder;

(2) First-degree rape or second degree rape;

(3) First-degree sexual offense or second degree sexual offense;

(4) Arson;

(5) Any violation of Article 5, Chapter 90 of the General Statutes that would constitute a felony if committed by an adult;

(6) First degree burglary;

(7) Crime against nature; or

(8) Any felony which involves the willful infliction of serious bodily injury upon another or which was committed by use of a deadly weapon.

Section 7B-1702. (Effective until December 1, 2019) Evaluation

Upon a finding of legal sufficiency, except in cases involving nondivertible offenses set out in G.S. 7B-1701, the juvenile court counselor shall determine whether a complaint should be filed as a petition, the juvenile diverted pursuant to G.S. 7B-1706, or the case resolved without further action. In making the decision, the counselor shall consider criteria provided by the Division. The intake process shall include the following steps if practicable:

(1) Interviews with the complainant and the victim if someone other than the complainant;

(2) Interviews with the juvenile and the juvenile's parent, guardian, or custodian;

(3) Interviews with persons known to have relevant information about the juvenile or the juvenile's family.

Interviews required by this section shall be conducted in person unless it is necessary to conduct them by telephone.

Section 7B-1702. (Effective December 1, 2020) Evaluation.

Upon a finding of legal sufficiency, except in cases involving nondivertible offenses set out in G.S. 7B-1701, the juvenile court counselor shall determine whether a complaint should be filed as a petition, the juvenile diverted pursuant to G.S. 7B-1706, or the case resolved without further action. In making the decision, the counselor shall consider criteria provided by the Department and shall conduct a gang assessment for juveniles who are 12 years of age or older. The intake process shall include the following steps if practicable:

(1) Interviews with the complainant and the victim if someone other than the complainant;

(2) Interviews with the juvenile and the juvenile's parent, guardian, or custodian;

(3) Interviews with persons known to have relevant information about the juvenile or the juvenile's family.

Interviews required by this section shall be conducted in person unless it is necessary to conduct them by telephone.

Section 7B-1703. Evaluation decision
(a) The juvenile court counselor shall complete evaluation of a complaint within 15 days of receipt of the complaint, with an extension for a maximum of 15 additional days at the discretion of the chief court counselor. The juvenile court counselor shall decide within this time period whether a complaint shall be filed as a juvenile petition.

(b) Except as provided in G.S. 7B-1706, if the juvenile court counselor determines that a complaint should be filed as a petition, the counselor shall file the petition as soon as practicable, but in any event within 15 days after the complaint is received, with an extension for a maximum of 15 additional days at the discretion of the chief court counselor. The juvenile court counselor shall assist the complainant when necessary with the preparation and filing of the petition, shall include on it the date and the words "Approved for Filing", shall sign it, and shall transmit it to the clerk of superior court.

(c) If the juvenile court counselor determines that a petition should not be filed, the juvenile court counselor shall notify the complainant and the victim, if the complainant is not the victim, immediately in writing with specific reasons for the decision, whether or not legal sufficiency was found, and whether the matter was closed or diverted and retained, and shall include notice of the complainant's and victim's right to have the decision reviewed by the prosecutor. The juvenile court counselor shall sign the complaint after indicating on it:

(1) The date of the determination;

(2) The words "Not Approved for Filing"; and

(3) Whether the matter is "Closed" or "Diverted and Retained".

Except as provided in G.S. 7B-1706, any complaint not approved for filing as a juvenile petition shall be destroyed by the juvenile court counselor after holding the complaint for a temporary period to allow review as provided in G.S. 7B-1705.

Section 7B-1705. Review of determination that petition should not be filed

No later than 20 days after the complainant and the victim are notified, the prosecutor shall review the juvenile court counselor's determination that a juvenile petition should not be filed. Review shall include conferences with the complainant, the victim, and the juvenile court counselor. At the conclusion of the review, the prosecutor shall: (i) affirm the decision of the juvenile court counselor or direct the filing of a petition and (ii) notify the complainant and the victim of the prosecutor's action.

Section 7B-1706. Diversion plans and referral

(a) Unless the offense is one in which a petition is required by G.S. 7B-1701, upon a finding of legal sufficiency the juvenile court counselor may divert the juvenile pursuant to a diversion plan, which may include referring the juvenile to any of the following resources:

(1) An appropriate public or private resource;

(2) Restitution;

(3) Community service;

(4) Victim-offender mediation;

(5) Regimented physical training;

(6) Counseling;

(7) A teen court program, as set forth in subsection (c) of this section.

As part of a diversion plan, the juvenile court counselor may enter into a diversion contract with the juvenile and the juvenile's parent, guardian, or custodian.

(b) Unless the offense is one in which a petition is required by G.S. 7B-1701, upon a finding of legal sufficiency the juvenile court counselor may enter into a diversion contract with the juvenile and the parent, guardian, or custodian; provided, a diversion contract requires the consent of the juvenile and the juvenile's parent, guardian, or custodian. A diversion contract shall:

(1) State conditions by which the juvenile agrees to abide and any actions the juvenile agrees to take;

(2) State conditions by which the parent, guardian, or custodian agrees to abide and any actions the parent, guardian, or custodian agrees to take;

(3) Describe the role of the juvenile court counselor in relation to the juvenile and the parent, guardian, or custodian;

(4) Specify the length of the contract, which shall not exceed six months;

(5) Indicate that all parties understand and agree that:

a. The juvenile's violation of the contract may result in the filing of the complaint as a petition; and

b. The juvenile's successful completion of the contract shall preclude the filing of a petition.

After a diversion contract is signed by the parties, the juvenile court counselor shall provide copies of the contract to the juvenile and the juvenile's parent, guardian, or custodian. The juvenile court counselor shall notify any agency or other resource from which the juvenile or the juvenile's parent, guardian, or custodian will be seeking services or treatment pursuant to the terms of the contract. At any time during the term of the contract if the juvenile court counselor determines that the juvenile has failed to comply substantially with the terms of the contract, the juvenile court counselor may file the complaint as a petition. Unless the juvenile court counselor has filed the complaint as a petition, the juvenile court counselor shall close the juvenile's file in regard to the diverted matter within six months after the date of the contract.

(c) If a teen court program has been established in the district, the juvenile court counselor, upon a finding of legal sufficiency, may refer to a teen court program, any case in which a juvenile has allegedly committed an offense that would be an infraction or misdemeanor if committed by an adult. However, the juvenile court counselor shall not refer a case to a teen court program if the juvenile is alleged to have committed any of the following offenses:

(1) Driving while impaired under G.S. 20-138.1, 20-138.2, 20-138.3, 2 0-138.5, or 20-138.7, or any other motor vehicle violation;

(2) A Class A1 misdemeanor;

(3) An assault in which a weapon is used; or

(4) A controlled substance offense under Article 5 of Chapter 90 of the General Statutes, other than simple possession of a Schedule VI drug or alcohol.

(d) The juvenile court counselor shall maintain diversion plans and contracts entered into pursuant to this section to allow juvenile court counselors to determine when a juvenile has had a complaint diverted previously. Diversion plans and contracts are not public records under Chapter 132 of the General Statutes, shall not be included in the clerk's record pursuant to G.S. 7B-3000, and shall be withheld from public inspection or examination. Diversion plans and contracts shall be destroyed when the juvenile reaches the age of 18 years or when the juvenile is no longer under the jurisdiction of the court, whichever is longer.

(e) No later than 60 days after the juvenile court counselor diverts a juvenile, the juvenile court counselor shall determine whether the juvenile and the juvenile's parent, guardian, or custodian have complied with the terms of the diversion plan or contract. In making this determination, the juvenile court counselor shall contact any referral resources to determine whether the juvenile and the juvenile's parent, guardian, or custodian complied with any recommendations for treatment or services made by the resource. If the juvenile and the juvenile's parent, guardian, or custodian have not complied, the juvenile court counselor shall reconsider the decision to divert and may authorize the filing of the complaint as a petition within 10 days after making the determination. If the juvenile court counselor does not file a petition, the juvenile court counselor may continue to monitor the case for up to six months from the date of the diversion plan or contract. At any point during that time period if the juvenile and the juvenile's parent, guardian, or custodian fail to comply, the juvenile court counselor shall reconsider the decision to divert and may authorize the filing of the complaint as a petition. After six months, the juvenile court counselor shall close the diversion plan or contract file.

NORTH DAKOTA
North Dakota Century Code Annotated
TITLE 27 Judicial Branch of Government (Chs. 27-01–27-26)
CHAPTER 27-20 Uniform Juvenile Court Act
(§§ 27-20-01–27-20-61)

§ 27-20-10. Informal adjustment.
1. Before a petition is filed, the director of juvenile court or other officer of the court designated by it, subject to its direction, may give counsel and advice to the parties and impose conditions for the conduct and control of the child with a view to an informal adjustment if it appears:

   a. The admitted facts bring the case within the jurisdiction of the court;

   b. Counsel, advice, and conditions, if any, for the conduct and control of the child without an adjudication would be in the best interest of the public and the child; and

   c. The child and the child's parents, guardian, or other custodian consent thereto with knowledge that consent is not obligatory.

2. The giving of counsel and advice and any conditions imposed for the conduct and control of the child cannot extend beyond nine months from the day commenced unless extended by the court for an additional period not to exceed six months and does not authorize the detention of the child if not otherwise permitted by this chapter. If the child admits to driving or being in actual physical control of a vehicle in violation of section 39-08-01 or an equivalent ordinance, the child may be required to pay a fine as a condition imposed under this section.

3. An incriminating statement made by a participant to the person giving counsel or advice and in the discussions or conferences incident thereto may not be used against the declarant over objection in any hearing except in a hearing on disposition in a juvenile court

proceeding or in a criminal proceeding against the declarant after conviction for the purpose of a presentence investigation.

27-20-19. Petition — Preliminary determination.

A petition alleging delinquency or unruliness under this chapter must be reviewed by the director, the court, or other person authorized by the court to determine whether the filing of the petition is in the best interest of the public and the child.

OHIO
Rules of Juvenile Procedure
RULE 9. Intake

(A) Court action to be avoided. In all appropriate cases formal court action should be avoided and other community resources utilized to ameliorate situations brought to the attention of the court.

(B) Screening; referral. Information that a child is within the court's jurisdiction may be informally screened prior to the filing of a complaint to determine whether the filing of a complaint is in the best interest of the child and the public.

Page's Ohio Revised Code Annotated
Title 21: Courts — Probate — Juvenile (Chs. 2101–2153)
Chapter 2152: Delinquent Children; Juvenile Traffic Offenders (§§ 2152.01–2152.99)

§ 2152.021 Complaint alleging that child is delinquent child or juvenile traffic offender; initiation of serious youthful offender proceedings. . . .
(F)

(1) At any time after the filing of a complaint alleging that a child is a delinquent child and before adjudication, the court may hold a hearing to determine whether to hold the complaint in abeyance pending the child's successful completion of actions that constitute a method to divert the child from the juvenile court system if the child agrees to the hearing and either of the following applies:

(a) The act charged would be a violation of section 2907.24, 2907.241, or 2907.25 of the Revised Code if the child were an adult.

(b) The court has reason to believe that the child is a victim of a violation of section 2905.32 of the Revised Code, regardless of whether any person has been convicted of a violation of that section or of any other section for victimizing the child, and the act charged is related to the child's victimization.

(2) The prosecuting attorney has the right to participate in any hearing held under division (F) (1) of this section, to object to holding the complaint that is the subject of the hearing in abeyance, and to make recommendations related to diversion actions. No statement made by a child at a hearing held under division (F)(1) of this section is admissible in any subsequent proceeding against the child.

(3) If either division (F)(1)(a) or (b) of this section applies, the court shall promptly appoint a guardian ad litem for the child. The court shall not appoint the child's attorney as guardian ad litem. If the court decides to hold the complaint in abeyance, the guardian ad litem shall make recommendations that are in the best interest of the child to the court.

(4) If after a hearing the court decides to hold the complaint in abeyance, the court may make any orders regarding placement, services, supervision, diversion actions, and conditions of abeyance, including, but not limited to, engagement in trauma-based behavioral health services or education activities, that the court considers appropriate and in the best interest of the child. The court may hold the complaint in abeyance for up to ninety days while the child engages in diversion actions. If the child violates the conditions of abeyance or does not complete the diversion actions to the court's satisfaction within ninety days, the court may extend the period of abeyance for not more than two additional ninety-day periods.

(5) If the court holds the complaint in abeyance and the child complies with the conditions of abeyance and completes the diversion actions to the court's satisfaction, the court shall dismiss the complaint and order that the records pertaining to the case be expunged immediately. If the child fails to complete the diversion actions to the court's satisfaction, the court shall proceed upon the complaint.

OKLAHOMA
Oklahoma Statutes, Title 10A. Children and Juvenile Code
(Arts. 1–2)
Article 2. Oklahoma Juvenile Code (Chs. 1–10)
Chapter 2. Custody and Court Proceedings (§§ 2-2-101–2-2-806)

§ 2-2-104. Preliminary Inquiries—Procedures—Informal Adjustment Without Petition—Agreement

A. A preliminary inquiry shall be conducted to determine whether the interests of the public or of the child who is within the purview of the Oklahoma Juvenile Code require that further court action be taken. If it is determined by the preliminary inquiry that no further action be taken and if agreed to by the district attorney, the intake worker may make such informal adjustment without a petition.

B. In the course of the preliminary inquiry, the intake worker shall:

1. Hold conferences with the child and the parents, guardian or custodian of the child for the purpose of discussing the disposition of the referral made;

2. Interview such persons as necessary to determine whether the filing of a petition would be in the best interests of the child and the community;

3. Check existing records of any district court or tribal court, law enforcement agencies, Office of Juvenile Affairs, and Department of Human Services;

4. Obtain existing mental health, medical and educational records of the child with the consent of the parents, guardian or custodian of the child or by court order; and

5. Administer any screening and assessment instruments or refer for necessary screening and assessments to assist in the determination of any immediate needs of the child as well as the immediate risks to the community. All screening and assessment instruments shall be uniformly used by all intake workers, including those employed by juvenile bureaus, and shall be instruments specifically prescribed by the Office of Juvenile Affairs.

C. Upon review of any information presented in the preliminary inquiry, the district attorney may consult with the intake worker to determine whether the interests of the child and the public will be best served by the dismissal of the complaint, the informal adjustment of the complaint, or the filing of a petition.

D. Informal adjustment may be provided to the child by the intake worker only where the facts reasonably appear to establish prima facie jurisdiction and are admitted and where consent is obtained from the district attorney, the parent of the child, legal guardian, legal custodian, or legal counsel, if any, and the child. The informal adjustment is an agreement whereby the child agrees to fulfill certain conditions in exchange for not having a petition filed against the child. The informal adjustment shall be completed within a period of time not to exceed six (6) months and shall:

1. Be voluntarily entered into by all parties;

2. Be revocable by the child at any time by a written revocation;

3. Be revocable by the intake worker in the event there is reasonable cause to believe the child has failed to carry out the terms of the informal adjustment or has committed a subsequent offense;

4. Not be used as evidence against the child at any adjudication hearing;

5. Be executed in writing and expressed in language understandable to the persons involved; and

6. Become part of the juvenile record of the child.

E. The informal adjustment agreement under this section may include, among other suitable methods, programs and procedures, the following:

1. Participation in or referral to counseling, a period of community service, drug or alcohol education or treatment, vocational training or any other legal activity which in the opinion of the intake officer would be beneficial to the child and family of the child;

2. Require the child to undergo a behavioral health evaluation and, if warranted, undergo appropriate care or treatment;

3. Restitution providing for monetary payment by the parents or child to the victim who was physically injured or who suffered loss of or damage to property as a result of the conduct alleged. Before setting the amount of restitution, the intake officer shall consult with the victim concerning the amount of damages; or

4. If the intake worker has reasonable cause to believe that the child has failed to carry out the terms of the adjustment agreement or has committed a subsequent offense, in lieu of revoking the agreement, the intake worker may modify the terms of the agreement and extend the period of the agreement for an additional six (6) months from the date on which the modification was made with the consent of the child or counsel of the child, if any.

F. If an informal adjustment is agreed to pursuant to subsection D of this section, the informal adjustment agreement may require the child to pay a fee equal to no more than what the court costs would have been had a petition been filed. The child shall remit the fee directly to the agency responsible for the monitoring and supervision of the child. If the supervising agency is a juvenile bureau, then the fee shall be remitted to a revolving fund of the county in which the juvenile bureau is located to be designated the "Juvenile Deferral Fee Revolving Fund" and shall be used by the juvenile bureau to defray costs for the operation of the juvenile bureau. In those counties without juvenile bureaus and in which the Office of Juvenile Affairs or one of their contracting agencies provides the monitoring and supervision of the juvenile, the fee shall be paid directly to the Office of Juvenile Affairs and shall be used to defray the costs for the operation of the Office of Juvenile Affairs.

§ 2-2-104.1. Diversion Services—Purpose—Procedures—Notice
A. Diversion services shall be offered to children who are at risk of being the subject of a child-in-need-of-supervision petition. Diversion services shall be designed to provide an immediate response to families in crisis and to divert children from court proceedings. Diversion

services may be provided by outside agencies as designated by the district courts, juvenile bureaus, court employees, or a combination thereof.

B. Diversion services shall clearly document diligent attempts to provide appropriate services to the child and the family of the child unless it is determined that there is no substantial likelihood that the child and family of the child will benefit from further diversion attempts.

C. Where the primary issue is truancy, steps taken by the school district to improve the attendance or conduct of the child in school shall be reviewed and attempts to engage the school district in further diversion attempts shall be made if it appears that such attempts will be beneficial to the child.

D. Efforts to prevent the filing of the petition may extend until it is determined that there is no substantial likelihood that the child and family of the child will benefit from further attempts. Efforts at diversion may continue after the filing of the petition where it is determined that the child and family of the child will benefit therefrom.

E. A child-in-need-of-supervision petition shall not be filed during the period that the designated agency, juvenile bureau, or court employee is providing the diversion services. A finding that the case has been successfully diverted shall constitute presumptive evidence that the underlying allegations have been successfully resolved.

F. The designated agency, juvenile bureau, or court employee shall promptly give written notice to the child and family of the child whenever attempts to prevent the filing of the petition have terminated and shall indicate in the notice whether the efforts were successful or whether a child-in-need-of-supervision petition should be filed with the court. A petition may or may not be filed where diversion services have been terminated because the parent or other person legally responsible for the child failed to consent to the diversion plan or failed to actively participate in the services provided.

OREGON
  Oregon Annotated Statutes
  Title 34 Human Services; Juvenile Code; Corrections (Chs. 409–424)
  Chapter 419C- Juvenile Code: Delinquency
  (§§ 419C.001–419C.680)
  Authorized Diversion Programs (§§ 419C.225–419C.226), Formal
  Accountability Agreements (§§ 419C.230–419C.245)

419C.225 Authorized diversion programs.
(1) Following a review of a police report and other relevant information, a county juvenile department may refer a youth to an authorized diversion program if the youth is eligible to enter into a formal accountability agreement under ORS 419C.230.

(2) An authorized diversion program may include a youth court, mediation program, crime prevention or chemical substance abuse education program or other program established for the purpose of providing consequences and reformation and preventing future delinquent acts.

(3) An authorized diversion program for a youth who is alleged to have committed an act that is a violation of ORS 813.010 must include an agreement that the youth will not use intoxicants while the youth is participating in the diversion program.

419C.230 Formal accountability agreements; when appropriate; consultation with victim.
(1) A formal accountability agreement may be entered into when a youth has been referred to a county juvenile department, and a juvenile department counselor has probable cause to believe that the youth may be found to be within the jurisdiction of the juvenile court for one or more acts specified in ORS 419C.005.

(2) Notwithstanding subsection (1) of this section, unless authorized by the district attorney, a formal accountability agreement may not be entered into when the youth:

(a) Is alleged to have committed an act that if committed by an adult would constitute:

(A) A felony sex offense under ORS 163.355, 163.365, 163.375, 163.385, 163.395, 163.405, 163.408, 163.411, 163.425 or 163.427; or

(B) An offense involving the use or possession of a firearm, as defined in ORS 166.210, or destructive device, as described in ORS 166.382; or

(b) Is being referred to the county juvenile department for a second or subsequent time for commission of an act that if committed by an adult would constitute a felony.

(3) The juvenile department must consult the victim before entering into a formal accountability agreement if:

(a) The victim has requested consultation in plea negotiations; and

(b) The formal accountability agreement involves an alleged act that if committed by an adult would constitute a violent felony.

PENNSYLVANIA
Pennsylvania Consolidated Statutes
Title 42. Judiciary and Judicial Procedure (Pts. I–VIII)
Chapter 63. Juvenile Matters (Subchs. A–F)
Subchapter B. Jurisdiction and Custody (§§ 6321–6328)

§ 6323. Informal adjustment.
(a) *General rule.*

(1) Before a petition is filed, the probation officer or other officer of the court designated by it, subject to its direction, shall, in the case of a dependent child where the jurisdiction of the court is premised upon the provisions of paragraph (1), (2), (3), (4), (5) or (7) of the definition of "dependent child" in section 6302 (relating to definitions) and if otherwise appropriate, refer the child and his parents to any public or private social agency available for assisting in the matter. Upon referral, the agency shall indicate its willingness to accept the child and shall report back to the referring officer within three months concerning the status of the referral.

(2) Similarly, the probation officer may in the case of a delinquent child, or a dependent child where the jurisdiction of the court is permitted under paragraph (6) of the definition of "dependent child" in section 6302, refer the child and his parents to an agency for assisting in the matter.

(3) The agency may return the referral to the probation officer or other officer for further informal adjustment if it is in the best interests of the child.

(b) *Counsel and advice.* — Such social agencies and the probation officer or other officer of the court may give counsel and advice to the parties with a view to an informal adjustment if it appears:

(1) counsel and advice without an adjudication would be in the best interest of the public and the child;

(2) the child and his parents, guardian, or other custodian consent thereto with knowledge that consent is not obligatory; and

(3) in the case of the probation officer or other officer of the court, the admitted facts bring the case within the jurisdiction of the court.

(c) *Limitation on duration of counsel and advice.* — The giving of counsel and advice by the probation or other officer of the court shall not extend beyond six months from the day commenced unless extended by an order of court for an additional period not to exceed three months.

(d) *No detention authorized.* — Nothing contained in this section shall authorize the detention of the child.

(e) *Privileged statements.* — An incriminating statement made by a participant to the person giving counsel or advice and in the discussions or conferences incident thereto shall not be used against the declarant over objection in any criminal proceeding or hearing under this chapter.

(f) *Terms and conditions.* — The terms and conditions of an informal adjustment may include payment by the child of reasonable amounts of money as costs, fees or restitution, including a supervision fee and contribution to a restitution fund established by the president judge of the court of common pleas pursuant to section 6352(a)(5) (relating to disposition of delinquent child).

PUERTO RICO
Laws of Puerto Rico Annotated
TITLE THIRTY-FOUR Code of Criminal Procedure (Pts. I–XIV)
PART XIII. Minors (Chs. 145–152), Chapter 151. Minors' Act
(§§ 2201–2238)

§ 2221. Removal of minors from judicial procedure
After a complaint has been filed and before the adjudication of the case, the Prosecutor may request the court to refer the minor to an agency or a public or private body if the following circumstances exist:

(1) If it is a Class I offense or a first time offender in a Class II offense.

(2) An agreement is signed between the Prosecutor, the minor, his parents or guardian and the agency or body to which the minor is referred.

(3) The social report of the Family Relations Specialist is taken into consideration.

(4) There is an authorization of the court.

The agency or body to which the minor is referred in accordance with this section shall report to the Prosecutor and to the court whether the minor is complying with or has complied or not with the conditions of the agreement. In case the minor has complied with said conditions, the Prosecutor shall request the court to dismiss the complaint. In case the minor has not complied, the Prosecutor shall request a hearing to determine if the procedure should continue.

RHODE ISLAND
[Rhode Island's statute is vague on diversion, which has been more fully implemented through its Rules of Juvenile Procedure]

Rule 4 - Informal Adjustment Procedure [Effective January 6, 2020], R.I. R. Juv. P. 4
(a) **Intake Department.** If the Intake Department decides to continue the intake process and to attempt informal adjustment, the Intake Department shall explain to the parties that the Intake Department intends to discuss plans for continuing contact with the child by the

Intake Department or by any public or private agency without the formal filing of the petition, and that the Intake Department wants to question the parties in regard to the child's general behavior, the child's school and home environment, and other similar factors bearing upon the proposed informal adjustment. The parties shall be informed that the parties need not answer questions, that the parties have the right to be represented by an attorney , that information obtained from the parties by the Intake Department during the adjustment process will not be admissible in evidence at an adjudicatory hearing, that the parties may withdraw from the adjustment process at any time, and that the efforts at informal adjustment shall not preclude the formal filing of the same petition at a future date. The Intake Department shall further inform the parties that informal adjustment shall not constitute an adjudication and that if the parties deny the allegations no effort will be made to arrive at an informal adjustment.

(b) **Specialized Calendars.** If the Intake Department determines that the informal adjustment of the petition may be achieved by referral to a specialized calendar within the court, the petition shall be referred to that calendar for further proceedings.

(c) **Referral to the Chief Judge.** If the proposed informal adjustment is unacceptable to the petitioner, the Intake Department shall present the petition to the chief judge of the court or a designated judicial officer, together with the Intake Department's recommendations, for determination by the chief judge or a designated judicial officer, as to whether the petition shall be formally filed.

Amended March 1, 2019, effective July 1, 2019; amended April 30, 2019, effective November 4, 2019; amended November 5, 2019, effective January 6, 2020.

SOUTH CAROLINA
South Carolina Code of Laws Annotated, Title 63. South Carolina Children's Code (Chs. 1–21), Chapter 19. Juvenile Justice Code (Arts. 1–23)
Article 9. Intake and Initiation of Proceedings (§§ 9–63-19-1040)

§ 63-19-1010. Intake and probation.
(A) The Department of Juvenile Justice shall provide intake and probation services for juveniles brought before the family courts of this

State and for persons committed or referred to the department in cooperation with all local officials or agencies concerned. The role and function of intake is to independently assess the circumstances and needs of children referred for possible prosecution in the family court. Recommendations by the department as to intake must be reviewed by the office of the solicitor in the circuit concerned, and the final determination as to whether or not the juvenile is to be prosecuted in the family court must be made by the solicitor or by the solicitor's authorized assistant. Statements of the juvenile contained in the department's files must not be furnished to the solicitor's office as part of the intake review procedure, and the solicitor's office must not be privy to these statements in connection with its intake review.

(B) Where circumstances do not warrant prosecution in the discretion of the solicitor, the intake counselor shall offer referral assistance for services as appropriate for the child and family. In the event that a juvenile is adjudicated to be delinquent or found by the family court to be in violation of the terms of probation, the intake counselor shall offer appropriate dispositional recommendations to the family court for its consideration and determination of the disposition of the case.

SOUTH DAKOTA
South Dakota Codified Laws Annotated
Title 26 Minors (Chs. 26-1–26-18)
Chapter 26-7A Juvenile Court (§§ 26-7A-1–26-7A-129)

26-7A-10. Preliminary investigation — Apparent, alleged or adjudicated abused or neglected child — Options available to state's attorney.
If a state's attorney is informed by a law enforcement officer or any other person that a child is, or appears to be, within the purview of this chapter and chapter 26-8A, 26-8B, or 26-8C, the state's attorney shall make a preliminary investigation to determine whether further action shall be taken. On the basis of the preliminary investigation, the state's attorney may:

(1) Decide that no further action is required;

(2) If the report relates to an apparent abused or neglected child and if additional information is required, refer the matter to

the Department of Social Services for further investigation and recommendations;

(3) If the report relates to a juvenile cited violation, proceed on the citation;

(4) If the report relates to an apparent child in need of supervision, an apparent delinquent child, or a juvenile cited violation, refer the matter to a court services officer for any informal adjustment to the supervision of the court that is practicable without a petition or refer the matter to a court-approved juvenile diversion program for any informal action outside the court system that is practicable without the filing of a petition; or

(5) File a petition to commence appropriate proceedings in any case that the youth does not meet the criteria provided in § 26-7A-11.1.

26-7A-11. Prerequisites to referral for informal adjustment or informal action.

A report of a preliminary investigation involving any apparent child in need of supervision, any apparent delinquent child, or any juvenile cited violation, may be referred to a court services officer for informal adjustment or to a court-approved juvenile diversion program for informal action pursuant to subdivision 26-7A-10(4) only if:

(1) The child and the child's parents, guardian, or other custodian were informed of their constitutional and legal rights, including being represented by an attorney at every stage of the proceedings if a petition is filed;

(2) The facts are admitted and establish prima facie jurisdiction; and

(3) Written consent is obtained from the child's parents, guardian, or custodian and from the child if the child is of sufficient age and understanding. Efforts to effect informal adjustment or informal action may extend no longer than four months from the date of the consent.

The state's attorney may include in the referral to a court-approved juvenile diversion program a requirement that restitution as defined in subdivision 23A-28-2(4) be imposed as a condition of the diversion program.

TENNESSEE
TN - Tennessee Code Annotated, Title 37 Juveniles
Chapter 1 Juvenile Courts and Proceedings
Part 1 General Provisions

37-1-110. Informal adjustment without adjudication — Pretrial diversion — No admission required.
(a)

(1) Before or after a petition is filed, a designated court officer may informally resolve a complaint containing delinquent or unruly allegations without adjudication by giving counsel and advice to the child if such informal resolution would be in the best interest of the public and the child, and the child and the child's parents, guardian, or other custodian consent to the informal adjustment with knowledge that consent is not obligatory. The informal adjustment shall not extend beyond three (3) months from the day commenced, unless extended by the court for an additional period not to exceed a total of six (6) months, and does not authorize the attachment or detention of the child if not otherwise permitted by this part.

(2) If the child and the victim agree to restitution, restitution may be paid independently of informal adjustment; however, financial obligations shall not be assessed or collected against a child as part of an informal adjustment pursuant to this section.

(b)

(1) After a petition has been filed and a designated court officer determines that an unruly or delinquent case is an appropriate case for diversion from adjudication, the parties may agree to pretrial diversion that suspends the proceedings and places the child under supervision on terms and conditions agreeable to the designated court officer and approved by the court. A child may not be placed on pretrial diversion if the delinquent act alleged is an offense described in § 37-1-153(b).

(2) A pretrial diversion agreement shall remain in force for a maximum of six (6) months unless the child is discharged sooner by the court. Upon application of any party to the proceedings, made

before expiration of the six-month period and after notice and a hearing, pretrial diversion may be extended by the court for an additional six (6) months.

(3) If, prior to discharge by the court or expiration of the pretrial diversion period, the child fails to fulfill the terms and conditions of the pretrial diversion agreement, the original petition may be reinstated and the case may proceed to adjudication just as if the agreement had never been entered.

(4) Attachment and detention of a child are not authorized for the violation of a pretrial diversion agreement unless otherwise permitted by this part.

(c) The petition shall be dismissed with prejudice once a child completes an informal adjustment pursuant to subsection (a) or pretrial diversion pursuant to subsection (b) without reinstatement of the original delinquent or unruly petition.

(d) No admission shall be required as part of informal adjustment or pretrial diversion, and any statements made by the child during the preliminary inquiry, informal adjustment pursuant to subsection (a), or pretrial diversion pursuant to subsection (b) are not admissible prior to a dispositional hearing.

TEXAS
Texas Statutes & Codes Annotated, Texas Family Code
Title 3 Juvenile Justice Code (Chs. 51–61)
Chapter 52 Proceedings Before and Including Referral to Court
(§§ 52.01–52.041)

Sec. 52.03. Disposition Without Referral to Court.
(a) A law-enforcement officer authorized by this title to take a child into custody may dispose of the case of a child taken into custody or accused of a Class C misdemeanor, other than a traffic offense, without referral to juvenile court or charging a child in a court of competent criminal jurisdiction, if:

(1) guidelines for such disposition have been adopted by the juvenile board of the county in which the disposition is made as required by Section 52.032;

(2) the disposition is authorized by the guidelines; and

(3) the officer makes a written report of the officer's disposition to the law-enforcement agency, identifying the child and specifying the grounds for believing that the taking into custody or accusation of criminal conduct was authorized.

(b) No disposition authorized by this section may involve:

(1) keeping the child in law-enforcement custody; or

(2) requiring periodic reporting of the child to a law-enforcement officer, law-enforcement agency, or other agency.

(c) A disposition authorized by this section may involve:

(1) referral of the child to an agency other than the juvenile court;

(2) a brief conference with the child and his parent, guardian, or custodian; or

(3) referral of the child and the child's parent, guardian, or custodian for services under Section 264.302.

(d) Statistics indicating the number and kind of dispositions made by a law-enforcement agency under the authority of this section shall be reported at least annually to the office or official designated by the juvenile board, as ordered by the board.

UTAH
Utah Code Annotated, Title 78A Judiciary and Judicial Administration (Chs. 1–12), Chapter 6 Juvenile Court Act (Pts. 1–14)
Part 6 Delinquency and Criminal Actions
(§§ 78A-6-601–78A-6-606)

78A-6-602. Petition — Preliminary inquiry — Nonjudicial adjustments — Formal referral — Citation — Failure to appear.
(1) A proceeding in a minor's case is commenced by petition, except as provided in Sections 78A-6-701, 78A-6-702, and 78A-6-703.

(2) . . .

  (b)

    (i) When the court is informed by a peace officer or other person that a minor is or appears to be within the court's jurisdiction, the probation department shall make a preliminary inquiry to determine whether the minor is eligible to enter into a written consent agreement with the probation department and, if the minor is a child, the minor's parent, guardian, or custodian for the nonjudicial adjustment of the case pursuant to this Subsection (2).

    (ii) Except as provided in Subsection (2)(k), the court's probation department shall offer a nonjudicial adjustment if the minor:

      (A) is referred with a misdemeanor, infraction, or status offense;

      (B) has no more than two prior adjudications; and

      (C) has no more than three prior unsuccessful nonjudicial adjustment attempts.

    (iii) For purposes of this Subsection (2)(b), an adjudication or nonjudicial adjustment means an action based on a single episode of conduct that is closely related in time and is incident to an attempt or an accomplishment of a single objective.

  (c)

    (i) Within seven days of receiving a referral that appears to be eligible for a nonjudicial adjustment pursuant to Subsection (2)(b), the probation department shall provide an initial notice to reasonably identifiable and locatable victims of the offense contained in the referral.

    (ii) The victim shall be responsible to provide to the division upon request:

      (A) invoices, bills, receipts, and other evidence of injury, loss of earnings, and out-of-pocket loss;

      (B) documentation and evidence of compensation or reimbursement from insurance companies or agencies of Utah, any other state, or federal government received as a direct result of the crime for injury, loss of earnings, or out-of-pocket loss; and

(C) proof of identification, including home and work address and telephone numbers.

(iii) The inability, failure, or refusal of the victim to provide all or part of the requested information shall result in the probation department determining restitution based on the best information available.

(d)

(i) Notwithstanding Subsection (2)(b), the probation department may conduct a validated risk and needs assessment and may request that the prosecutor review the referral pursuant to Subsection (2)(h) to determine whether to dismiss the referral or file a petition instead of offering a nonjudicial adjustment if:

(A) the results of the assessment indicate the youth is high risk; or

(B) the results of the assessment indicate the youth is moderate risk and the referral is for a class A misdemeanor violation under Title 76, Chapter 5, Offenses Against the Person, or Title 76, Chapter 9, Part 7, Miscellaneous Provisions.

(ii) Except as provided in Subsection (2)(k), the court's probation department may offer a nonjudicial adjustment to any other minor who does not meet the criteria provided in Subsection (2)(b).

(iii) Acceptance of an offer of nonjudicial adjustment may not be predicated on an admission of guilt.

(iv) A minor may not be denied an offer of nonjudicial adjustment due to an inability to pay a financial penalty under Subsection (2)(e).

(v) Efforts to effect a nonjudicial adjustment may not extend for a period of more than 90 days without leave of a judge of the court, who may extend the period for an additional 90 days.

(vi) A prosecutor may not file a petition against a minor unless:

(A) the minor does not qualify for nonjudicial adjustment under Subsection (2)(b) or (d)(ii);

(B) the minor declines nonjudicial adjustment;

(C) the minor fails to substantially comply with the conditions agreed upon as part of the nonjudicial adjustment;

(D) the minor fails to respond to the probation department's inquiry regarding eligibility for or an offer of a nonjudicial adjustment after being provided with notice for preliminary inquiry; or

(E) the prosecutor is acting under Subsection (2)(k).

(e) The nonjudicial adjustment of a case may include the following conditions agreed upon as part of the nonjudicial closure:

(i) payment of a financial penalty of not more than $250 to the juvenile court subject to the terms established under Subsection (2)(f);

(ii) payment of victim restitution;

(iii) satisfactory completion of community or compensatory service;

(iv) referral to an appropriate provider for counseling or treatment;

(v) attendance at substance use disorder programs or counseling programs;

(vi) compliance with specified restrictions on activities and associations;

(vii) victim-offender mediation, if requested by the victim; and

(viii) other reasonable actions that are in the interest of the child or minor, the community, and the victim.

(f) A fee, fine, or restitution included in a nonjudicial closure in accordance with Subsection (2)(e) shall be based upon the ability of the minor's family to pay as determined by a statewide sliding scale developed as provided in Section 63M-7-208 on and after July 1, 2018.

(g) If a prosecutor learns of a referral involving an offense identified in Subsection (2)(k), if a minor fails to substantially comply with the conditions agreed upon as part of the nonjudicial closure, or if a minor is not offered or declines a nonjudicial adjustment pursuant to Subsection (2)(b), (2)(d)(ii), or (2)(d)(vi), the prosecutor shall review the case and take one of the following actions:

(i) dismiss the case;

(ii) refer the case back to the probation department for a new attempt at nonjudicial adjustment; or

(iii) subject to Subsection (2)(i), file a petition with the court.

(h) Notwithstanding Subsection (2)(g), a petition may only be filed upon reasonable belief that:

(i) the charges are supported by probable cause;

(ii) admissible evidence will be sufficient to support adjudication beyond a reasonable doubt; and

(iii) the decision to charge is in the interests of justice.

(i) Failure to pay a fine or fee may not serve as a basis for filing of a petition under Subsection (2)(g)(iii) if the minor has substantially complied with the other conditions agreed upon in accordance with Subsection (2)(e) or those imposed through any other court diversion program.

(j) Notwithstanding Subsection (2)(i), a violation of Section 76-10-105 that is subject to the jurisdiction of the juvenile court may include a fine or penalty and participation in a court-approved tobacco education program, which may include a participation fee.

(k) Notwithstanding the other provisions of this section, the probation department shall request that a prosecutor review a referral in accordance with Subsection (2)(g) if:

(i) the referral involves a violation of:

(A) Section 41-6a-502, driving under the influence;

(B) Section 76-5-112, reckless endangerment creating a substantial risk of death or serious bodily injury;

(C) Section 76-5-206, negligent homicide;

(D) Section 76-9-702.1, sexual battery;

(E) Section 76-10-505.5, possession of a dangerous weapon, firearm, or short barreled shotgun on or about school premises; or

(F) Section 76-10-509, possession of dangerous weapon by minor, but only if the dangerous weapon is a firearm; or

(ii) the minor has a current suspended order for custody under Subsection 78A-6-117(5)(a).

(l) If the prosecutor files a petition in court, the court may refer the case to the probation department for another offer of nonjudicial adjustment.

(m) If a minor violates Section 41-6a-502, regardless of whether a prosecutor reviews a referral under Subsection (2)(k)(i)(A), the minor shall be subject to a drug and alcohol screening and participate in an assessment, if found appropriate by the screening, and if warranted, follow the recommendations of the assessment. . . .

VERMONT
VT - Vermont Statutes Annotated
TITLE THREE. EXECUTIVE
PART 1. GENERALLY, CHAPTER 7. ATTORNEY GENERAL

Section 163. Juvenile court diversion project
(a) The Attorney General shall develop and administer a juvenile court diversion project for the purpose of assisting juveniles charged with delinquent acts. In consultation with the diversion programs, the Attorney General shall adopt a policies and procedures manual in compliance with this section.

(b) The diversion program administered by the Attorney General shall support the operation of diversion programs in local communities through grants of financial assistance to, or by contracting for services with, municipalities, private groups, or other local organizations. The Attorney General may require local financial contributions as a condition of receipt of project funding.

(c) All diversion projects receiving financial assistance from the Attorney General shall adhere to the following provisions:

(1) The diversion project shall only accept persons against whom charges have been filed and the court has found probable cause, but are not yet adjudicated.

(2) Alleged offenders shall be informed of their right to the advice and assistance of private counsel or the public defender at all stages of the diversion process, including the initial decision to participate, and the decision to accept the diversion contract, so that the candidate may give his or her informed consent.

(3) The participant shall be informed that his or her selection of the diversion contract is voluntary.

(4) Each State's Attorney, in cooperation with the Attorney General and the diversion program, shall develop clear criteria for deciding what types of offenses and offenders will be eligible for diversion; however, the State's Attorney shall retain final discretion over the referral of each case for diversion. The provisions of 33 V.S.A. Section 5225(c) and Section 5280(e) shall apply.

(5) All information gathered in the course of the diversion process shall be held strictly confidential and shall not be released without the participant's prior consent (except that research and reports that do not require or establish the identity of individual participants are allowed).

(6) Information related to the present offense that is divulged during the diversion program shall not be used in the prosecutor's case. However, the fact of participation and success, or reasons for failure may become part of the prosecutor's records.

(7) The diversion project shall maintain sufficient records so that the reasons for success or failure of the program in particular cases and overall can be investigated by program staff.

(8) Diversion projects shall be set up to respect the rights of participants.

(9) Each participant shall pay a fee to the local juvenile court diversion project. The amount of the fee shall be determined by project

officers based upon the financial capabilities of the participant. The fee shall not exceed $ 150.00. The fee shall be a debt due from the participant, and payment of such shall be required for successful completion of the Program. Notwithstanding 32 V.S.A. Section 502(a), fees collected under this subdivision shall be retained and used solely for the purpose of the Court Diversion Program.

(d) The Attorney General is authorized to accept grants and gifts for the purposes of this section, such acceptance being pursuant to 32 V.S.A. Section 5.

(e)

(1) Within 30 days after the two-year anniversary of a successful completion of juvenile diversion, the court shall provide notice to all parties of record of the court's intention to order the expungement of all court files and records, law enforcement records other than entries in the juvenile court diversion program's centralized filing system, fingerprints, and photographs applicable to the proceeding. The court shall give the State's Attorney an opportunity for a hearing to contest the expungement of the records. The court shall expunge the records if it finds:

(A) two years have elapsed since the successful completion of juvenile diversion by the participant and the dismissal of the case by the State's Attorney;

(B) the participant has not been convicted of a subsequent felony or misdemeanor during the two-year period, and no proceedings are pending seeking such conviction;

(C) rehabilitation of the participant has been attained to the satisfaction of the court; and

(D) the participant does not owe restitution related to the case under a contract executed with the Restitution Unit.

(2) The court may expunge any records that were sealed pursuant to this subsection prior to July 1, 2018 unless the State's Attorney's office that prosecuted the case objects. Thirty days prior to expunging a record pursuant to this subdivision, the court shall provide written notice of its intent to expunge the record to the State's Attorney's office that prosecuted the case.

(3)

A) The court shall keep a special index of cases that have been expunged pursuant to this section together with the expungement order. The index shall list only the name of the person convicted of the offense, his or her date of birth, the docket number, and the criminal offense that was the subject of the expungement.

(B) The special index and related documents specified in subdivision (A) of this subdivision (3) shall be confidential and shall be physically and electronically segregated in a manner that ensures confidentiality and that limits access to authorized persons.

(C) Inspection of the expungement order and the certificate may be permitted only upon petition by the person who is the subject of the case. The Chief Superior Judge may permit special access to the index and the documents for research purposes pursuant to the rules for public access to court records.

(D) The Court Administrator shall establish policies for implementing this subsection (e).

(f) Except as otherwise provided in this section, upon the entry of an order expunging files and records under this section, the proceedings in the matter shall be considered never to have occurred, all index references thereto shall be deleted, and the participant, the court, and law enforcement officers and departments shall reply to any request for information that no record exists with respect to such participant inquiry in any matter. Copies of the order shall be sent to each agency or official named therein.

(g) The process of automatically expunging records as provided in this section shall only apply to those persons who completed diversion on or after July 1, 2002. Any person who completed diversion prior to July 1, 2002 must apply to the court to have his or her records expunged. Expungement shall occur if the requirements of subsection (e) of this section are met.

(h) Subject to the approval of the Attorney General, the Vermont Association of Court Diversion Programs may develop and administer programs to assist persons under this section charged with delinquent, criminal, and civil offenses.

(i) Notwithstanding subdivision (c)(1) of this section, the diversion program may accept cases from the Youth Substance Abuse Safety Program pursuant to 7 V.S.A. Section 656 or 18 V.S.A. Section 4230b. The confidentiality provisions of this section shall become effective when a notice of violation is issued under 7 V.S.A. Section 656(b) or 18 V.S.A. Section 4230b(b), and shall remain in effect unless the person fails to register with or complete the Youth Substance Abuse Safety Program.

(j) Notwithstanding subdivision (c)(1) of this section, the diversion program may accept cases pursuant to 33 V.S.A. Sections 5225-5280.

VIRGINIA
  VA - Code of Virginia (Annotated), TITLE 16.1. COURTS NOT OF RECORD
  CHAPTER 11. JUVENILE AND DOMESTIC RELATIONS DISTRICT COURTS
  ARTICLE 2. ORGANIZATION AND PERSONNEL

Section 16.1-237. Powers, duties and functions of probation and parole officers
In addition to any other powers and duties imposed by this law, a probation or parole officer appointed hereunder shall:

A. Investigate all cases referred to him by the judge or any person designated so to do, and shall render reports of such investigation as required;

B. Supervise persons placed under his supervision and shall keep informed concerning the conduct and condition of every person under his supervision by visiting, requiring reports and in other ways, and shall report thereon as required;

C. Under the general supervision of the director of the court service unit, investigate complaints and accept for informal supervision cases wherein such handling would best serve the interests of all concerned; . . .

WASHINGTON
Annotated Revised Code of Washington
Title 13 Juvenile Courts and Juvenile Offenders (Chs.
13.04–13.90)
Chapter 13.40 Juvenile Justice Act of 1977 (§§ 13.40.005–13.40.900)

13.40.070. Complaints — Screening — Filing information — Diversion — Modification of community supervision — Notice to parent or guardian — Probation counselor acting for prosecutor — Referral to community-based, restorative justice, mediation, or reconciliation programs.
(1) Complaints referred to the juvenile court alleging the commission of an offense shall be referred directly to the prosecutor. The prosecutor, upon receipt of a complaint, shall screen the complaint to determine whether:

(a) The alleged facts bring the case within the jurisdiction of the court; and

(b) On a basis of available evidence there is probable cause to believe that the juvenile did commit the offense.

(2) If the identical alleged acts constitute an offense under both the law of this state and an ordinance of any city or county of this state, state law shall govern the prosecutor's screening and charging decision for both filed and diverted cases.

(3) If the requirements of subsection (1)(a) and (b) of this section are met, the prosecutor shall either file an information in juvenile court or divert the case, as set forth in subsections (5), (6), and (8) of this section. If the prosecutor finds that the requirements of subsection (1) (a) and (b) of this section are not met, the prosecutor shall maintain a record, for one year, of such decision and the reasons therefor. In lieu of filing an information or diverting an offense a prosecutor may file a motion to modify community supervision where such offense constitutes a violation of community supervision....

(6) Where a case is legally sufficient the prosecutor shall divert the case if the alleged offense is a misdemeanor or gross misdemeanor or violation and the alleged offense is the offender's first offense or violation. If the alleged offender is charged with a related offense that may

be filed under subsections (5) and (8) of this section, a case under this subsection may also be filed.

(7) Where a case is legally sufficient to charge an alleged offender with:

(a) Either prostitution or prostitution loitering and the alleged offense is the offender's first prostitution or prostitution loitering offense, the prosecutor shall divert the case;

(b) Voyeurism in the second degree, the offender is under seventeen years of age, and the alleged offense is the offender's first voyeurism in the second degree offense, the prosecutor shall divert the case, unless the offender has received two diversions for any offense in the previous two years;

(c) Minor selling depictions of himself or herself engaged in sexually explicit conduct under RCW 9.68A.053(5) and the alleged offense is the offender's first violation of RCW 9.68A.053(5), the prosecutor shall divert the case; or

(d) A distribution, transfer, dissemination, or exchange of sexually explicit images of other minors thirteen years of age or older offense as provided in RCW 9.68A.053(1) and the alleged offense is the offender's first violation of RCW 9.68A.053(1), the prosecutor shall divert the case.

(8) Where a case is legally sufficient and falls into neither subsection (5) nor (6) of this section, it may be filed or diverted. In deciding whether to file or divert an offense under this section the prosecutor may be guided by the length, seriousness, and recency of the alleged offender's criminal history and the circumstances surrounding the commission of the alleged offense.

(9) Whenever a juvenile is placed in custody or, where not placed in custody, referred to a diversion interview, the parent or legal guardian of the juvenile shall be notified as soon as possible concerning the allegation made against the juvenile and the current status of the juvenile. Where a case involves victims of crimes against persons or victims whose property has not been recovered at the time a juvenile is

referred to a diversion unit, the victim shall be notified of the referral and informed how to contact the unit.

(10) The responsibilities of the prosecutor under subsections (1) through (9) of this section may be performed by a juvenile court probation counselor for any complaint referred to the court alleging the commission of an offense which would not be a felony if committed by an adult, if the prosecutor has given sufficient written notice to the juvenile court that the prosecutor will not review such complaints.

(11) The prosecutor, juvenile court probation counselor, or diversion unit may, in exercising their authority under this section or RCW 13.40.080, refer juveniles to community-based programs, restorative justice programs, mediation, or victim offender reconciliation programs. Such mediation or victim offender reconciliation programs shall be voluntary for victims.

(12) Prosecutors and juvenile courts are encouraged to engage with and partner with community-based programs to expand, improve, and increase options to divert youth from formal processing in juvenile court. Nothing in this chapter should be read to limit partnership with community-based programs to create diversion opportunities for juveniles.

WEST VIRGINIA
Michie's ™ West Virginia Code, Chapter 49. Child Welfare. (Arts. 1–8)
Article 4. Court Actions. (Pts. I–IX)
Part VII. Juvenile Proceedings. (§§ 49-4-701–49-4-725)

§ 49-4-702. Prepetition diversion to informal resolution; mandatory prepetition diversion program for status offenses and misdemeanor offenses; prepetition review team.
(a) Before a juvenile petition is formally filed with the court, the court may refer the matter to a case worker, probation officer or truancy diversion specialist for preliminary inquiry to determine whether the matter can be resolved informally without the formal filing of a petition with the court.

(b)

(1) If the matter is for a truancy offense, the prosecutor shall refer the matter to a state department worker, probation officer or truancy diversion specialist who shall develop a diversion program pursuant to subsection (d) of this section.

(2) If the matter is for a status offense other than truancy, the prosecutor shall refer the juvenile to a case worker or probation officer who shall develop a diversion program pursuant to subsection (d) of this section.

(3) The prosecutor is not required to refer the juvenile for development of a diversion program pursuant to subdivision (1) or (2) of this subsection and may proceed to file a petition with the court if he or she determines:

(A) The juvenile has a prior adjudication for a status or delinquency offense; or

(B) There exists a significant and likely risk of harm to the juvenile, a family member or the public.

(c) If the matter is for a nonviolent misdemeanor offense, the prosecutor shall determine whether the case can be resolved informally through a diversion program without the filing of a petition. If the prosecutor determines that a diversion program is appropriate, it shall refer the matter to a case worker or probation officer who shall develop a diversion program pursuant to subsection (d) of this section.

(d)

(1) When developing a diversion program, the case worker, probation officer or truancy diversion specialist shall:

(A) Conduct an assessment of the juvenile to develop a diversion agreement;

(B) Create a diversion agreement;

(C) Obtain consent from the juvenile and his or her parent, guardian or custodian to the terms of the diversion agreement;

(D) Refer the juvenile and, if necessary, his or her parent, guardian or custodian to services in the community pursuant to the diversion agreement.

(2) A diversion agreement may include:

(A) Referral to community services as defined in section two hundred six [§ 49-1-206], article one of this chapter for the juvenile to address the assessed need;

(B) Referral to services for the parent, guardian or custodian of the juvenile;

(C) Referral to one or more community work service programs for the juvenile;

(D) A requirement that the juvenile regularly attend school;

(E) Community-based sanctions to address noncompliance; or

(F) Any other efforts which may reasonably benefit the community, the juvenile and his or her parent, guardian or custodian.

(3) When a referral to a service provider occurs, the service provider shall make reasonable efforts to contact the juvenile and his or her parent, custodian or guardian within seventy-two hours of the referral.

(4) Upon request by the case worker, probation officer or truancy diversion specialist, the court may enter reasonable and relevant orders to the parent, custodian or guardian of the juvenile who have consented to the diversion agreement as is necessary and proper to carry out the agreement.

(5) If the juvenile and his or her parent, custodian or guardian do not consent to the terms of the diversion agreement created by the case worker, probation officer or truancy diversion specialist, the petition may be filed with the court.

(6) Referral to a prepetition diversion program shall toll the statute of limitations for status and delinquency offenses.

(7) Probation officers may be authorized by the court to participate in a diversion program.

(e) The case worker, probation officer or truancy diversion specialist shall monitor the juvenile's compliance with any diversion agreement.

(1) If the juvenile successfully completes the terms of the diversion agreement, a petition shall not be filed with the court and no further action shall be taken.

(2) If the juvenile is unsuccessful in or noncompliant with the diversion agreement, the diversion agreement shall be referred to a prepetition review team convened by the case worker, probation officer or the truancy diversion specialist: Provided, That if a new delinquency offense occurs, a petition may be filed with the court.

(f)

(1) The prepetition review team may be a subset of a multidisciplinary team established pursuant to section four hundred six [§ 49-4-406], article four of this chapter.

(2) The prepetition review team may consist of:

(A) A case worker knowledgeable about community services available and authorized to facilitate access to services;

(B) A service provider;

(C) A school superintendent or his or her designee; or

(D) Any other person, agency representative, member of the juvenile's family, or a custodian or guardian who may assist in providing recommendations on community services for the particular needs of the juvenile and his or her family.

(3) The prepetition review team shall review the diversion agreement and the service referrals completed and determine whether other appropriate services are available to address the needs of the juvenile and his or her family.

(4) The prepetition review shall occur within fourteen days of referral from the state department worker, probation officer or truancy diversion specialist.

(5) After the prepetition review, the prepetition review team may:

(A) Refer a modified diversion agreement back to the case worker, probation officer or truancy diversion specialist;

(B) Advise the case worker, probation officer or truancy diversion specialist to file a petition with the court; or

(C) Advise the case worker to open an investigation for child abuse or neglect.

(g) The requirements of this section are not mandatory until July 1, 2016: Provided, That nothing in this section prohibits a judicial circuit from continuing to operate a truancy or other juvenile treatment program that existed as of January 1, 2015: Provided, however, That any judicial circuit desiring to create a diversion program after the effective date of this section and prior to July 1, 2016, may only do so pursuant to this section.

WISCONSIN
Wisconsin Annotated Statutes
Juvenile Justice Code (Ch. 938)
Chapter 938. Juvenile Justice Code (Subchs. I–XX)
Subchapter V Procedure (§§ 938.24–938.32)

938.245. Deferred prosecution.
(1) When available. An intake worker may enter into a written deferred prosecution agreement with all parties as provided in this section if all of the following apply:

(a) The intake worker has determined that neither the interests of the juvenile nor of the public require filing of a petition for circumstances relating to s. 938.12, 938.125, 938.13, or 938.14.

(b) The facts persuade the intake worker that the jurisdiction of the court, if sought, would exist.

(c) The juvenile, parent, guardian and legal custodian consent.

(1m) Victims; right to confer with intake worker. If a juvenile is alleged to be delinquent under s. 938.12 or to be in need of protection or services under s. 938.13 (12), an intake worker shall, as soon as practicable but before entering into a deferred prosecution agreement under sub. (1), offer all of the victims of the juvenile's alleged act who have so requested an opportunity to confer with the intake worker concerning the proposed deferred prosecution agreement. The duty to offer an opportunity to confer under this subsection does not limit the obligation of the intake worker to perform his or her responsibilities under this section.

(2) Contents of agreement.

(a) Specific conditions. A deferred prosecution agreement may provide for any one or more of the following:

1. 'Counseling.' That the juvenile and the juvenile's parent, guardian or legal custodian participate in individual, family or group counseling and that the parent, guardian or legal custodian participate in parenting skills training.

2. 'Compliance with obligations.' That the juvenile and a parent, guardian, or legal custodian abide by such obligations, including supervision, curfews, and school attendance requirements, as will tend to ensure the juvenile's rehabilitation, protection, or care.

3. 'Alcohol and other drug abuse assessment.' That the juvenile submit to an alcohol and other drug abuse assessment that meets the criteria under s. 938.547 (4) and that is conducted by an approved treatment facility for an examination of the juvenile's use of alcohol beverages, controlled substances, or controlled substance analogs and any medical, personal, family, or social effects caused by its use, if the multidisciplinary screen under s. 938.24 (2) shows that the juvenile is at risk of having needs and problems related to the use of alcohol beverages, controlled substances, or controlled substance analogs and its medical, personal, family, or social effects.

4. 'Alcohol and other drug abuse treatment and education.' That the juvenile participate in an alcohol and other drug abuse outpatient treatment program or a court-approved alcohol or other drug abuse education program, if an alcohol and other drug abuse assessment under subd. 3. recommends outpatient treatment, intervention, or education.

5. 'Restitution.'

a. That the juvenile participate in a restitution project if the act for which the agreement is being entered into resulted in damage to the property of another, or in actual physical injury to another excluding pain and suffering. Subject to subd. 5. c., the agreement may require the juvenile to repair the damage to property or to make reasonable restitution for the damage or injury, either in the form of cash payments or, if the victim agrees, the performance of services for the victim, or both, if the intake worker, after taking into consideration the well-being and needs of the victim, considers it beneficial to the well-being and behavior of the juvenile. The agreement shall include a determination that the juvenile alone is financially able to pay or physically able to perform the services, may allow up to the date of the expiration of the agreement for the payment or for the completion of the services, and may include a schedule for the performance and completion of the services. Any recovery under this subd. 5. a. shall be reduced by the amount recovered for the same act under subd. 5. am.

am. That the parent who has custody, as defined in s. 895.035 (1), of the juvenile make reasonable restitution for any damage to the property of another, or for any actual physical injury to another excluding pain and suffering, resulting from the act for which the agreement is being entered into. Except for recovery for retail theft under s. 943.51, the maximum amount of any restitution ordered under this subd. 5. am. for damage or injury resulting from any one act of a juvenile or from the same act committed by 2 or more juveniles in the custody of the same parent may not exceed $5,000. Any order under this subd. 5. am. shall include a finding that the parent is financially able to pay the amount ordered and may allow up to the date of the expiration of the agreement for the payment. Any recovery under this subd. 5. am. shall be reduced by the amount recovered for the same act under subd. 5. a.

b. In addition to any other employment or duties permitted under ch. 103 or any rule or order under ch. 103, a juvenile under 14 years of age who is participating in a restitution project provided by the county or who is performing services for the victim as restitution may, for the purpose of making restitution, be employed or perform any duties under any circumstances in which a juvenile 14 or 15 years of age is permitted to be employed or to perform duties under ch. 103 or any rule or order under ch. 103. A juvenile who is participating in a restitution project provided by the county or who is performing services for the victim as restitution is exempt from the permit requirement under s. 103.70 (1).

c. An agreement under this subdivision may require a juvenile who is under 14 years of age to make not more than $250 in restitution or to perform not more than 40 total hours of services for the victim as total restitution.

6. 'Supervised work program.' That the juvenile participate in a supervised work program or other community service work in accordance with s. 938.34 (5g).

7. 'Volunteers in probation.' That the juvenile be placed with a volunteers in probation program under conditions the intake worker determines are reasonable and appropriate, if the juvenile is alleged to have committed an act that would constitute a misdemeanor if committed by an adult, if the chief judge of the judicial administrative district has approved under s. 973.11 (2) a volunteers in probation program established in the juvenile's county of residence, and if the intake worker determines that volunteer supervision under that program will likely benefit the juvenile and the community. The conditions an intake worker may establish under this subdivision may include a request to a volunteer to be a role model for the juvenile, informal counseling, general monitoring, monitoring of the conditions established by the intake worker, or any combination of these functions, and any other deferred prosecution condition that the intake worker may establish under this paragraph.

8. 'Teen court program.' That the juvenile be placed in a teen court program if all of the following conditions apply:

a. The chief judge of the judicial administrative district has approved a teen court program established in the juvenile's county of residence and the intake worker determines that participation in the teen court program will likely benefit the juvenile and the community.

b. The juvenile is alleged to have committed a delinquent act that would be a misdemeanor if committed by an adult or a civil law or ordinance violation.

c. The juvenile admits to the intake worker, in the presence of the juvenile's parent, guardian, or legal custodian, that the juvenile committed the alleged delinquent act or civil law or ordinance violation.

d. The juvenile has not successfully completed participation in a teen court program during the 2 years before the date of the alleged delinquent act or civil law or ordinance violation.

9m. 'Youth report center.' That the juvenile report to a youth report center after school, in the evening, on weekends, on other nonschool days, or at any other time that the juvenile is not under immediate adult supervision, for participation in the social, behavioral, academic, community service, and other programming of the center. Section 938.34 (5g) applies to any community service work performed by a juvenile under this subdivision.

(b) No out-of-home placement; term of agreement. A deferred prosecution agreement may not include any form of out-of-home placement and may not exceed one year.

(c) Alcohol or other drug abuse treatment; informed consent. If the deferred prosecution agreement provides for alcohol and other drug abuse outpatient treatment under par. (a) 4., the juvenile and the juvenile's parent, guardian or legal custodian shall execute an informed consent form that indicates that they are voluntarily and knowingly entering into a deferred prosecution agreement for the provision of alcohol and other drug abuse outpatient treatment.

(2g) Graffiti violation. If the deferred prosecution agreement is based on an allegation that the juvenile violated s. 943.017 and the juvenile has attained 10 years of age, the agreement may require that the juvenile participate for not less than 10 hours nor more than 100 hours in a supervised work program under s. 938.34 (5g) or perform not less than 10 hours nor more than 100 hours of other community service work, except that if the juvenile has not attained 14 years of age the maximum number of hours is 40.

(2v) Habitual truancy violation. If the deferred prosecution agreement is based on an allegation that the juvenile has violated a municipal ordinance enacted under s. 118.163 (2), the agreement may require that the juvenile's parent, guardian, or legal custodian attend school with the juvenile.

(3) Obligations in writing. The obligations imposed under a deferred prosecution agreement and its effective date shall be set forth in writing. The written agreement shall state whether the juvenile has been adopted. The intake worker shall provide a copy of the agreement and order to the juvenile, to the juvenile's parent, guardian, and legal custodian, and to any agency providing services under the agreement.

(4) Right to terminate or object to agreement. The intake worker shall inform the juvenile and the juvenile's parent, guardian, and legal custodian in writing of their right to terminate the deferred prosecution agreement at any time or to object at any time to the fact or terms of the agreement. If there is an objection, the intake worker may alter the terms of the agreement or request the district attorney or corporation counsel to file a petition. If the agreement is terminated the intake worker may request the district attorney or corporation counsel to file a petition.

(5) Termination upon request. A deferred prosecution agreement may be terminated upon the request of the juvenile, parent, guardian, or legal custodian.

(6) Termination if delinquency petition filed. A deferred prosecution agreement arising out of an alleged delinquent act is terminated if the district attorney files a delinquency petition within 20 days after receipt of notice of the deferred prosecution agreement under s. 938.24 (5). If a petition is filed, statements made to the intake worker during the intake inquiry are inadmissible.

(7) Cancellation by intake worker.

  (a) If at any time during the period of a deferred prosecution agreement the intake worker determines that the obligations imposed under it are not being met, the intake worker may cancel the agreement. Within 10 days after the agreement is cancelled, the intake worker shall notify the district attorney, corporation counsel, or other official under s. 938.09 of the cancellation and may request that a petition be filed. In delinquency cases, the district attorney may initiate a petition within 20 days after the date of the notice regardless of whether the intake worker has requested that a petition be filed. The court shall grant appropriate relief as provided in s. 938.315 (3) with respect to any petition that is not filed within the time period specified in this paragraph. Failure to object to the fact that a petition is not filed within the time period specified in this paragraph waives any challenge to the court's competency to act on the petition.

(b) In addition to the action taken under par. (a), if the intake worker cancels a deferred prosecution agreement based on a determination that the juvenile's parent, guardian, or legal custodian is not meeting the obligations imposed under the agreement, the intake worker shall request the district attorney, corporation counsel, or other official under s. 938.09 to file a petition requesting the court to order the juvenile's parent, guardian, or legal custodian to show good cause for not meeting the obligations. If a petition under this paragraph is filed and if the court finds prosecutive merit for the petition, the court shall grant an order directing the parent, guardian, or legal custodian to show good cause, at a time and place fixed by the court, for not meeting the obligations. If the parent, guardian or legal custodian does not show good cause, the court may impose a forfeiture not to exceed $1,000.

(8) When obligations met. If the obligations imposed under the deferred prosecution agreement are met, the intake worker shall so inform the juvenile and a parent, guardian, and legal custodian in writing. No petition may be filed or citation issued on the charges that brought about the agreement and the charges may not be the sole basis for a petition under s. 48.13, 48.133, 48.14, 938.13, or 938.14.

(9) Written policies. The intake worker shall perform his or her responsibilities under this section under general written policies promulgated under s. 938.06 (1) or (2).

WYOMING
  Wyoming Statutes Annotated
  Title 14 Children (Chs. 1–13)
  Chapter 6 Juveniles (Arts. 1–5)
  Article 2. Juvenile Justice Act (§§ 14-6-201–14-6-252)

§ 14-6-211. Complaints alleging delinquency; investigation and determination by district attorney.
(a) Complaints alleging a child is delinquent shall be referred to the office of the district attorney. The district attorney shall determine whether the best interest of the child or of the public require that judicial action be taken. The department, the county sheriff and the county probation departments shall provide the district attorney with any assistance he may require in making an investigation. The district attorney shall prepare and file a petition with the court if he believes action is necessary to protect the interest of the public or child.